A Harry Stack Sullivan Case Seminar
Treatment of a Young Male Schizophrenic

By Harry Stack Sullivan

CLINICAL STUDIES IN PSYCHIATRY

CONCEPTIONS OF MODERN PSYCHIATRY

THE FUSION OF PSYCHIATRY AND SOCIAL SCIENCE

THE INTERPERSONAL THEORY OF PSYCHIATRY

PERSONAL PSYCHOPATHOLOGY

THE PSYCHIATRIC INTERVIEW

SCHIZOPHRENIA AS A HUMAN PROCESS

ROBERT G. KVARNES, M.D., Editor
GLORIA H. PARLOFF, Assistant Editor

A Harry Stack Sullivan
Case Seminar

Treatment of a Young Male
Schizophrenic

With Comment, Twenty-five Years Later, by
JOHN C. DILLINGHAM
STANLEY JACOBSON, ED.D.
ROBERT G. KVARNES, M.D.
IRVING M. RYCKOFF, M.D.

W·W·NORTON & COMPANY·INC·*New York*

Library of Congress Cataloging in Publication Data

Main entry under title:
A Harry Stack Sullivan case seminar.

1. Schizophrenia—Cases, clinical reports,
statistics. 2. Sullivan, Harry Stack, 1892–1949.
I. Sullivan, Harry Stack, 1892–1949. II. Dillingham,
John C. III. Kvarnes, Robert G. IV. Parloff,
Gloria H.
RC514.H34   616.8'982'09   76–7005
ISBN 0-393-01130-5

Dedicated to
James Inscoe Sullivan

Often overlooked or unacknowledged are the interpersonal support systems that make the work of originative people possible. As Harry Stack Sullivan's foster son, Jimmie Sullivan self-effacingly but efficiently maintained for Sullivan a supportive environment that helped this somewhat irascible, rather temperamental genius to engage productively in a wide range of creative activities.

Contents

Preface

During the past thirty-five years, Harry Stack Sullivan has become known as the foremost American psychiatric theoretician. Although Sullivan died of a heart attack in 1949 at the age of fifty-six, his influence is still growing. Trained in the psychoanalytic tradition of the 1920s, Sullivan presented his early papers along traditional psychoanalytic lines and in typical psychoanalytic language. However, after prolonged work with schizophrenics, he began formulating his insights in terms of interpersonal relations, emphasizing that the emotional difficulties in living stemmed from and occurred in the relationships between people. This led him away from the intrapsychic formulations of Freud and most of his followers. Sullivan's contributions can be seen as being principally in the realm of ego psychology, a field to which Freud felt he could not devote ample attention if he were to continue his important work on id and superego psychology. Sullivan also pioneered in developing liaisons between the field of psychiatry and the social and biological sciences, especially as they related to culture and personality. During his lifetime, Sullivan's major publication was *Conceptions of Modern Psychiatry*. Following his death, a series of books was prepared from his notes and recorded lectures under the editorship of Helen Swick Perry, Mary Ladd Gavell, Martha Gibbon, and Gloria Parloff: *The Interpersonal Theory of Psychiatry*, *The Psychiatric Interview*, *Clinical Studies in Psychiatry*, *Schizophrenia as a Human Process*, *The Fusion of Psychiatry and Social Science*, and *Personal Psychopathology*.

To my knowledge, the seminar presented here is the richest clinical illustration available both of Harry Stack Sullivan's perceptivity about schizophrenia and of his ability as a teacher. The seminar was organized during 1946–47 for the psychiatric residents at Sheppard and Enoch Pratt Hospital by Dr. Harry Murdock and Dr. Will Elgin, the hospital's Medical Director and Assistant Medical Director at the time. As with many of the Sullivan teaching sessions, the seminar occurred on Sunday mornings in the recreation room of Dr. Dexter M. Bullard's home on the grounds of Chestnut Lodge Sanitarium in Rockville, Maryland. First- and second-year residents from Sheppard were joined in the seminar by staff members from Chestnut Lodge and by some advanced students from the Washington School of Psychiatry.

Although Sullivan did not regard himself as a talented clinician or teacher, he did have unusual sensitivity to, experience with, and empathy toward young male schizophrenics, whom he had studied extensively in his special ward at Sheppard and Enoch Pratt Hospital during the late 1920s. Sullivan's delicacy in perceiving and reacting to anxiety in therapeutic interactions is reflected in this seminar, where essentially he was talking to young residents who in their hospital case loads were encountering young male schizophrenics, not infrequently in a state of acute panic. Obviously, the sturdier the patient's ego (or the resident's ego) and the stronger the doctor-patient relationship, the freer Sullivan felt in confronting anxiety-fraught material.

This publication was prepared primarily to provide a demonstration of Harry Stack Sullivan at work as a teacher. It is fortunate that an unusually articulate patient provided the seminar with a wealth of material with which to work. However, because much of the patient's personal data (with identifications disguised but with dynamic ingredients intact) is an essential part of the seminar account, the question of how to avoid a breach of confidentiality delayed publication of the seminar for many years. With the death of the central figure, the problem was abruptly resolved.

A special note is also in order regarding the recording of the seminar. In the 1940s, a few highly skilled medical secretaries could take shorthand notes of an entire case conference, even with a manic patient talking at a very rapid pace. For this seminar, Dr. Murdock and Dr. Elgin assigned a superior hospital secretary, Louise King. On the Mondays following the sessions she transcribed her notes, and if she had missed a few words, I was usually able to supply them, sometimes with the help of other participants. She automatically omitted all interruptive vocal sounds—such as coughs, "uh's," and interjections, which are accurately but distractingly recorded by modern machines, and which add nothing to the meaning of a report. Louise King deserves special commendation for her unusual skill, competence, and devoted participation, both as a listener and as the recorder.

Sullivan's participation in the seminar has been included virtually without editing. The contributions of the other participants have been edited somewhat in the interests of greater clarity and minimal repetition. All such editing has been approved by the seminar members.

I would like to suggest that in the course of reading this book the reader undertake an experiment. Sullivan was an effective speaker, with a slight Irish brogue providing additional grace to his words. Since this seminar represents Sullivan talking extemporaneously, I would like to suggest that the reader occasionally try reading aloud passages that are especially meaningful. This procedure may give a better sense of the impact of Sullivan's personal style.

The contemporary discussions that follow each of the original seminar sessions were initially organized to help determine how the material might best be prepared for publication. This occupied our attention only briefly, however, because at the first meeting we decided to enlist the services of Gloria Parloff, managing editor of *Psychiatry: Journal for the Study of Interpersonal Processes* (founded by Sullivan in 1938). Subsequently, the discussions considered the seminar content itself, and they have been included to show the differences that twenty-five years have made in the various trends in therapy and in salient social problems. They also include some additional historical material about the seminar, the participants, and Sullivan.

Finally, I would like to add that no other learning experience in psychiatry and psychoanalysis has had so great an impact on me as my participation in this seminar. My numerous rereadings of the seminar over the years and during the course of the preparation of the manuscript for publication have enriched my original understanding of Sullivan's expositions, especially in the light of my clinical experience during the intervening twenty-five years. This intensive study of the seminar—in part enforced —has deepened my appreciation of the enduring nature of Sullivan's contributions.

R.G.K.

Acknowledgments

The editor of what is in effect someone else's creative work fully deserves to be modest, and "acknowledgments" become even more important than usual. There were many along the way who urged and assisted in the publication of this seminar. In the 1940s, at the Sheppard and Enoch Pratt Hospital, Towson, Maryland, Dr. Harry Murdock, Dr. Will Elgin, Louise King, my fellow seminar members, and others on the staff helped prepare the original manuscript. Some fifteen years after the seminar, Jerry Styrt (one of the original seminar participants) and his wife, Mary, in an effort to foster publication, had the manuscript retyped in more publishable form; however, both consideration for the patient and questions of appropriate style of presentation delayed further work on the manuscript at that time. The current Medical Director of Sheppard Pratt, Dr. Robert Gibson, has extended Sheppard's permission for publication of the seminar.

My sincere thanks go to the seminar members and the estates of deceased seminar members for permission to identify their contributions. Thanks also go to the other members of the "Comment Seminar"—John Dillingham, Stanley Jacobson, and Irving Ryckoff, resident faculty members at the Washington School of Psychiatry, Washington, D.C. Their work sustained the momentum. The skillful organizing and editorial work by Gloria Parloff, the assistant editor, pulled the disparate parts together to produce the final manuscript.

Significant also were the enthusiastic support and suggestions of my wife, Miriam, both at the time the original seminars were held in 1946–47 and, more recently, as the manuscript was being prepared for publication. Special thanks are also due Ann Salzman and Katherine Henry for research and editing associated with the preparation of the manuscript.

R.G.K.

Seminar Participants

Case Seminar, 1946–47

Robert A. Cohen, M.D.

Director, Division of Clinical and Behavioral Research, National Institute of Mental Health. Training and Supervising Analyst, Washington Psychoanalytic Institute. President, Washington School of Psychiatry.

Larry Cooper, M.D.

Pseudonym.*

Edna G. Dyar, M.D.

Deceased.

Mary White Hinckley, M.D.

Staff Psychiatrist, Brattleboro Retreat, Brattleboro, Vermont.

W. Deaver Kehne, M.D.

Private practice, psychiatry and psychoanalysis, Washington, D.C. Teaching Psychoanalyst, Washington Psychoanalytic Institute. Associate Clinical Professor of Psychiatry, George Washington University Medical School.

Robert G. Kvarnes, M.D.

Private practice, psychiatry and psychoanalysis, Washington, D.C. Director, Washington School of Psychiatry.

* In two instances, the editors were unable to locate participants and were unable to obtain permission to identify their contributions to the seminar.

Robert R. Morris, M.D.

Private practice, psychiatry and psychoanalysis, Marin County, California.

Samuel Novey, M.D.

Deceased. Private practice, psychoanalysis. Director of Training, Sheppard and Enoch Pratt Hospital, Towson, Maryland. Associate Professor of Psychiatry, Johns Hopkins University School of Medicine.

Stanley Peal, M.D.

Psychiatrist, Pittsburgh, Pennsylvania.

Joseph Rom, M.D.

Deceased.

Leon Salzman, M.D.

Professor of Clinical Psychiatry, Georgetown Medical School. Clinical Professor of Psychiatry, Albert Einstein College of Medicine.

Herbert Staveren, M.D.

Deceased.

Jerome Styrt, M.D.

Private practice, psychoanalysis and psychotherapy, Baltimore, Maryland. Associate Clinical Professor, University of Maryland School of Medicine. Teaching Consultant, Sheppard and Enoch Pratt Hospital, Towson, Maryland.

Philip S. Wagner, M.D.

Psychiatrist, Chino Reception Center, California Institution for Men, Chino, California. Private practice, psychiatry and psychoanalysis, Irvine, California.

Charles Wheeler, M.D.   Pseudonym.*

Mary White, M.D.   See Mary White Hinckley.

Otto Allen Will, Jr., M.D.   Medical Director, Austen
                               Riggs Center, Inc., Stock-
                               bridge, Massachusetts.

John P. Witt, M.D.   Private practice, psycho-
                               analysis, Baltimore,
                               Maryland, Teaching:
                               Baltimore–D.C. Institute for
                               Psychoanalysis; Sheppard
                               and Enoch Pratt Hospital,
                               Towson, Maryland; Phipps
                               Clinic, Johns Hopkins Hos-
                               pital.

Comment Seminar, 1971–72

John C. Dillingham   Philosopher. Director,
                               Metropolitan Mental Health
                               Skills Center, Washington
                               School of Psychiatry.

Stanley Jacobson, Ed.D.   Clinical Psychologist. Direc-
                               tor, School Mental Health
                               Services, and Dean of Stu-
                               dents, Washington School of
                               Psychiatry.

Robert G. Kvarnes, M.D.   See above.

Irving M. Ryckoff, M.D.   Private practice, psychiatry
                               and psychoanalysis, Wash-
                               ington, D.C. Chairman of
                               the Faculty, Washington
                               School of Psychiatry.

* In two instances, the editors were unable to locate participants and
were unable to obtain permission to identify their contributions to the
seminar.

A Harry Stack Sullivan Case Seminar
Treatment of a Young Male Schizophrenic

I

Case Seminar, November, 1946

This Sunday-morning case seminar, arranged primarily for residents of the Sheppard and Enoch Pratt Hospital, Towson, Maryland, had met once prior to the first session presented here. At that initial session, Robert Kvarnes, a psychiatric resident at Sheppard, volunteered to present clinical data about his psychotherapeutic work with a young male patient at the hospital, and the five subsequent sessions of the case seminar, which are presented here, focus on that patient. This session, like the others, illustrates some of Harry Stack Sullivan's teaching methods— with the presenter, with the other individual participants, and with the group as a whole. Following the interchanges with the seminar members, Sullivan adds a lengthy explication of some of the clinical and treatment aspects of the case.

In addition to Kvarnes, the Sheppard residents present were Larry Cooper (pseudonym), Joseph Rom, Jerome Styrt, Charles Wheeler (pseudonym), and John Witt. The others who attended this session were Philip Wagner, of the Sheppard staff; Robert Cohen, Edna Dyar, and Herbert Staveren, of the Chestnut Lodge staff; and Robert Morris, Leon Salzman, and Otto Will, from the Washington School of Psychiatry.

KVARNES: This is the case of a twenty-five-year-old boy from New York City. His illness dates from February, 1946, mainly a gradually increasing self-recriminatory pattern with tension and anxiety, leading to hospitalization in July, and subsequently to Sheppard Pratt, where our relationship began.

The family background is unstable. The father's people came from Russia; the paternal grandfather was a scrupulous Orthodox

Jew. There were eight children in the family, one of whom developed a manic-depressive psychosis. The paternal grandmother died in Russia, and subsequently her husband came to the U.S. The patient's father was nine at this time and was left by his father in Russia, to be cared for by relatives. Apparently, while working as an apprentice he ran away and lived a difficult existence until he was called to this country by his father when he was fifteen. In the ensuing ten years the patient's father finished college and took a law course at night, teaching during the day. He finished his law course at the age of twenty-five, developed a "nervous breakdown" which was apparently a severe exhaustion state, required hospitalization for a couple of weeks, and then lived on a farm for a year. After his recovery, he obtained employment in the state civil service. Shortly thereafter he ran for office in the state legislature, and served for ten years during the 1920s.

The father described himself as being an aggressive, friendly, sociable person. He became a leading figure in social and educational legislation and introduced much of that type of legislation.

The mother's parents were also born in Russia and migrated to the U.S., where her father became a successful shirt manufacturer. The patient's father described him as being of a nervous temperament, headstrong, impatient, shrewd, dominating, and jealous of his children. The maternal grandmother was a steadying influence. The patient had little contact with his grandparents on either side. His mother had four siblings, and one of these, the youngest, a girl, is hospitalized with paranoid schizophrenia.

The mother is an ambitious, energetic person. Prior to marriage she had taught school for mental defectives and throughout her marriage has been engaged in many activities. She ran a political campaign for her husband, served as a hospital organizer, was engaged in much charity work. She also owns a business which she runs herself. The father said that she should have been the politician, that she was much more aggressive and determined than he. She had a "nervous breakdown" following one of these campaigns, again apparently an exhaustion. She was hospitalized for a couple of weeks and made her recovery without untoward incident.

This couple had four children, the first of whom was injured in high forceps delivery and died at birth. Originally, arrangements had been made for the mother to give birth in a hospital, but she became convinced that babies were something natural and should be delivered in the home by a general practitioner, and decided to run the pregnancy that way. The patient has some feeling about that delivery and the handling of it, which I will bring up later. The second child was the patient. The third was a stillborn child that apparently had been dead about a month before delivery. The fourth is a boy about three years younger than the patient. Early in his development this brother began to stutter and became a severe problem, requiring much attention from parents, housekeepers, and special nurses, and finally entered a special school. He had trouble adjusting to kindergarten and to school, and later was inducted into military service and discharged because of "nervousness."

The early history of the patient shows the pregnancy and delivery to be normal. He was breast-fed for two or three months and then bottle-fed when he did not gain. The mother did not know whether it was lack of milk or "improper" milk. He was cared for by his mother for the first year or two, and the father describes her as being very scientific, saying that she raised the child "according to the book." There is no history of behavior problems in infancy or early childhood. The patient was born in 1921. The father sustained a fracture in 1922 and was in a cast for six months. During this time the patient's mother ran the political campaign that enabled him to be elected. The care of the child fell to the nurse who was attending the father. Other nurses followed, and finally a Czechoslovakian housekeeper who apparently took care of both the patient and his younger brother. The story has it that she spent much time on the younger child. Everybody considered the patient a normal, independent child, and both parents felt he was neglected because of that.

His schooling was uneventful except that on the basis of a teacher's recommendation he was skipped from 5A to 6A because he seemed to catch on more quickly than the other children and was more inclined to be restless in class. He skipped another grade in junior high school, also on a teacher's recommendation, after the parents took him to a psychologist who discovered a high IQ. Subsequently the patient had trouble with mathematics and required a tutor. The patient describes himself as a "failure" in mathematics, and adds that he failed a year, but the parents reported that while he failed the mid-semester examinations, he did pass the course. His progress in high school was uneventful, with better than average, but not outstanding, grades. He applied to an Ivy League school for a pre-law course, was denied admission, but was told that he would be admitted if he first took a course at City College. This he did and then entered his first-choice school.

He was in college from 1938 to 1942, was appointed editor of the school paper, and with the onset of World War II entered the civilian pilot training program as a college student. After some hours in the air, he asked to be eliminated because of extreme nervousness. He was very tense, airsick much of the time, and felt he was undependable at the controls.

His father describes him as being a very bookish child, conscientious and diligent in his studies, shy but not unusually so. His parents did not feel that he was shy with girls, and yet in retrospect they realize that he did not have many dates or many female associates.

In August, 1942, the patient volunteered for military service, entered the Navy V7 training program, and was commissioned as an ensign. His first choice was submarine service. He admits that he had to prove himself, and that he volunteered mostly on that basis. He was not chosen, apparently because he lacked sufficient engineering training. He was assigned to his second choice, service on a destroyer escort. After a few months of school, he went to sea, initially in the Aleutians. When he returned, he again went to a special school, and was assigned to a division then in the Pacific. There he found it necessary to ask for a transfer to another division or to another type of ship, on the basis of his feelings of insecurity and of being much threatened. I have not been able to get this picture more clearly. However, he was assigned as a gunnery officer on an amphibious personnel destroyer and was engaged in landing operations. His ship saw combat, was damaged considerably, and on one occasion the patient apparently attempted to perform some heroic deed. He tried to go down below decks and rescue some of the personnel. They were all dead, but he was commended by his superior officer. He progressed to lieutenant (sg) before he left the Navy, serving in Japan and Korea. He returned to the U.S. in December, 1945, and shortly thereafter was discharged. In January he had already entered law school.

The feeling is that the patient's difficulties began after he entered law school. The parents had considered him normal until this time. He was there about a month and during this time became more and more tense, was unable to concentrate, and was recriminating in his attitude toward his own ability in school. Ultimately he had to consult a doctor because of his difficulties. The doctor recommended his leaving school.

The parents describe the boy as being not particularly aggressive with girls, as having some dates but seeming uninterested. However, there was no suspicion that he was having trouble. While in college he had become reacquainted with a girl he had known in summer camp when he was about eighteen and she was fourteen or fifteen. When he was in the service, he wrote his parents asking that they meet her. He wrote to the girl with increasing affection, and when he returned from the Aleutians in the fall of 1944 he dated her a few times, and continued to correspond with her while he was in the Pacific; by the time he came home, he had arranged an engagement and decided to go ahead and marry her. The girl is a brilliant student who immediately after graduation from college got a job on the editorial staff of a liberal magazine. She is described as being pretty, quite high-pressured, liberal in her viewpoint, and modern in her attitude toward sex. With his return to college, the patient began dating her every night, and eventually came to feel that he was neglecting both the girl and his studies. They went on with their plans for marriage and the date was set for June of 1946. By March the patient was very tense and upset about the whole affair. He felt intellectually inadequate in comparison with the girl, as well as having grave feelings of sexual inadequacy. He denies intercourse, although the girl was willing, but they did play with each other's genitals.

Prior to his military service the patient had had no relations with women. While in the Navy, wanting to test himself, he had on several occasions taken girls to hotel rooms. These were usually girls he picked up in taverns, generally older than he. He always had orgasm, but felt inadequate, had premature ejaculation, and never felt that he satisfied the woman, although apparently none of them had complained.

After he quit school he was very threatened by the thought of marriage, and although the engagement had been announced in the paper, it was called off and the patient decided to take an automobile trip. A boyfriend volunteered to go with him. They started out on a trip which was to take them to California, but in Kansas, while the patient was driving, they had an accident that caused considerable damage to the car, necessitating their waiting for five weeks for repairs. They called off the trip and returned. On the way back they were involved in another accident, but this time the friend was driving.

During this trip the patient frequently stopped at book stores to buy psychiatric or psychological textbooks and spent a great deal of time talking about his difficulties. He felt completely dependent on his friend, who did all the planning on the trip.

Upon his return he felt he had to see a psychiatrist, and his father took him to a friend of his, a Dr. F. The doctor saw him a couple of times, and attempted to buck him up by patting him on the back. But since he seemed no better he was finally admitted to Springhill in July. Shortly afterwards, since he was reluctant to talk about his problems, they decided on a course of electroconvulsive therapy and he had three shocks. After this he became more communicative and seemed to form a relationship to a Dr. W, proceeding to talk about some of his problems; however, he gradually slipped back into his uncommunicative state. It was not a stupor or muteness, but he just did not talk about things that bothered him. He was given another series of shocks, perhaps six or seven. Again there was some diminution of tenseness, but this only lasted a month or two. About this time the sanitarium underwent some administrative difficulty, during which several doctors left, and the patient urged his parents to take him home, which they did in August. He continued almost daily visits with Dr. W, who attempted to begin an analysis. The patient concerned himself almost exclusively with self-disparagement, and the situation at home became more and more involved. The patient started to cry out about his parents, their mishandling of his youth, and his dependence on his father, and yet he felt more and more dependent—to the point where at times he wanted to get into bed with his parents to be comforted. This went on for about six weeks, until ultimately the doctor suggested that the boy move in with him in an effort to relieve the bad home situation. The parents objected, and out of their discussions with Dr. W came the decision to send him to Sheppard. He was brought to the hospital on September 14 by the psychiatrist, preceded by several hours by the father, who made the arrangements for the admission and gave the history.

Initially the boy was communicative with me. He concerned himself almost exclusively with self-recrimination. In all of the initial talks there was much use of psychiatric terminology. He talked about his "masochism," his "destructive, self-destructive tendencies," his "resistiveness to his analyst" and to the hospital, his evasion, his "psychoneurosis" and the "neurotic elements" in the family, and the "power plays" he used to handle the environment at home. On admission he expressed some feeling that he was being railroaded in spite of the fact that arrangements had been made with his knowledge. Apparently he was told that he could look the place over, but instead he was admitted the same day. He has expressed some suicidal fantasies, but has never made a known suicidal gesture.

I was unable to find any evidence of delusions or hallucinations early in his stay, and his orientation was good. In the six weeks since his admission we have had almost daily office talks and occasional talks on the ward. Throughout he has been communicative. In our talks he would be the one to start and continue the conversation throughout the time. From the very beginning and right up to now the main issue is the real inferiority he feels. He early spoke of his feelings of sexual inadequacy, and it was from him that I obtained the story of the heterosexual experiences and the difficulties with his girlfriend. He recriminates himself in everything. He felt that the only way he got through school was by the use of cribs and copying, that when it was time to write a theme he invariably got the material out of books from his father's library. He put passages from books into letters to friends and took books from the library with the intention of impressing people. He said he had difficulty in debates or other situations where he had to make a speech. He always felt inadequate and insecure.

The story from the parents suggests that he did very well in school. He felt that he had accepted the job as editor of the college paper entirely for its prestige value. He was unable to apply himself to the journalistic side of the job. He frequently speaks of his failure in mathematics, and one day we pursued that subject until he admitted that he had not actually failed. He added, "What's the difference, I didn't learn properly." That is one of the predominant attitudes—his failure to grasp any of the material he was reading, to get any knowledge or information from it. He said something to the effect that he did it solely for its emotional purposes, but this I am unable to clarify. He said his pattern was constantly one of building himself up and that he frequently would incorporate other people's experiences into his story and claim them for his own. He mentioned that over the years he has changed his handwriting to appear more sophisticated.

The patient condemns himself and calls himself a kleptomaniac. He says he has stolen money from his parents and has done some shoplifting, picking up a tie on one occasion and a piece for his camera on another.

His whole approach to the Navy experience was that he was inadequate, that he put on a mask of efficiency by which he was not fooled but which got him by. He was promoted twice but it means nothing to him. He says any attempt he made at "this heroic stuff" was entirely on the basis of needing to prove himself. He mentioned many times how he always allowed his father to get him out of jams in school with the principal or the teachers. He was able to give only one instance of this—the math difficulty that prompted his father to talk with the principal, which in turn resulted in arrangements for a tutor—but he implies that his father helped him out of everything.

He objects to his own secretiveness, saying he has never allowed other people to read his mail and was always secretive about things he thought. He never wanted anybody to know him. When he talks of himself he frequently uses such terms as "demented," "completely insane," "pathological liar," "psychoneurotic," or "kleptomaniac." In another phase he talks of his difficulties as being in relation to physical feelings—that he doesn't want to be touched by people and shrinks away from close contact. In the hospital he does not like to have his hair cut or to be shaved, feeling tense on such occasions. I inquired about the subways that he had taken to school, and he said that he did not feel physically aloof at that time; yet shortly afterward he said he has felt that way all his life.

Also pervading his talk is the feeling that something is going to be done to him, that the whole environment of the hospital is a threatening one. Part of this is a fear of medication and treatment. When he came in he had a rather severe case of athlete's foot and also some calluses which he had picked down to the skin; in addition, his nails had been chewed down, and he had bitten his lip. I treated the athlete's foot but there was some reluctance to accept treatment. He mentioned several times his fear of cold showers. He does not like to take showers on the ward, and if they are at all cool he becomes especially tense and apprehensive. He has not been to hydrotherapy because of his fear of showers and cold water. One day when he was talking about his physical fears, he told me with considerable difficulty of the fear he had of having his temperature taken rectally; he said when it had been done recently he had thought of the possibility of the thermometer breaking in his rectum—the phrase "glass in the ass, glass in the ass" kept going through his mind. He also becomes upset when he thinks of having an enema. Innumerable times he has said, "I wonder what is coming next?" or "What are they going to do?"

During the conversation about the physical aspects of his problem, the feeling that he was physically inferior came up. I pointed out that he is 5'10" tall, the proper weight, and above-average in development. After some discussion he focused on the fact that he had a small penis; on subsequent occasions he mentioned comparing penises with a boy friend and discovering that his was smaller. Also there has been a vague mention of what he considers Jewish physical traits. I have tried several times to clarify that, but he has steered the talk away from it. He recently mentioned being squeamish about odors and touch, and an inability to feel comfortable in school laboratories, either chemical or biological.

He looks back on the shock treatment as an entirely gruesome and threatening experience. He remembers the treatments as being done in a small shack on the corner of the grounds; in fact it was a one-room cottage, with beds at one end, where the patients stayed a couple of hours before being walked back to their rooms. He describes the shock by saying that he was "bound, gagged, and then knocked out." Several times I have had to reassure him that he will not receive shock from us. It has been a preoccupation with him.

He has occasionally talked about the family situation, calling it indescribable. He says that during the period between leaving Springhill and coming to Sheppard he was "neurotically coloring the whole environment." He did not want to let his father out of his sight and made so many demands on him that he interfered with his father's work. He accused his mother of abusing him as a child. When she left home for a few weeks' vacation during this period between hospitalizations, he seemed to be better.

Now he talks about his feeling of complete loss of control of his environment. He feels we are watching him, that he cannot go anywhere without somebody watching him or being with him. The eyes are on him at all times. He can do nothing that is not observed and recorded. He has sometimes mentioned his feelings of hostility, but there have been no overt evidences of this. He says he feels like telling one of the other patients on the ward to shut up. One day when he was more tense than usual, he kicked at chairs and tables, but mildly, not upsetting them. A couple of times he has said, "No, I don't want to go to this activity and I will get out of here"—and that has been about his strongest wording.

Two weeks ago Saturday, after we had been getting along pretty well in our interviews, he was quite agitated and tense, and I felt it might be advisable to try a sedative tub. Realizing his feeling about hydro, I made an effort to tell him what the procedure would be, accompanied him to the tub room, and waited until he got in. I came back twice during the two-hour period that he was in the tub; he was quite tense throughout. Very little sedation was received. I didn't see him then until the following Monday, and apparently there was a gradually increasing tension over the weekend. On Saturday night he was a little more careless in covering himself, walking around the room and the ward with his pajama pants open. He was at that time quite tense and requested a checker game with somebody, although usually requests are made of him. In the course of the game he demonstrated one of his fancy trick moves and seemed to feel good about that. On Sunday night his tenseness was marked. Monday morning the nurse called me and said he wanted to see me, that he had something to tell me. I was in the process of interviewing some relatives of a new patient, but I went up to the ward and discovered that during Sunday night and Monday morning he had chewed the inside of his mouth and developed a Vincent's infection on the abraded area, with markedly swollen cheek and submaxillary gland. He was not concerned about that but had the feeling that he had to get something off his chest. I told him I was not able to spend a great deal of time with him and explained why, and said that I would be able to come back in the afternoon and spend all the time he wanted. We talked about his cheek. His attitude was: "I don't give a damn. What the hell is the difference?" I spent about fifteen minutes with him and he seemed to quiet down some, lay down on the bed, and requested not to go to dinner, but just to be allowed to rest. I ordered some medication, which he accepted without particular protest. When I went back later he only mentioned that the tub had sponsored a whole series of thoughts but he had no great urge to talk out the problem.

On another occasion since then, it became obvious that he was trying to tell me something in the office, and ultimately he said that he had the feeling that he had passed from being a severe psychoneurotic to being a schizophrenic. Apparently this was a frightening idea to him.

The office interview pattern is that we sit down and talk. He carries the conversation. I ask him a question once in a while, and usually my position is to define more clearly what he means by various words. At the beginning he used all kinds of psychiatric terminology and I tried to clarify what he meant. After forty-five minutes or an hour I get ready to terminate the interview, and I usually stand up and say that I will see him the next day at 2:30. He becomes tense, starts out on a new subject, and might say, "What is in store for me, what is this about my father's visiting?" He seems to want to cling to the interview and I have trouble getting him out. Sometimes I will give him five or ten minutes, but at other times I get the feeling that what he wants to say is more important and would require a half hour or more of talking and I am not able to carry on. Ultimately, after I have made a speech about having to go about my work, he will go with the attendant.

Yesterday his parents visited him after not having seen him for about a month. I requested that they not visit because it upset him and them. He had talked about some of the mutually upsetting things and said that their attitude made him much more agitated. On yesterday's visit they were apparently on friendlier terms. He was anxious to see them but said, 'I don't know what I am going to say to my father." He seldom mentions his mother.

Some of the content involved a feeling that in the Navy he had kept inaccurate records, and although he will not be more specific, he apparently feels that he committed some crime through his book work. He has also at times expressed the notion that the federal government was after him for incorrect income tax forms. He has intimated that his crimes will catch up with him and that somebody will come and get him.

I talked to his parents yesterday and the mother said that while they were sitting outside, the patient jerked his shoulders, at which she said, "Look what you're doing." He jerked them again and she said, "You did it again and you just read that in the book." Again he jerked them, again she said, "See, you did it again," and he smiled, which confirmed in her the notion that she had given him some insight.

In the interview Friday something happened which I don't understand. We had talked over their visit, and he seemed a little less tense and more comfortable. On leaving he said, "Do you sleep?" I said, "What do you mean?" He said, "Oh, I guess I realize that I am not the only patient in the hospital." He seemed on Friday to be much more outgoing and more relaxed on the ward.

SULLIVAN: What is he like?

KVARNES: He is 5'10", average weight. Pleasant-looking fellow. Short haircut and at times remains unshaven. He does not have a strikingly Jewish appearance. At times in his talk he gets a wild, hunted look.

SULLIVAN: I am trying to figure out what he would be like if he were not a patient. Trying to arrive at the obvious assets and liabilities.

KVARNES: He has been labeled handsome by some of the people around the place.

SULLIVAN: What I would like to know about anybody is largely missing. Some of it can be inferred, but none of it can be inferred very reliably. Starting from the present backward, which is certainly not the way I like to proceed, but it is sometimes necessary, we do gather that he has had some genital contact with women. That he came near, I gather, to marrying one. If he had any genital contact with her it was mutual manipulation, but anyway during his Navy career he did have some contact with loose women. He thought it was all unsatisfactory to them, I gather. He had some instances of precocious ejaculation, which would make him a member of the human race, male type. That he had an idea that his genitals were small and he has seen somebody else's. I suppose one's experience can be that private that one can have seen only one other penis in growing to this age. The next step— has he been able to establish any intimate relations with one of his own sex, and by intimate I mean the thing suggested on the auto trip, namely a great deal of free and revealing talk of himself and the other fellow. Then I have only to guess. I hear he made the trip with a chum. If he had a chum, that is jolly, but I would certainly be most enthusiastic to know about this phase that precedes his interest in women, when he would be either a success or a failure in establishing free and easy relations with another man. Even if I had no particular faith in developmental history (and I have very great faith in it), I could not overlook the fact that he was male, his friend was male, and therefore just to give an idea of what might be a wise basis for progress, I would like to know what experience he had in being frank, free and easy with members of his own sex. It is inferrable that he had a chum, but those inferences are risky. The whole history of his relationship with this man with whom he took the auto trip stands out as an exceedingly important field on which I have little data. Still, he did make the trip and they got as far as Kansas and they had an accident. I hope you know a lot about that accident. The shock of an accident to an unstable person would vary a good deal depending on whether the accident involved people other than the driving party and whether it seriously imperiled the life of his companion and finally himself, and the same with the accident on the return trip. These two people who had at least a speaking acquaintance were together three weeks or so, far, indeed, from home, and because it was a human contact not long before the appearance of a severe mental disorder, it would interest me deeply.

I hope you see why the interest in this. I am attempting to explore what I can expect to do as a man with a man, quite aside from the developmental importance of such events.

Then, before that, all I hear of his school years is scholastic with a little comment about his father's talking to the principal when the boy failed in something. But I suppose to most people in the school the scholastic aspects were of less importance than the social. Then I am permitted a very faint inference sometime or other, perhaps when he was in college, that he was acquainted enough with a girl so that he developed a love affair moving to engagement, mostly by mail. But all the competition and bullying and development of skills in maintaining some degree of peace and quiet and rest from the other boys in his earlier school, I hear nothing of that. Again I can infer something because there is some talk of sports, but I am pretty foggy about that.

Then below that, in childhood, I gather he had a Czechoslovakian nurse. I can't help but wonder whether she was Czech or Slovak, or something else. Seems to have been a wonderful boy only his kid brother developed a speech disorder. That looks like two or three Roman candles going off in the childhood situation. Anyway I can infer there is something important and because he was such a wonderful boy he seems to be throwing bricks at his father and mother throughout the course of his disturbed period, so I gather that adjustment to authority in the family and skill in manipulating the parents would be worthy of knowing something about. Might, in fact, be terribly important. Why? Because according to his hints and anything in the history, nothing has gone any too usual in this boy's development from his school entrance. He was a very bright boy there seems no doubt. In retrospect he does not seem particular about it, and in fact produces data which I distrust. I distrust it not because I think it is false, but seriously misleading, all this comment about plagiarism and such, I don't know what it means. It looks like things did not go so well but here again I don't know whether we are listening to pre-legal education, high school, grammar school, or what the hell. An exceedingly important development time factor is missing without which I won't have the foggiest notion which I am hearing about.

Those are the deficiencies in the information I was able to pick up which impressed me forcibly. There is a great deal of what one would like to know that seems to be denied us.

Just to take an amusing, except for the atrociousness connected with it, incident, he gets shock treatment at Springhill. He seems to describe it as being bound, gagged, and knocked out. That suits me fine, but he survived and what about the period afterwards? Well, to anybody who has fallen on their head or been punched in the jaw, there are some quite exciting incidents connected with recovering consciousness. That may be an abnormal interest of mine, since I was dropped on my head on the concrete steps the first year of my schooling.

You told one of the saddest stories I have heard in some time of trying to extricate yourself from an emotionally charged visit to the patient, taking fifteen minutes during which he had something on his mind that he wanted to tell you which faded when your convenience suited. I want to mention that because I want to remember it. That is one of the most tragic things in dealing with some disturbed patients, that if and when they do have something on their minds, it is improbable that we will get it because God knows there is no reason to suppose they will hold it for our convenience.

You see what I wish I knew about this boy. Maybe you can supply some of the data.

KVARNES: Back at the time that the attention was being directed to the younger boy, he was apparently a lone wolf in his playing, something he recriminates himself for. That would be the period from eight to ten.

SULLIVAN: He would then have been in grammar school?

KVARNES [nods yes]: He said that his games were playing ball with himself in the house, bouncing the ball against the wall, and he felt there was very little control of him by his parents, that he was allowed free coming and going as he wished, but at the same time there was a great protest against the lack of attention given him.

SULLIVAN: He then suffered a real feeling of neglect. Let us be sure about this. He now says that at that time—*at that time,* as he recalls it, he suffered a real feeling of neglect.

KVARNES: He says that, and says at that time he had some feeling of superiority in having as much freedom as he had.

SULLIVAN: As a person he has a feeling of superiority—in spite of hell and high water it has to be superiority over somebody else, and as he was in school at that time, does he mean by this feeling of superiority that he was glad that he was much less managed than most of the children he knew?

KVARNES: I don't know if he was glad. He does mention that he was aware at that time that he was.

SULLIVAN: Less managed than other children he knew?

KVARNES [nods]: And another reference to his younger brother.

SULLIVAN: I would not be surprised. I am asking you now specifically does he draw comparisons between his freedom of parental control and other boys he knew who were of his age?

KVARNES: Only by inference.

SULLIVAN: Let me say you don't know by inference. You can speculate but you don't know. Here the boy presents to you an experience which seems to be curious, at least interesting. That limits the apparent neglect of his parents, but you don't like the words "is proud of," but let's see, he comments on his superior freedom from management. Insofar as he is talking about having actually lived through these years, he is probably talking about something that can be made clear, and I don't know what the neglect by the parents and so on may have been compared with, and I am far from sure what his superiority about the comparative freedom refers to as a comparison. You may think that I am just harping on some little detail where you would have been content to speculate, but I am not. I am very anxious to know about such things as that. Do you see why? He now seems to be balled up about his parents and there are hints that he has been balled up about himself and other people of comparable position, and here we hear something about it and we are content to guess what he means by this neglect, but if one just thinks of oneself it becomes evident that these are comparisons—with whom? with what? At the age of eight his relationship with his younger brother is not the most important relationship in his life or if it is he is pretty sick already. The home situation is rather stipulated by the attitude of the parents, but the school situation has a considerable element of freedom if only from the contrasting background of many people in school. If his comparison can be referred to what he knew about others, then he knows what he is talking about.

What else have you?

KVARNES: You mentioned sports. He is an accomplished tennis player, but I don't think he has been in any team sport. I have not asked specifically. His relationship to his chums I have some data on. Apparently he has had friends with whom he was fairly intimate. He was able to talk over some problems of puberty with the boy with whom he compared penises. His parents describe a couple of relationships with school chums and college friends, and the boy who accompanied him was an intimate friend in college. The friendship carried through the war, and when the patient developed difficulty, the friend withdrew from his school course in order to accompany the boy on the trip. On the trip they frequently spoke of some of the patient's feelings. It was a reiteration, largely, of his disparaging attitude.

SULLIVAN: You have just the patient's statement. It was evident that he was well along in his disturbance. Therefore I would hear this but still wonder what went on. Just casually let me say that if a patient who sounds as well equipped for life in genetic factors as this boy, with his background that would give him a springboard into anything, I would think the outcome was fair, which is about as far as I can go, and to hear of a person as intensely interested in this young man as this so-called chum seems to be— *seems to be*—I can imagine people interrupting their school to take long trips to California without any love for the person who provides the transportation, but as long as there *seems to be*, there might be a valuable source of collateral information. Why? Because he can't possibly have as much at stake for concealing, distorting, and fixing information as the parents certainly will have. I would have my eye on this personal friend as a valuable source of data.

KVARNES: He says he has talked at times of his sexual inadequacy with other people. I have not tracked down specifically to whom, but in the Navy he said he talked to others about the feelings he had had.

SULLIVAN: What are the feelings? All I have heard is that he had intercourse with loose women and that it does not satisfy them and that he has a small penis. What are the feelings? Tell me about them. Do you know what he is talking about?

KVARNES: No, I don't.

SULLIVAN: If I say I think you have sexual inadequacy, have you the foggiest notion what I am talking about? If a patient talks about having a rotten spot in the back of his skull, I feel I am near to discussing something, but I don't know what he means. Statistically half the human race is sexually inadequate in feeling that their penis is not as large as some other penis that they know of, and if half the human race had those feelings they would feel inadequate to satisfy a woman, only they don't care, most of them. It seems to be pretty important to him. It might be worthwhile finding out what he is talking about.

KVARNES: The situation arose after he had been fortified by alcohol.

SULLIVAN: That makes him a regular member of the human race. Don't you think that most well people who decide to have a heterosexual experience and know anything about alcohol find it a great help? If he thinks it is sexual inadequacy, he is uninformed. Well, go ahead.

KVARNES: I don't know that I have other data on that.

SULLIVAN: Does this man impress you as the sort of a person who takes kindly to legal thinking? Have you been fairly well acquainted with a competent attorney? Have you noticed the difference in the way he approaches problems and the way a doctor does? Does he impress you as being comfortable in the legal, abstract way of thinking?

KVARNES: I would say not particularly comfortable. If I ask specific questions when I try to clarify what he means, he will switch off and get into another subject. The direct question and answer has not borne too much fruit.

SULLIVAN: Do you know that he's chosen one of the most difficult law schools in the world?

KVARNES: No. He was just there a month.

SULLIVAN: At the school, do you know whether there was any particular thing in that month that was especially difficult? Was he called upon for a recitation and made to feel like the droppings of a worm by the professor?

KVARNES: He mentioned that he was very fearful of being called upon.

SULLIVAN: Perhaps he heard somebody else called on. That does not seem to be particularly unusual.

He was seen by a doctor for what?

KVARNES: The first doctor he saw was a private practitioner.

SULLIVAN: But why did he see him? My interest about this law school business is to be understood in that this is the place where it seems any residual doubt about this man's adequacy for what he was trying to do disappeared. Everybody, including him, seems to be reasonably agreed that there is where he clearly broke down. So I get intensely curious as to what was going on there. Even though you believe in heredity, precipitating factors are sometimes quite revealing, and I wonder what happened to him in law school or what happened to other people so that he could imagine what was going to happen to him, what ailed him and whether he went to the doctor under his own steam or not, and whether he could tell the doctor what he was there for, because people who wind up in mental hospitals are not able to tell the doctor just what ails them.

I have taken a lot of time on this. What I have neglected to do is to thank you for this comprehensive and well-organized presentation. All of you get very little of that because there is so much else to do. I do not believe that one can avoid the necessity of making pretty good sense to a patient like this as to one's way of trying to satisfy one's interest, especially with a person who, like this patient, seems to be volunteering a great deal in the psychotherapeutic situation. The sooner one follows a certain method for getting clear on his present ideas or recollections of the past, there under consideration, the sooner one communicates to him that one is interested in how he grew and the sooner one decides the distortions of the current mental state. While there are probably a great many other ways of doing it, this business of dividing life into infancy, childhood, grammar school, up to the time when one gets interested in a chum and gets close to that person, much closer than anyone else, unless one can track through these stages then there are unresolved uncertainties as to what he means by a great deal of what he says later on.*

I am afraid you think here is a man with high intelligence, overprivileged family, and a good scholastic record despite his present views of himself, and a really successful career in the Navy, that he has broken down by a problem of heterosexual adjustment, and so far as I am concerned you might be right, but I would never know how this broke him down until I knew a great deal about the underpinnings which made the heterosexual adjustment such an unfortunate last straw. That is why I have gone to some trouble to emphasize these gaps in what would make me happy about my acquaintance with his history.

Now I am going to ask someone to summarize what has been heard. I am going to pick on Dr. Staveren. What are you sure of in the situation?

STAVEREN: He seems to come from a home where the parents are pretty insecure people who have felt it necessary to bolster themselves up with a good deal of ambition and a great deal of

* For an explication of Sullivan's concept of the developmental eras and their interpersonal significance, see Harry Stack Sullivan, *The Psychiatric Interview* (New York: W. W. Norton, 1954), pp. 142–146.

activity, but we don't know very much about them as people so
far. He was the older of two living children and seems to have
been neglected, that much is certain. Whether it was a matter of
just not enough to go around for two or something in the relationship between the parents at the time he was conceived or
born, I don't know. I would have to know something about the
relationship between the parents and him during the first few
years before the other brother was born. The whole story is one
of extremely low self-esteem. It may be the thing that accounts
for his dissatisfaction with his success. Although friendships have
been reported here and there, nothing has been said about real intimacy. Steps were made by him at discussing himself with some
of his friends, but the whole story sounds like a fairly isolated life.

KVARNES: He states at this time that he has never had anybody
with whom he could really talk about himself.

SULLIVAN: That despite this companion on the automobile trip.
Did you ask specifically if that included his friend on the trip?

KVARNES: No, I did not ask.

STAVEREN: From the observation that, for instance, he does
volunteer a good deal of information which is not informative, I
would say he probably has had very little experience in talking
about himself in a significant way. I notice a great lack of discussing his home and his family in any terms that would have something to do with living. I don't know whether he is completely
unclear about it or whether he is just too anxious to see his parents
as people and how they act and function and deal with him. The
thing that he must have observed, their own striving for success
and climbing, seems to be the technique he has adopted to deal
with his own low self-esteem. The thing that is missing is why he
has such a low opinion of himself.

SULLIVAN: Dr. Cohen, let's get your views of what we have
here.

COHEN: I would agree with what Dr. Staveren said. The outstanding thing is that he has told how much of a bastard he is
without telling what sort of a bastard he really is because none of
the things are really supported by the evidence. Yet we do know
he has a rather low opinion of himself and, as Dr. Staveren said,
that must have developed in the setting of the family, and certainly the parents seem to have been much more important to each
other. The hint is that the father must have been competing with

the mother in order to maintain a certain position in his own right and that neither of them had very much time for the children, except for the younger son when he drew them up by becoming a stammerer and did not bring much credit to the family.

A few of Dr. Kvarnes' remarks indicate some of the patient's hostility. One thing was the change in the Navy from destroyer escort to destroyer duty. First, I am inclined to push the onset of his overt illness back to about that period because I think that in the Navy, as contrasted to the Army, promotions were more on the basis of length of service. You would go up with the group, and most young officers would prefer destroyer escort because they have more responsibility and might even have had command of a ship. He chose the other duty. Something might have come up that was close to knocking him over at that time. I suppose it has something to do with underlying rage and hostility that he felt he was able to express as a gunnery officer whereas if he had been in more physical contact he might have been upset by actual direct hostility and might have broken down; this longer range thing made it possible for him to go through.

SULLIVAN: I don't know who else was in the Navy. I am particularly interested in having someone who was in the Navy comment on the interpersonal relationships that prevailed in which he had certain things required of him during the Aleutians part of his career, which was the early part. Who had naval service? Anyone besides Dr. Cohen?

WILL: I happened to be on the same type of ship which this young man transferred to. As far as the situation with people went, he did transfer from a ship which was somewhat comparable to a ship which is known to be an auxiliary. On a number of these small ships it is possible to show a considerable degree of emotional disturbance and be accepted. It was interesting to me to note how some of the officers were able to maintain a life almost completely separate from any close contact with associates aboard ship and not be considered abnormal. It was considered quite appropriate for an individual to be extremely hostile, outspokenly so, to all of his associates after a few months at sea, to have nothing to do with them even at mealtimes if the captain permitted, even aboard a small ship with nine or ten officers. An individual might be depressed and isolated socially and it was explained away as a protective measure against the extreme monotony. The transfer from the destroyer escort to the APD would be of some interest. Both duties were considered fairly good duties, and you could receive promotion in both. I would be interested to know whether he had personal difficulty aboard the DE because terrific antagonisms occur aboard that small a ship and if an individual is not quite comfortable with other people and can't quite lose himself in the healthy expressions of pleasure that are occasionally permitted a crew of a small ship, then any tendency toward isolation is increased.

SULLIVAN: Dr. Morris, I would like to have comment at this moment from you. The reason for my interest is that he comes from the Navy to law school where everybody would agree things were pretty bad. The Navy has a singular distinction from most of the types of life that people have been prepared for in overprivileged urban homes such as this—or for that matter, practically any urban home. I would like to hear Dr. Morris's views about the Navy life and about the patient's problem.

MORRIS: I was on a Liberty transport for a year and a half in which we went to various Pacific islands carrying troops, occasionally in combat areas but not too much combat. There were about fourteen officers and two hundred men. We found that many of the young ensigns who just came out of training found it very difficult to adjust, not knowing just what their role was. There would be the old-time Navy enlisted men and the chiefs, who often would take it out on the young ensign, and he would be a point of ridicule and it would be difficult to adjust to that situation. Some of them would sort of retire and let the chiefs run their department. Others would be on the defensive and try to take over the situation and seemed very miserable because of the ridicule and knowing the chiefs thought little of them. Perhaps one of the ways they were able to adjust was to join with the group in expressing hostility toward the skipper or the captain, who everyone thought was a son-of-a-bitch. One particular man, a rather quiet person, at first seemed to minimize such difficulty by spending much time in the communications office reading up on the manuals, and having little contact with others. He was found later on top of the Golden Gate Bridge thinking about suicide.

SULLIVAN: I will ask one question of all the Navy personnel

present. Would you be keenly interested in personalities and circumstances under which he had sought help about his personality difficulties on board? That might be an extremely risky adventure. That would occur to you as worth investigating?

COHEN: I would think so. It might be a point of departure. It might be an easier starting point than the family.

SULLIVAN: That is probably connected with great tension and might be most disastrous.

ROM: What was going on in the Aleutians?

SULLIVAN: Well, in the Aleutians it was nothing like urban life. It is an extremely depressing climatic situation. In some ways, since it was early in the war, the undercurrent of fear in the personnel was greater than much later.

WILL: I would say that some of these questions could be most aptly answered by referring to a little book called *Mr. Roberts*. If you glance through that you will find the state of mind of many officers who served on these ships. They did not have the pride that comes of being on a thoroughly virile combat vessel and yet the officers were subjected to considerable danger. However, in the little experience I had in the floating Navy, I saw few people who demonstrated fear of shipwreck or enemy action, except those people who night after night went on combat patrol. Other people suffered from a severe, chronic boredom. It required very little ability to perform, and they were forced to associate for long periods of time, day and night, with a small group of people. A man who was an ensign was never able to live alone because the Navy rewards advance in rank by increased isolation. The man in the lowest rank associates with the most people. On an APD an ensign lives with one other man. Aboard a small ship of that nature with long periods at sea, a man has a remarkable opportunity to spend a great deal of time considering himself and considering any failures on his part to adequately get along with other people. It seems that all your abilities fade away and your disabilities seem to be magnified. I should think for sensitive individuals it is a serious and difficult period of adjustment.

SULLIVAN: In developing useful contact with the patient, if one has some of these hunches, it often gives the patient a feeling that you are really making sense, that you are looking for things that matter and that you understand them. Since I have never been in the Navy, but have been interested in it chiefly because it is a part of the war where just the physical congestion of people can be very great, it is good to have some hunches about it so that one can enter into anything that comes up in that connection. As I say, I don't believe we are anywhere near the most important thing in this man's personality problem by concentrating on the capacity for heterosexual adjustment. That is the last and most easily discussed, but it is not going to tell the story.

WITT: One part I would be interested in learning more about is what the patient thought his parents would like to have him be—whether there is any connection between his ideas of what his parents would like and their overt or unpleasant ways of telling him, and between his father's record and his idea that he was so inferior. Also along with that and his feeling of having inferior genitals, what the reaction in the family was to puberty—whether any notice was taken of it and what their acceptance of it was.

KVARNES: The patient complained that there was no freedom of talk on sexual matters in the family. He has reviled the family because of that.

SULLIVAN: Have you gone to town on that topic? Tried to find out what he really was talking about? It is a general statement. Has he illustrated at all, told you about attempting to talk with his father and what happened?

KVARNES: Not specifically.

SULLIVAN: What I am getting at is that he has a blanket statement, "I am no good. I have never been any good." Then he goes on to say that it is his parents' fault, and everybody else's fault, and then occasionally he says, "For example, there isn't any freedom for talking about sexual topics in the home." That sounds as if it illustrated something. You have got to find out what he means by that.

KVARNES: Whether or not he made an attempt to talk?

SULLIVAN: Somebody must have. You want to know what this means. What I would have seen if I had been there. As long as it stays so general, one has the shocking experience later of discovering that one was wholly misled by this stream of generalities—that you did not get anything about the who or what he was talking about. Not demanding, not pinning them down, but just in the conversation asking the questions that will give you the notion of what it would seem like if you had been there, and then you have something you can trust. That is why we spent so much time on this damn Navy, but you have to be enough at home, and recall enough of experiences and development to ask them natural questions to expand the data. You might say, "Well, for example, did you ever ask your father about masturbation?" A natural inquiry. And he says yes or no, and then you want to hear about it.

STYRT: The thing that interests me in watching him is the question of team games. He plays baseball well, in a way that indicates he has had a fair amount of experience, and yet while playing he intimates that his performance is no good. He hits the ball well in a situation in which others cannot hit it, and yet he does not run out, not because he is tired or indifferent to the game, but because what he does is not of any moment. He will hit the ball out of reach and yet throw the bat down as though he had hit out.

Also, prior to his entering the service his father was probably a constant source of direction and perhaps stimulus. In the Navy he was under the direction of a more impersonal father. I am curious about how he reacted to that—whether he could go ahead and make his own acquaintances, and to what extent his father directed his acquaintances in the early years. This type of father frequently points out the best boy to be friendly with. It comes then to a situation where he must rely on his own choice.

COOPER: Earlier in the history Dr. Kvarnes mentioned that the patient had some feeling toward the dead sibling, and said that he would refer to it later, but he failed to bring it up.

KVARNES: When the father gave the sequence of siblings he got it backward and had the patient as the first child. When I discussed it with the patient, he talked about his mother's overactivity and said she lost another baby by running around too much, but he started to tear up and immediately went off of that to another subject.

WHEELER: I have wondered whether these other two siblings were boys or girls. Another thing, he has said nothing whatever about masturbation, either in childhood or now. I wonder about the silence and whether it may point to one of the things that have especially concerned him.

KVARNES: He has many times spoken of compulsive masturbation and has condemned himself for it. In answer to the first question, the firstborn was a boy and the stillborn I don't know.

SULLIVAN: When did this masturbation start and what do you mean by compulsive?

KVARNES: The masturbation started after he had been comparing penises with the other boy at the onset of puberty, and by compulsive he means the necessity of doing it more than once, or feeling compelled to masturbate on occasion.

DYAR: One thing which I was interested in was the attitude his mother had when the parents came to visit and she said to her son, "There, you did it again." A great many patients would take a comment like that as criticism and I wonder whether that's an example of the critical attitude that this mother has had all her life toward her son, and how much it explains his condition.

KVARNES: The parents have been hypercritical throughout. The father will constantly correct him at the table even now, and still they say there was little pressure on the child throughout his childhood. The patient's response to his mother, I think—and I base it on something previous—is, "My God, look how dumb they are." He brought a letter from his father to the office and read me the first page, which was generalities about the illness and included a suggestion that he keep trying to get well, and he made no comment, but his actions seemed to imply, "What a stupid remark." Also in the letter the father said, "We know you are somewhat improved," and he looked at me with a pleading look as if to say, "My God, why all the misinformation?"

ROM: The way this patient responds to greetings, my feeling is that he is thoroughly scared. He really recoils in terror when I greet him and then he looks at one as though about to ward off an attack. It is the same sort of thing I have seen in soldiers returning from Guadalcanal, an impending panic. I would give more weight to his Navy experiences than things that operated earlier.

SULLIVAN: You feel anybody who had the Navy career must be suffering from serious personality strain regardless of what he went in with?

ROM: At least the situation would have been different if he had not been in the Navy.

SULLIVAN: My God, we can all agree to that—that it would. Any long situation dealing with the same sex group. Everybody is somewhat different from having been in the Navy and you are inclined to think there is a lot to be found there, quite regardless of the earlier years. It immediately awakens in me the question, do you expect the mental disability rate among ex-Navy personnel to be very high?

ROM: Yes.

SULLIVAN: There is a chronic argument as to whether anyone, meaning everyone, has a point of stress at which they will break. I tend to sympathize with Dr. Rom as to the extraordinary character of much of the Naval life as compared with the Army service, but I don't believe the Navy has been terribly hard on its personnel, not to the extent that I would concentrate tremendously on it. I would think the Navy service here is of importance because it is a testing ground before serious disturbance and gave one time for recognition and harassment about one's inadequacies with very little opportunity to compensate or to have very good advice about them.

WAGNER: In listening to the story and trying to sense the disabling contact and events, I felt that the parents were insufferable, narcissistic, unstable people who had psychotic episodes and found their careers early of more importance than their children, so that the child was weaned at two months. This might have been the first shocking incident, followed perhaps, as Dr. Kvarnes related, by his surmise that being born following a stillbirth and being followed by another catastrophe meant that life was not very safe. The absence of information during childhood and puberty in a negative sense suggests that already he was finding fantasy more satisfying than realistic experience. He seems to have been a rather articulate patient. He relates profusely but in that area he has little to tell.

KVARNES: He has mentioned that he thinks he spent most of his childhood in fantasy. He does not tell me what or how.

WAGNER: He was wobbly in the Navy but he was successful. He was able to be a hero and was able to compete with his father and losing the support of the Navy was difficult for him. He was sustained by the hope that someday a satisfactory heterosexual adjustment would make life meaningful, and early found that this was socially imposed as a requirement.

I am very much interested in the early throes of the illness where he cried from time to time for his father and wanted to get in his father's bed. I wondered if in that there is some indication that a man can be saved. It seems to me that a schizophrenic who can cry for someone might be able to crawl back.

His sensitivity to cold and the shower and his feelings that the world round him is intruding on him make me feel his current protest is a need to deny body and self and whether the integrative experience to follow would be that you find his body and self acceptable. I wonder if any schizophrenic who has not had any secure relationship in the past on which he could count ever acquires that in the therapeutic relationship. Should he get well on that basis?

SULLIVAN: Have we a consensus on what ails this man or is there an open mind in some of you? And secondly, do you think that he has any sequelae from the shocks that he had? Does anyone feel that this is not at all a typical case of schizophrenic disturbance? If so, I wish you would say what you think about it.

SALZMAN: I am not at all sure that it is schizophrenia. I did not feel that he uses schizophrenic mechanisms in handling his difficulties except for the withdrawal and the tendency to avoid contact with other people and intimate relationships with other people, but that so often is a history of severe neurosis as well as schizophrenia.

SULLIVAN: Anyone else? The thumbnail sketch of his complaints is that he has an extraordinarily disparaging attitude. No one entertains the idea that he might be an affective disorder? . . . I hear comments about his having tension and agitation. The person that reports is, and has to be, somewhat of a target person, which is not fair, but you are all more interested in learning something than suffering. I really want to know what you mean by his being *tense*. It is one of those nasty words that may or may not be capable of being described.

KVARNES: When seen in the office he is in constant motion. He is picking at his fingernails or moving in his seat or he gets up and moves around the room. There is much sucking on his lip. On the ward he is in constant motion, pacing back and forth in his room or up and down the corridor. When the telephone rings he jumps. He tells me he almost panics when his name is called.

SULLIVAN: There is an approach to everything in psychiatry of importance which I wish I could ingrain in all of you so that it would always be very handy to your awareness when dealing with patients. Everything begins. Everything begins, and if it has gone on perfectly smoothly then that is one thing, but if there has been change, that change has been dated and is capable of being placed if there is any promise of attempt to work with a patient. In other words, where there has been an insidious change over a period of years, my experience, and even proxy experience, suggests that there is stupendous difficulty in making a therapeutic attack, but everything that one wants to talk about with this patient can probably be dated, and this sensitiveness to things like the telephone and to being greeted gives a classic example, as "When did you begin to notice being so tense about the telephone?" I am not just trying to get things strung on a line of time to make a nice record, but if I can get him to look back at a significant change, then I can ask a good deal about the circumstances and quite often by that simple expedient one can learn a great deal of data in which you can make valid inferences, valid guesses of what might be the significant pressure to which he was exposed at that time. A number of things strike you, namely, this business of cold showers. There must have been times when he had to take cold showers. What were the circumstances of that? When did it occur? With this simple-minded type of inquiry one can get started on a markedly personal discussion. Does he suppose it might be because of so and so in this story? If you ask fairly sensible questions, fairly commonplace questions, he will probably be able to give you some hints as to what matters. What does matter? In a very broad way, what ails him is that he has not felt that he was an adequate human being. We all agree to that. He felt he was nowhere near that. Two aspects, and one of them I am especially glad to remember to mention. No matter how inadequate a human being he has been convinced at various times and stages of development he might be, he has actually gotten away with a great deal as if he were an adequate being. That is to no one's discredit. It is offered as an attack against his position. "You say you have been no good, but actually you did so and so." Put him on the spot to prove it, and he comes to see that you esteem the performance. We don't want patting on the back. With a politician father and mother he must have been born into pats on the back, but he has to defend himself so far as I am concerned on having several years of naval work and having gotten through the university. He is going to discover that he has not been as total a loss as he may at the moment feel, and in defending himself he is apt to tell you a lot about what ails him. There is a distinct difference in trying to defend a position and merely supporting a position, and the attitude you take is, "Hell, you are not such a total loss," which relieves the anxiety.

Step by step, with this man—first the developmental scheme, his life data, is important because it gives you an idea when to inquire about things, and with this double orientation of knowing what you are after and inquiring about it at the right time the patient gets the impression we know a hell of a lot more than we do. It is helpful in organizing one's inquiry and impressing upon the patient that the personal history makes sense. That life is not as incomprehensibly deplorable as it may seem in his present state.

Dr. Wagner has brought up a terribly important consideration, namely, what can be the therapeutic effect of patient and physician. I can't touch greatly on that but we can pick up another point in that connection, namely this Dr. W who tangled with him, more or less, at Springhill. You have data from Springhill and I am frank to say I wonder how good it is, but what do they say? They must have noticed something before they gave him shock. What did they claim ailed him?

KVARNES: General resistance to talking, not a muteness, but a hostile, objecting attitude toward the whole hospitalization, plus the tenseness and agitation, plus the lack of willingness to talk out his problem.

SULLIVAN: That might show his superior intelligence, too. Is any comment made about what was attempted in this alleged psychotherapy, this intensive work supposedly, which wound up with his being invited to the doctor's home? Any note about that man's opinion? Tell us what you surmise about it.

KVARNES: I can't suggest the doctor-patient relationship in that case. Somewhere in the course of our talks, he said he had talked with Dr. W about things, mostly nebulous things. He talked in psychiatric terms about anxieties and pressures and his responses, and said he did not gain anything from it.

SULLIVAN: In these notes, is there any comment about homosexuality? Seems almost too good to be true that it was not gone into. No comment about latent homosexuality?

KVARNES: No comment. They labeled him schizophrenic.

SULLIVAN: I surmise one or two things about his intensive psychotherapy by Dr. W. Either it was so utterly obscure for a variety of reasons that nothing much happened except that the patient became more disturbed as to his prospects and worried himself to death about whether he was going to rapidly get worse, or was deeply puzzled about what he could do to help himself. Or the other one is that Dr. W's thinking aimed at and perhaps obscurely wandered around the problem of whether this patient was a homosexual.

I think a good many of you probably do wonder whether this man has been, is, or will be homosexual. I think there are few better topics for precipitating an aggravation of a schizophrenic illness than galloping into that field. Yet he seems to be very uncomfortable and I gather not only with the doctor but with the ward personnel, and with practically every contact he has, with perhaps the notable exception of this game of checkers where apparently he did not show quite the same performance that he does at other times.

STYRT: I was on that evening and when I came up he told me he wanted to have one of the other patients in this four-bed room moved into another room. He said he was afraid of him. He couldn't stand still and he looked scared. I told him I would see what I could do. I went back to the ward office and when I walked past the door again the patient was lying across the bed with his pajama pants half off and the other patient was sitting on his bed groaning. The next day the patient was so disturbed that I gave him a sedative. I made no attempt to talk to him other than to reassure him and he made no attempt to talk to me.

SULLIVAN: There is no ideal psychiatric tool that one person can pick up, but a fairly safe question in a thing like that is "How does he bother you?"

STYRT: That was about the way I asked it and he became agitated and walked away.

SULLIVAN: I am afraid, as is the case with a good many of the younger patients, behind the screen of his more or less continuous restlessness and tension, there is an approach to a pretty panicky feeling, and it is not at all uncommon to find if one can enter the field with safety that what with bum hunches, with books, and with contact with other mental patients and possibly with actual experiences, the patient has become greatly disturbed about some-

thing he refers to as his homosexuality, or fear of it, and this incident that Dr. Styrt mentions sounds like one of these unhappy
schizophrenic adventures into something like fascination with
homosexual possibilities. It is a very obscure business, anything
but simple, and easily translated into a system of motivation. I am
poking around here trying to show the background and some of
the risks to what I very much want this patient to tell me.

Now, what the hell worries him? He says "I am no good, I have
never been any good." Well, all right, but why are you restless
and frightened by the telephone? There is no relation between
that content and the evident muscular restlessness and so on. His
statement of what ails him and what we can see ails him, we are
wholly inadequate to explain.

I must be prepared to meet a pretty grave crisis in our relationship when I ask this because if he immediately starts referring to
his very much more disturbing ideas of sexual inadequacy, then
I must be able to handle this or the therapeutic situation might be
completely ruined or the patient may go into panic, and one must
be prepared with a lively plan of action before one attacks the
problem of finding out what really ails this patient. One of the
great virtues is that you can get good hunches about this in
situations where this demand is not made. As long as somebody
is telling you about their past there is a feeling that that is easier
than what I am panicky about now. You get a world of information out of that. Now, what really is haunting you all the time?
Let us suppose that the patient says, "Doctor, I am a homosexual."
What do you do then? The relationship during the panic may
cause lamentable entanglements with other people, may be
wrecked at the patient's leisure, or close the door to recovery.
What does one do?

Well, here is something that is done. You can hear what is said.
You can presume it does not mean what you think. You can
notice it is damn important to the patient and you can say something which indicates you have survived the blow. That you
don't think it is as awful as he thinks you might think. If you
realize you don't know what the patient is talking about, then
your views are not significant. Still the patient may assume that
your thinking agrees—that is the horrible thing about you. So,
this is a risky business that the patient thinks he is homosexual, or
knows he is homosexual. The next move has to be as automatic

and spontaneous as—"Now, what in the world makes you think so?" You will have to work your own way out of that. You must be prepared for the statistically most frequent response: "Well, you know damn well I am, Doctor." What do you do then? There must not be stuttering and stammering and obscure retreats into asking irrelevant questions. There has to be something done now which reduces the anxiety. So, as the patient comes back at me, "You know I am homosexual," I say, "Well, I don't know what you mean by being homosexual—it had not occurred to me. What makes you think you are? Do you know anything that points that way?" And the patient always does. I am trying to put them on the spot so that they can defend their position. Set up any reason in the world for this queer idea that you are homosexual. There is no telling what I will hear. I will hear that he has had 4,572 unquestionably homosexual entanglements with men. I must still do something, and what? It is irrelevant in this patient, but suppose I actually did hear about a homosexual experience, then I would proceed to inquire about the circumstances. Did he seek it, or was it forced on him? Just commonplace inquiries before the final movement, but in this boy all I can say is that he finds himself interested in other people's genitals, and wishes they were interested in his, and feels funny sensations in his mouth and every time anybody lights a cigarette he has to rush to the toilet. I must get in now because I want my last act to work. The last act is when I think I have got enough, when the person does not seem to be as tense as he was at the great admission, then I gaze into the future and say, "Oh, yes, I can see how it looks that way to you now." Then I am through. I feel I have done everything I can to meet a great risk in a fashion that will protect my relationship with the patient and prevent him from going into a panic over now we know he is a homosexual and it is horrible. If I have something to talk about that does not deny, but which indicates that he may be wrong, I feel that is sufficient. That carries the implication that we will talk some more.

Now I want to say something because I am inclined to think that either fear of homosexuality or something almost as bad will come out if he is really honest. I want to talk a little further about the whole notion of the awful things that ail patients, particularly schizophrenics. I know no reason to believe that schizophrenics—any particular schizophrenic in front of me—are startlingly different from anybody else. It is going to be a matter of timing of events, and if a person is really repeatedly restricted to sexual relations with members of his own sex only, then in all reasonable probability the therapeutic problem is what blocks his freedom to the other sex, and if a person is convinced that he is an unprincipled scoundrel concerned only with such acts, what has stopped him from developing beyond that.

Again from the developmental standpoint—all these things that represent appalling mistakes in the overprivileged—my attack will be in that direction. In other words, I can conceive of nothing being accomplished by studying homosexuality from some of the fashionable notions that it is more or less inborn and how can you make a good adjustment to it. I am not telling you you can cure every case by any technique I have ever discovered but I am telling you now if a person is schizophrenic or very disturbed over alleged peculiarities of sex life then the attack on that person who obviously has not been able to fit into life on an adult pattern is to find out why they could not get further.

WITT: Where you spoke of this build-up to nondirect and perhaps therefore more meaningful assurance that you don't think he is simply horrible because of his admission of homosexuality, is there any place for saying that perhaps there is in this homosexuality some implicit arrest in development and that it is possible to go ahead with it and that things like homosexuality are not viewed by everybody in all society as necessarily bad?

SULLIVAN: If a person is coming for treatment because of difficulties in living outside a mental hospital in which one's sexuality is alleged to be important, rather than having views about homosexuality, my approach is that it is not the only thing that is making you have difficulty with people—it never is. I want to know all the difficulties one has, as well as the fact that one follows a homosexual pattern of life. Generally there are glaring defects in living as well as this homosexual pattern of life, and quite frequently these are closely related to the why and wherefore of the homosexual pattern, but when it comes to disturbed people, I never enter into this business of homosexuality and what about it, until the patient has accepted it as part of a relatively commonplace problem. Everything you have in mind can be handled only by indirection. It may be the basis of your statement to the patient, but it can never be presented in such a way because it is obviously at great variance to the patient's moral conscious attitude and therefore with schizophrenics it may be taken as eyewash or evidence of your unworthiness or lack of understanding. I have never found anything that is safe in these critical situations with schizophrenics who pop this out of the bag. You have all these views and they may come in handy after the topic has lost all its anxiety. We have to be pretty skillful to keep them on a topic and to know that they are following us, and with the schizophrenic, particularly with such a topic, that is a trick. It has got to get down to be something like lifesize. Then the technique should be brought up in questions, and the patient says: ". . . this loathsome thing that I do." Then I say: "Loathsome—powerful word. What are you trying to tell me about this loathsome practice?" If the patient will go along with me, and says, "Well, Doctor, doesn't everybody feel it is loathsome?" I feel here is a genuine inquiry, then I can volunteer the sort of thing you have in mind.

Comment on First Session,
Twenty-five Years Later, December, 1971

About twenty-five years after the original case seminar met, four faculty members of the Washington School of Psychiatry— John Dillingham, Stanley Jacobson, Robert Kvarnes, and Irving Ryckoff—met to study the seminar as "original Sullivan material" and to consider how the seminar might be prepared for publication. After the first "comment seminar," Gloria Parloff was invited to help work the material into publishable form. The discussion seminars took on a life of their own, including questions, disagreements around some of the original seminar material, and the addition of supplemental historical and personal data that helped to clarify the original seminar sessions. Since the members of the comment seminar discussed the original sessions in sequence, the appropriate comments have been appended to the transcripts of each of the original sessions.

KVARNES: At the first meeting of the seminar in October, Dr. Staveren presented a case. For the second meeting I volunteered to present this case, because it was a good articulate schizophrenic, and we decided to proceed with it. I presented in the last five of the six meetings of the seminar.

RYCKOFF: The material we now have includes the five meetings? I've got five separate chapters. The material you are handing us is——

KVARNES: Is one Sunday meeting. We stayed with the case for five meetings. In the course of it I got more anxious and less free in divulging material. The last meeting was a series of questions we prepared for Sullivan, and they're interesting.

JACOBSON: Very interesting in so many different ways. First of all the cast of characters in this seminar—I assume Philip Wagner and Sam Novey——

KVARNES: And Edna Dyar and Herb Staveren, and Bob Cohen and Mary White——

JACOBSON: Who's Cooper?

KVARNES: Larry Cooper and Jerry Styrt; John Witt, Stan Peal, Joe Rom—they were Sheppard residents. There were about a half dozen of us. Charlie Wheeler was another.

We could either talk here about our reactions to what we're reading or talk about what to do further with this series of meetings. I really think I'm going to try to do something with it. I think it needs a substantial editing job, both on my stuff and on everybody else's—knock out some that's not significant, and also edit Sullivan a bit if necessary. The verbal flow doesn't seem to come off very well in the reading, but I think that could be improved with Gloria's help. If the seminar is published we should indicate that in order to make it flow as written material we edited it, not to change the thrust or the form or anything like that but just to bring it into readable form.*

RYCKOFF: A lot of it should be condensed, people making these single comments——

KVARNES: Some of those are useful only in demonstrating how a guy reacts anxiously to Sullivan's questioning under fire. They are vague and uncertain.

JACOBSON: Like after your long introduction, he says, "What is he like?" It's amazing to me that anybody could put himself in the position you put yourself in, could present that intensively in——

* Sullivan has in fact been edited very little, but otherwise the general editing procedure suggested here has been followed.

RYCKOFF: Didn't you know Sullivan at this point?

KVARNES: I only knew of him; I had only seen him at the previous meeting of the seminar. As time went on I got constricted to some extent in what I would present. I think I got "nervous in the service." But also I didn't come away feeling butchered. Even in the incident which he calls "one of the most tragic stories," of my trying to extricate myself from the emotionally charged patient. I did not resent that because it was helpful. The interesting part of it was that I didn't mention to him that I had smelled homosexual panic; and I went around the hospital—both during the work day and after hours when we were drinking beer in the bachelors' quarters—sounding people out about how to handle this, admittedly in a very tentative fashion. I was quite uncertain how to deal with it, but I couldn't get any help. Nobody picked up my concern, and what struck me in the rereading of this seminar was that Sullivan sensed it. He answered my question even though I didn't ask it because I was scared to. I came away feeling that that was an immensely significant learning experience. In that particular instance he gave me a framework for dealing with the panic situation, in which one says, in effect: "Well, what are you talking about? You know, I hear what you are saying but let's put it into an understandable framework." Once you can do that your own anxiety goes down and it becomes manageable. Second thing was the significance of building a bridge to the next time of meeting, after a schizophrenic has told you something he thinks is awful; one of the things you do is to indicate it isn't so awful you won't see him again. He lives with that kind of "all or nothing" anxiety. I had sensed that but never heard it put into those kinds of words. That was very useful. I have always tried to do that since.

JACOBSON: I felt—I don't know how you reacted but I felt Sullivan dealt with that whole thing very sensitively for the whole group.

KVARNES: Absolutely.

JACOBSON: Everybody stayed clear of it until the end, when Sullivan——

KVARNES: "Homosexual panic" hadn't been stated. There is one thing that seemed more apparent to me before than it is now. I had had the feeling that he was laying for somebody who would make a diagnosis of a "homosexual panic"—that he was just waiting for somebody to say that so he could jump all over him. Now when I read it this time, I didn't get that feeling. Did you others?

RYCKOFF: I can see your basis for feeling that way because he puts a great deal of emphasis on getting facts and history. You can hear Sullivan pinning you down—"Do you know this? What happened then?" He keeps pinning you down all the time. It would make me leery of sticking my neck out to make a broader generalization based on an intuitive sense of what was going on. Because the implication of this kind of emphasis on history is that he would then say, "Where the hell is your data?" I came out of it with two kinds of thoughts: One is that he does believe that there is something to be gotten out of careful history-taking— that it helps you to delineate the developmental phases of the patient, get a notion of where he's at in terms of general development. But the second one, which interests me more, is that he uses history as a way of making a connection with the patient, as a way of demonstrating to the patient that you have taken the effort to try to understand what's happened to this man in the course of his lifetime, and that that's a coin of exchange, a means by which he gains a little bit of confidence in your attempting to reach out to him, to understand what's going on. In the second case, the facts per se become less important than the use to which they are put in the ongoing relationship.

DILLINGHAM: He says that rather explicitly in the second session. He talks about inquiring about the patient's feelings, and he says, "I don't care much what is said, but as long as I am seriously trying to get something said, it is possible that he will begin to draw comparisons that are free from these jittery background feelings and . . . there is something for a discussion." But I think that also is an implication that it is a way of reducing panic in you, that you then get some hard data you can use.

KVARNES: Les Farber had a phrase about therapy that I felt was a good one—that you help the patient write his own history, in effect.

DILLINGHAM: Perfect.

KVARNES: His own life, and it comes out in the way Sullivan asks his questions. One of the things, I don't know if it's explicit here, but he was always talking about making it clear to the patient where you are going with your inquiries. That the questions are not just shots in the dark and anxiety-provoking things but they are going someplace. That comes back to your point, Irv, I think, that it's a method of building the relationship.

RYCKOFF: I just remembered, you mentioned Sam Novey. Did you know that just before he died Sam had written a book on history? This was about five years ago now, and I guess it comes back to me because it had some of the overtones vis-à-vis some of the things we are talking about now—Sullivan's use of history.

JACOBSON: I was interested in how much he emphasized the Navy experience, and I wonder to what extent he was doing that for the sake of all those guys around the room who happened to have been in the Navy, and was being a sensitive kind of supervisor—giving them an opportunity to come on board where they could come on board. It surprised me that so many of the men in the room had had Navy experience.

RYCKOFF: It was 1946, right after the war.

KVARNES: But many more Navy than others—not Air Force, not Army.

DILLINGHAM: I was impressed with the effort he put into—I don't know whether it is just another dimension of what you are describing—of really trying to isolate the Navy experience as opposed to the Army or the Air Force, the Marine Corps. He really had a sense—which I certainly didn't have, and don't have very clearly—that it was a very different experience from the other services and that its difference maybe was important.

KVARNES: I had a hunch on that, too—the homosexual problem is greater in those tight quarters.

RYCKOFF: I thought another value of his doing that—whether he had it in mind or not—was to make it clear to the fellows who were there, who had been in the Navy, that their experience, their sense of what Navy life was like, could be used as a relevant way of getting in touch with this patient. Even now, after all these years, I tend to think when I listen to a patient describing his world that mostly has nothing to do with my world, my experience, that there is considerable distance one has to overcome. And he demonstrates that the patient's being in the Navy had something to do with the experiences of many of those in the seminar.

JACOBSON: I think that comes through in lots of ways. I would be hard put to pick them out, but that is really a simple, philosophical notion of his, that we are all part of the same bag.

KVARNES: Where he asks, "What is he like?" my response is

I think an interesting one because I had gone on presenting a history without any clear idea of what I was doing, certainly not how it was to be responded to. Then when he says, "What is he like?" I went into a very concrete response, I think partly because I didn't understand the question and partly because I was anxious about it, and maybe because I thought I had already said what he was like—which I hadn't. I had responded as I had done in Air Force write-ups on people I saw. We would give a physical description, and then tell what kind of a guy he was, how he was coming across to you as a person, trying to arrive at some of the obvious assets and liabilities; you know, say, "He's been labeled handsome"——

JACOBSON: Once you introduced the notion that Sullivan had the homosexuality in mind all along, giving everyone a chance to bring it out, which they might very well have because it's a special issue on shipboard, then I began to wonder whether the question "What is he like?" was reaching for some of those dimensions too—is he effeminate—a virile guy? How does he come on as a human being?

KVARNES: His response was to go into the sexual history right then—about difficulty in contact with women, premature ejaculation. The young typist read this section and said she was surprised that the homosexual thing hadn't come up earlier, because that's what she thought right away. Now, a whole generation later, it is very easy, but goddammit, we didn't talk about it then, and he himself, as you can see, is tentative.

RYCKOFF: It is striking, the fact that it is a generation later; it does have a dated sound, and part of it comes from what you are implying, that the kind of perspective which is now common wasn't available—it was just beginning to be thought of.

DILLINGHAM: When you are talking about this Czechoslovakian nurse, "I can't help but wonder whether she was Czech or Slovak" —that kind of thing really frustrates me—the particularization, the focusing down on such data.

KVARNES: I don't know what he himself would do with that, except that he would be interested, might have some ideas about the difference, and probably the same point of the value of inquiry again. That conveys a considerable degree of respect for one's experience, when you ask that kind of question. Then, his phrase here, right in that line, "Seems to have been a wonderful boy, only his kid brother developed a speech disorder. That looks like two or three Roman candles going off in the childhood situation."

JACOBSON: Couple of places where I thought he used rather nice metaphors—where he had more of that kind of flair than I had anticipated.

RYCKOFF: You mean that kind of freer, more poetic kind of——

JACOBSON: Yeah. Also, there's an interesting personal note in one paragraph above where Sullivan comments, "I was dropped on my head on the concrete steps the first year of my schooling" —wouldn't that make him five years old? Who is dropping him on his head when he is five years old? Another kid? Father playing with him? Some kind of horseplay? He's not an infant dropped on his head.

KVARNES: Referring again to his style of expression, remember when the patient is talking about the small penis—Sullivan says, "Statistically half the human race is sexually inadequate in feeling that their penis is not as large as some other penis that they know of, and if half the human race had these feelings they would feel inadequate to satisfy a woman, only they don't care, most of them. . . .

[Laughter]

DILLINGHAM: But still it ends on that sardonic kind of thing, "It might be worthwhile finding out what he is talking about."

KVARNES: Then this next point was a good one, about being fortified by alcohol, where Sullivan says, "Don't you think that most well people who decide to have a heterosexual experience and know anything about alcohol find it a great help?" Lots of people don't.

JACOBSON: But that's another example of the way he includes himself and the patient in the same universe.

KVARNES: Another thing in this that's of significance is that there was a real attempt to pin down where the illness got started, and I didn't know that at the time. I wasn't thinking in those terms. Was it at law school? Was it while he was in the Navy? Was it while he was on this trip to California? And he would come in and try to narrow it to where it actually got kicked off because he wants to know what the events were immediately preceding it, and it's quite true that they are not here. I'm not sure that they ever came out.

RYCKOFF: That's the kind of thing that I find hard to deal with. That is, it often sounds to me as if in Sullivan's preoccupation with being specific and scientific and sticking to data, and so on and so forth, that he is demanding more of the phenomenon of human behavior and human illness than it can produce. That is, is it that specifiable? I mean, can you say when the illness began in objective terms? I feel that he pushes. Most of us, I would guess, nowadays, or even then, would not, might not try to push the material to that point of specificity, to say the boy is well on day 6, but on day 7, this is the situation.

KVARNES: I think one of the points here is that where you've got somebody who seems to be an acute schizophrenic, you would look to that. Most of the people we see have gradual onsets of neuroses and we don't see these acute, abrupt illnesses. But the other thing that was emphasized is that "everything begins," which is a very good formulation—if you don't know how to deal with some symptom or phenomenon, start sorting it out on a historical chain.

RYCKOFF: I suppose it's part of the feeling I have that nowadays my own general approach would be somewhat more in terms of the experiential than the chronological. This sticks to finding facts, to detailing history. Nowadays don't people approach this kind of work more in terms of detailing the experience, not solely the facts? The whole process of involvement with a patient, it seems to me, could be described more as tuning in on the patient's experience, not——

DILLINGHAM: But what if the patient can't do that? Isn't that a form of, sort of teaching the therapist how to teach the patient how to sort out some of the realities about the shape of his experience? Like you are saying later on that you need to recite some facts to the patient, something that he can't dispute—in terms of reassurance, so that you first have to state it as a fact, as nothing one can argue about.

JACOBSON: I'm still having trouble with what you are saying. For one thing, I think Sullivan is not dealing with a patient here but with a therapist, and when he tries to sort out the onset of the illness I would assume for him the onset of the illness has a diagnostic significance. If the illness begins in the middle of the long trip with the friend, or begins when he is in a situation where the major psychological stress is competition with other people, it has one or another kind of significance to it. I assume that's the kind of thing he's trying to get to.

RYCKOFF: I was contrasting the question of getting to it by finding out how the patient experienced these——

DILLINGHAM: I think that what he is saying in effect is that you can't very effectively or responsibly ask him how he felt about the trip unless you have some real sense of the trip. That you don't know where you are going unless you get some sort of map points that are factual too, and he says that the patient feels very anxious when he feels you are asking questions in the dark, that you don't know why you are asking.

JACOBSON: This little sentence: "At the age of eight his relationship with his younger brother is not the most important relationship in his life or if it is he is pretty sick already," you know, has a lot in it. One way of looking at what Sullivan does sometimes is to see it as generalizing—another way might be to see it as stereotyping. For example, when he says, "Does this man impress you as the sort of person who takes kindly to legal thinking? Have you been fairly well acquainted with a competent attorney? Have you noticed the difference in the way he approaches problems and the way a doctor does? Does he impress you as being comfortable in the legal, abstract way of thinking?"

KVARNES: Sullivan was in touch with that because some of his best friends were lawyers. One of his big supporters was Randolph Paul, who was the foremost legal tax expert at the time, and Paul brought onto the board of the Washington School of Psychiatry Abe Fortas and Justice Douglas, also acquaintances of Sullivan's at that time. And I know on several occasions when patients consulted with Sullivan about something like a marital problem he made it very clear that they didn't need a psychiatrist, they needed a lawyer for the way they were going about it, the way they were thinking about it.

But let's jump to another good passage, much later, where Sullivan says, "I think a good many of you probably do wonder whether this man has been, is, or will be homosexual"—one nice way of introducing, "I think there are few better topics for precipitating an aggravation of a schizophrenic illness than galloping into that field." I've always felt so damn grateful for the part where Sullivan says, ". . . the patient says, 'Doctor, I am a homosexual.' What do you do then?" and so on. "Well, here is something that is done. You can hear what is said. You can presume it does not mean what you think." What the patient thinks *you* think is damned important. You can say something to the patient which indicates that you have survived. Without false reassurance or lessening the significance of the information.

JACOBSON: That's a point that I think is still not really universally understood in helping people, the importance of saying something that might not get any kind of significant response but saying it only to indicate that you've survived the blow.

RYCKOFF: The patient has said something which to him is awesome and you have said OK on it.

JACOBSON: I'm still here. Right.

DILLINGHAM: And it's a great ending, too. "Oh yes, I can see how it looks that way to you now."

KVARNES: It respects the reason for communicating without necessarily agreeing with the patient's conclusions.

DILLINGHAM: Also a marvelous illustration, a sort of microscopic illustration of what he is talking about—something having a beginning, a middle, and an end.

JACOBSON: There seems to be an assumption with everybody in the seminar—with Sullivan—that there is plenty of time, that it takes time, that you move slowly. What brings it to mind, Cohen says about his Navy experience that "it might be an easier starting point than the family," and Sullivan says, "That is probably connected with great tension and might be most disastrous." Seems to be saying, stay away from that kind of thing for now. And that brings to my own mind the current thinking that treatment takes too long, that there just is not time.

RYCKOFF: Should be shorter.

JACOBSON: Yes, should be shorter. But whether it *can* be shorter is a current issue in psychotherapy, I think.

RYCKOFF: Even in the situations where there is more justification for thinking of short-term therapy, it still is an issue. There is a question of how much time is needed. The experiential kind of therapy, encounter group therapy, poses an opposite kind of question—I'm fascinated by how much opposite it is because it's based not on sorting out, understanding, putting together, and so on, but on transformation, some kind of internal experience by which everything is changed, and I suppose everybody is fascinated by even the idea that that can be done; it's as close to magic as anybody can think of. I myself keep feeling that it is very deceptive, but I'm even more suspicious of my own negative reaction. Because it scares me to think it can be done. Scares me about myself personally—not to mention my profession for all these years.

JACOBSON: Well, I don't have your doubts about it. I mean, having been deeply involved in a lot of short-term intensive group work, I think it has a lot of significance. But I don't think it has anything to do with the therapy we're discussing. Lots of events in life can make dramatic changes for you at some level, but you're still the same kind of human being with the same kinds of dispositions to react.

RYCKOFF: Well, this isn't the time to try to do it, but sometime for my own benefit I'd like to specify what those levels are—for example, ego capacity to effect ego change. All these families of schizophrenics I have spent some years with—the evidence is that the families are just as crazy as the patient, thought disorders are just the same; all this documentation that we get from Laing and so on is old hat—a lot of us have known about it for a long time, that really within the family the schizophrenic is quite normal. But how do you account for the fact that the father, the mother, and the siblings are not in the same hospital in the same ward? They are doing everything they are supposed to do—these crazy people—that same ego capacity enables them to do that, to somehow contain the thought disorders.

KVARNES: We're running out of time.

II

Case Seminar, December, 1946

This session follows the format previously established—the case presentation by Kvarnes, the posing of a discussion question by Sullivan, his exchanges with each of the participants, and his extended closing comments on major clinical issues that he picked out of the morning's seminar.

In Session II, new members were Samuel Novey, of the Sheppard staff; Mary White [Hinckley], of the staff of Chestnut Lodge; and Stanley Peal, a resident at Sheppard. Also present were Larry Cooper, Robert Morris, Joseph Rom, Leon Salzman, Herbert Staveren, Jerome Styrt, Philip Wagner, Charles Wheeler, Otto Will, and John Witt.

KVARNES: I have continued to see the patient on an average of five times a week for anywhere from forty-five minutes to one and three-quarters hours, mostly office visits, with only an occasional ward visit. I thought I would review the case by adding new material which would bring the old material to mind. I have tried to follow the questions that were asked, in an effort to fill in the history.

The earliest other-than-family relationship that I can establish is with a boy who lived in the apartment below. Apparently the friendship started at three or four and has continued to the present, with occasional correspondence. This boy, Jim, was also of Jewish parentage and there is a rather interesting family relationship as Bill, the patient, sees it. They played almost exclusively at the playmate's home. Bill seemed to be very interested in going to Jim's house and engaging in various games and using Jim's toys. Jim's father was a rather jolly man who played along with the children at times and the patient apparently came to feel that this man was different from his own father, who was more aloof, with less tendency to be interested in the boys' play activities. I have not been able to establish clearly as yet why there was reluctance to bring Jim to the patient's home. He said his home was so disorderly, there was no organization, nobody ran the home, and he did not have the right kind of toys; and yet there is a great deal said about the father's being indulgent in that respect. The patient could have had anything he wanted. He told me about going to movies with Jim and how they frequently would act out the movie, playing the various parts, and even the love scenes. There was some difficulty in telling this, suggesting that he felt it was unusual for two boys to be acting out a love scene.

When the patient was nine, the parents moved to another apartment, several blocks away. The friendship continued but perhaps lessened in intensity.

Also during this early period the family doctor spent a lot of time with the patient on a friendship basis. He liked to take the patient with him on his calls, and Bill said he did such things as "had me smoke a cigar at five," but the patient never got the idea that he would like to be a doctor.

Other significant people through his growing years include four cousins, sons of his mother's sister. They lived in the suburbs, a relatively rural home compared with the apartment in which the patient lived. I am not able to get him to talk about these boys as individuals—he will not even respond to my request to supply me with their first names. They seem to operate as a group. There was considerable envy throughout of their country life, as compared to his restricted city living.

The maternal grandparents would occasionally take him for rides, and he was indulged by them, but there was never any warmth of feeling associated with either, particularly the grandfather, who was stubborn, insistent, and difficult to get along with.

He told me on several occasions that he had tried to run away a few times when he was eight or nine, apparently a turbulent period for him. He is not sure why he ran away. He thinks it was because he didn't get his own way and yet later he told me he got his way whenever he wanted it. He was able to wheedle his mother sometimes but generally he turned to and got everything he wanted from his father. He remembers once telling his mother he was going to run away, and then going down the street until she called him back.

He thought he had more freedom than the other children in the neighborhood, but he was not especially proud of it. When he talked about that, there was more of a feeling of neglect, followed with the comment of lack of discipline in the home, lack of organization in the family. He would tell the nurse or his parents where he was going and then he would go. He was able to call his cousins and visit them but he would always inform his parents. There are some stories about going to the movies alone across the street, not telling his parents, and occasionally coming home late. He said his father would call the police, but on further questioning he is not sure whether his father actually did that.

He mentions in that same period that he very frequently got carsick; his mother was a poor driver, reckless and preoccupied, had been in several accidents, and had been in the hospital, but he refused to give any details when I pursued the subject.

The association with Jim goes on into pre-adolescence, although he also had a rather similar attraction to another boy in the neighborhood, Barney. He told of having a falling out with Jim for a few months at the age of thirteen or fourteen, based on some disagreement that was never very clear to me. It involved a girl, and Bill became irritated with his friend, who dated the girl while Bill at the same time had only a kind of fantasy affair with her. She didn't even know that Bill liked her. Finally, at a party, the friend "made a noble gesture," extending his hand and wanting the unpleasantness to be over. The patient consented and they continued in an off-and-on acquaintanceship from then on.

Jim apparently grew larger than the patient and it was he with whom Bill compared penises and with whom there was some mutual attempt at masturbation; they masturbated in the presence of each other but neither of them was successful. After that the patient went home, went into the bathroom, and masturbated to orgasm for the first time. He remembers vividly having a great deal of guilt about the experience, but why is not clear. He was not guilty about his parents' attitude, but was fearful of being discovered in this situation.

Subsequently, Jim became interested in aeronautical engineering. His father fostered this interest, taking him up for airplane rides; he got his degree in that field, married, and now has several children. Bill compares himself to Jim in his own lack of success.

Barney also continued as an occasional friend. He became interested in medicine, was not able to get into a Class A school, ended in a Class B school, and when it closed, went to work in a factory. Bill is inclined to admire Barney's interest in medicine and to consider him a success, losing sight of the fact that he did not complete school nor accomplish his objective.

Bill started in Hebrew school but went without a great deal of interest. He always tended to play it down, to make a joke of it, and to this day does not know enough about the rituals to be comfortable. He stopped going to the temple except for one occasion in the Navy when he went to meet a friend and felt restless and insecure.

The patient went to an exclusively male junior high school. When he was to enter high school, he went to the school nearest to his home, stayed one day, felt uneasy, and arranged to transfer to an all-male school with seven thousand students, about a thirty-minute subway ride from his home. I asked him what made him uncomfortable at the first school, and he said maybe it was the girls, maybe it was the building, but he would not amplify that.

Puberty was attended by a great deal of feeling on his part that he was slow in development. Apparently he compared himself with his older cousin and with Jim. The cousin apparently went through changes earlier than the patient. He also compared himself with boys at the swimming pool at the Y and with the fellows in his class. In both instances he did not take into account the difference in ages. He had skipped two grades and consequently was one of the youngest boys in the class, but he expected to be scholastically and physically up to the older boys.

About that time he began to show an interest in girls, but had considerable difficulty in developing any relationship. He fantasied love affairs with many girls, and would even secretly go to their homes, being careful not to be seen in his attempts to find out something about them. He would also do this with some of his boyfriends who went to other schools. He said that was very compulsive behavior. When I asked him what he meant, he said it was like the criminal who returns to the scene of his crime, that he had to find out, but he could not reveal the fact that he was there.

During the puberty period, the exact age he is not able to state, he was invited to go into the woods by a young girl and was quite certain it was for lovemaking; he pleaded that his hay fever was too bad, and now feels that he missed his earliest opportunity to get somewhere with girls.

During this period he felt it was impossible to talk to his father about his problems and made no attempt to do so. He did not inquire about masturbation, but learned from his school chums. He had known about the possibility of nocturnal emission and was not frightened, but did not talk to his father about it. He did not talk with his mother either, even though he described their relationship as being completely free with each other. He would often sit on the toilet seat while his mother was taking a bath, and this has continued up to the present time. He described it as "a oneness with her." He brought up an early experience when he had been sitting on the front porch, and when his mother came out, he had impulsively picked up her skirt and then felt upset and ran into the house expecting something to happen, but nothing was said. He also remembers that once when he was four or five he went to a baby carriage and peeked under the child's skirt and had guilt feelings about that.

With regard to the pattern of play and his relationship with other boys at that period, he described himself as always being on the fringe, never being in any specific group. He did play with a gang on the street, football and other games, but there was no stress on the gang type of activities, the pranks and fights with other gangs. He was afraid of a group of tough Polish boys who lived on one edge of his neighborhood; he was once accosted by them but refused to fight. More than that I have not been able to obtain. He insists that whenever it became necessary for him to put up resistance he thought of his tendency to get a bloody nose and generally would run away. He believes, however, that he had some fights and thinks it was with his cousins and with Jim, but he doesn't remember what they were fighting about.

One day he told me about having some trouble being too frequently singled out by homosexuals. He said it happened to him very often on the subway—somebody would question him and he knew they were homosexual. Also, he had a rather effeminate schoolteacher who seemed to make a pet of the patient; on one occasion—he was reluctant to date it but probably while in the

Navy—he visited the teacher, who was in the company of several other teachers, and this man had put his arms around the patient from behind and pulled him up close. The patient felt that this was an obviously homosexual gesture. He was unable to push the man off at the moment, but he didn't make any particular response and nothing more came of it.

He said that during puberty and early adolescence he felt that his hips were wider than other boys' hips, and when he put powder on his face after shaving and took special care in accentuating the wave in his hair he felt sure that these were feminine things to do.

He feels he has been quite aware, at least since high school, of operating under a double sense of values. The first was living up to what his father thought he should be—the son of a prominent man. He was known to be a good boy and felt he had to live up to it. He was not able to clarify the other set of values—whether he meant his own feelings of rebellion against his parents or not.

He has mentioned many times the strictly male atmosphere he grew up in, and I tried to track down what it meant to him but he does not amplify the story. He doesn't say that something bad happened to him because of that. He just suggests it.

I went into the Navy experiences some more, particularly his time on the APD, because I felt it was a clear period to work on. The patient said that the reason for the transfer was that the ship to which he was assigned was run by an officer well known as a severe disciplinarian, and he was quite afraid of him and knew him to be anti-Semitic. When he was assigned they already had a gunnery officer, and he immediately took steps to be transferred. His commanding officer agreed and there was no unpleasantness. Since there was also a gunnery officer on the APD already, he had to take a job for which he had no training. He was apparently in charge of maintenance of the machines on the ship. His group left for the Far East almost the same day that he joined the ship. In one action in which many minesweepers were sunk, his ship was directing rescue operations. Another officer and he were standing on deck as a boat was being prepared to go to one of the sinking ships, and he turned to the commanding officer and asked who was to go, unconsciously knowing that he would not be chosen. I asked him if it was his duty more than the other man's and he said, "Well, no, I suppose not." I asked him who the other officer was and he said the ship's officer. A Jewish sailor hauled most of the men out and when the rescue crew came out they were commended and given medals and he felt envious of them. When a short time later they sent out another boat, he impulsively jumped on and went along; a man whom he tried to haul out of the minesweeper turned out to be dead, but subsequently he found that the skipper had written a commendation. Later, a piece of timber hit the Jewish sailor on the head and killed him. An investigation was held and the patient did everything to shift the responsibility off himself. He said he felt very guilty about that and I asked him if it was about the accident or about shifting the responsibility and he said both. If there had been an investigation by other officers, he said, "I would have been guilty." I asked why, and he said, "We covered up for each other." I asked him if he had been on good terms with the other officers and he said, "I guess so. I had several friends." I asked him if he had been able to talk with them freely and he said he never had anyone he could talk freely with. He mentioned that he ate with the others, spent a good deal of time talking, and was always friendly with his roommate on any of the ships, and I got the impression that his life had not been as isolated as he had initially described it.

I have used that story several times when he gets to be self-derogatory to illustrate that here was a period in which he had little training for his job, that he had to learn how to do it on the way to combat, and that during the rescue operations he had merited a commendation. I then asked if he had ever had a reprimand while on the ship and he thought he had, but it turned out that he had never had one. He was accepted as a useful member of the crew.

Another time he told me about his tendency to avoid responsibility on this ship, and when I asked him to explain, he thought a minute and said, "Well, navigation, for instance," adding that he had never been able to get anything out of his navigation studies and had no mathematical talents. When I asked him when he had been asked to navigate, he said he had not been asked. Then I asked him where the shifting of responsibility was and he said if he had been asked he would have shifted the responsibility. I tried to point out that there had been no test of his ability and that he was making judgment without trial.

One day when he spoke about the Navy he told me of an experience of going to a whorehouse in Panama. He was trying to say the word, and when I supplied it, he said it was a peculiar place, laughed in a friendly way, and went on to tell me more. He was impressed with the girls who invited him, and later he asked the officer who had been with him if he felt any guilt, but was not able to remember the other man's reply.

He told me about one of the girls he had some relations with. He had met her in a tavern and she was drunk and he was pretty dizzy. He remembers her apartment because of all the female paraphernalia. He said he forced himself on her. She wanted him to leave but he was reluctant to go and it ended by their having sexual relations. I said something to the effect that apparently she made you leave by going to bed with you. He laughed a little and passed on to something else. He said he had seen her subsequently but it was a casual acquaintance without any more visits to her apartment. He felt guilty about that also.

In law school, the day that he called his father up as he was feeling more and more insecure—feeling that he was not learning rapidly enough and that he was behind the other students—he told his father he was having a severe headache and that he was intensely fearful of being called on. He had not been previously called on but admitted that the school was very tough, and that he had seen several boys who had been called on and had been taken apart. He told his father he thought he should see a doctor for a physical check-up. He didn't tell his father about what he was feeling other than that. His father arranged a visit with a private practitioner who tried to talk to the patient a little, but he refused to tell anything other than that he was having headaches. The doctor suggested he was probably doing too much in relation to his schoolwork and his girlfriend and recommended that he go on a trip. This trip was arranged by the father and Bill and his friend left a week or two later, after he broke up with the girlfriend.

I went into his story of his traveling companion, Steve. He was a boy whom the patient had met while at college, the son of an advertising executive. Steve was a top student and, like the patient, entertained liberal views. Their friendship was pretty much on the basis of talking politics and political science. Steve was not much of a hand with the girls and very little given to talking about himself in that sphere. Their conversations, it seems, were always on a rather high intellectual level. They had great respect for each other. Steve had later gone into the Air Force, worked himself up to radio gunner in the Air Force, had sixteen missions over Germany, was shot down on the last mission and wounded, came to and bailed out, pulling his rip cord at five thousand feet, and was rescued and taken prisoner by the Germans. The patient had been corresponding with Steve, and on finding out that he was missing in action, he wrote to Steve's parents. He said he wrote the letter for effect, that he did not know what his real feelings were. When he found out that Steve was alive, he resumed correspondence with him, and later he went to visit him. He puts it that he went to visit the parents' home. Steve had also come to the city, where they double-dated with a friend of the patient's girlfriend, going to shows and nightclubs.

Apparently it was Bill's father who had interested Steve in accompanying the patient on the trip. The patient did very little planning for the trip, and I am not yet clear as to why Steve, who was in law school, was so willing to leave school and go on the trip. On the trip they largely talked about intellectual things and the patient's own self-condemnatory attitudes. There was some pressure by Steve to get the patient interested in physical exercises when they stopped for the night; he would try to tell him, "You can do anything you want to do." There was no discussion by either about their relations with girlfriends. The patient doesn't remember whether he mentioned his girlfriend with whom he had just broken off. There was no suggestion of any intimacy between the two boys at any time; it was all on an intellectual level rather than a more intimate, emotional one. Incidentally, Steve didn't return to law school but entered the political science department of one of the universities instead.

About a week ago, we talked about the fear of cold showers. He said he didn't know when the fear started, but that he always got panicky in the cold shower, even as a small child, when he would jump up and down and go through a lot of activity. I asked him if he considered that unusual, and he said he thought so. He remembered an incident at fifteen or sixteen when he was ridiculed while taking a cold shower, for jumping around a lot and running away from it. When I asked him if he remembered who did this, at first he said no but then he looked ashamed and said that it was out at the beach with Jim and Jim's father and the father was kidding them about not being able to take it. I said,

"Did you think that the strong didn't jump around in the shower and the weak did?" He said yes, that he had that idea quite clearly. He said that was different from the panicky feelings, which were intensely fearful. It seemed that this was not panic at all, but a normal jumping around in a cold shower that he was talking about, putting the judgment on it that it was panic because he felt he could not take it. He has not himself brought up this fear since. I don't know whether this is the bottom of that story, but it has been dropped from the list of derogatory feelings at the moment.

He mentioned something more about the accident out in Kansas. He was driving, and as they approached an intersection another car plowed into them. Nobody was hurt except the patient, who sustained some small lacerations on the forehead. He was not criticized by the other driver, and I am not at all sure that the patient was at fault, as he insists. In the second accident nobody was injured and he has not said much about it.

Something that he has brought up a couple of times, and which has been attended by a great feeling of discouragement and great restlessness in the office, has been his attitude toward his illness. He started out by talking about how badly he had regressed, and how he was content to stay as a child and that all the childhood fears and terrors were coming back. I pressed him on the meaning of regression. He said, "Lack of development." I said, "What do you mean by regression?" and he said, "Well, I have still under-development of sex characteristics." I said, "What specifically?" and he said, "Small penis." I told him that probably 50 percent of the male population had smaller penises, but they did not necessarily make comparisons. Then he said he thought it meant loss of function and loss of desire to do anything or to get well, to do physical activity, and I asked what that meant to him and he said, "I see myself as psychotic, regressing in a schizophrenic pattern, being shocked back, then slipping and getting shocked, and slipping until I die in an institution." Then we got to talking about how he was using "schizophrenia," and "psychotic," and "regression," and other words in his own specific meanings and that we would have to try to come to some understanding of the use of these terms. I pointed out that he was labeling himself schizophrenic, implying a malignant prognosis, and seeing the future in that light, and that there were some things in his picture that made it better than that—his ability to form some meaningful relationships, his ability to verbalize his problems, and his above-average intelligence were all in his favor—and he accepted that fairly well that day.

Another day he came into the office very disturbed, shaking his head and flushed, with a rather wild look in his eye. When I asked him what was wrong, he said he had been chewing a nut, had felt a pain in his tooth, had kept on chewing, and had cracked the tooth, which was evidence of his self-destructive tendencies. I was able to point out that almost everybody had cracked a tooth at one time or another, that it was not so unusual, and he quieted down after about ten or fifteen minutes and spoke no more about it.

I should mention that he often talks about his submissiveness, saying that he accepted everything they did at Springhill, took the shock without knowing anything about it, and he mentions his running away from fights and not doing anything to defend himself. On one occasion recently, when he was going into the bathroom, another patient hit him in the stomach and Bill did nothing about it; after he got to thinking about it, analyzed it, and realized he was being submissive again, he went back, hit the other patient in the face, and then had great guilt feelings about it, feeling that he was going to be punished. We talked about incidents like this not being unusual for people in cramped quarters, and concluded that he might as well forget it. He did ask the other boy why he had done it, and the other patient said, "No reason, that's all. You can go now." So the patient came out and lifted his hands up in a what-the-hell manner, the whole thing has not been repeated, and he doesn't talk about it any more.

About his relationship to me I am not very clear. He has said several times that undoubtedly something has happened. He told me I was the first one who had cracked through his shell. I told him that was fine, that the shell had not been doing much good. He also told me that it was only in the office when he was talking to me that things in the hospital made sense, that things on the ward were detrimental to him, and suggested it was useful to him to continue talking.

One day he talked about his feelings of rage and aggression against the other patients on the ward and his refusal to talk to them. He mentioned a bald-headed man and said he wanted to flick ashes on the man's bald head, then rushed out of the office, leaving all the doors open, went into the toilet and urinated, and came back, shut the doors, and made no more mention of it.

That is essentially what has been going on up to the present time.

SULLIVAN: Can you illustrate this head-shaking after breaking the tooth?

KVARNES: It was negation, as if "there is something wrong with me." I have tried to write down the interviews as we have had them. I have extensive notes, and perhaps we can get a picture of what is going on.

SULLIVAN: Do you make your notes after the interview?

KVARNES: Yes, right after he leaves.

SULLIVAN: I would like to hear from each of you what you feel you now understand about why this man is sick. I am far from certain that we know why he is sick but I think the picture of developmental history is rather remarkably good. He has been quite productive, and since part of psychiatry consists of forming good hunches and carefully investigating to see whether they are good and at other times revising them so that they are better, I think in view of the large amount of data we got before, and as I see this rather astonishing filling in, I would like each of you to express some view as to your hunch as to what ails this man and I don't mean diagnosis. I mean what do you suppose has gotten him down? The notion being your idea of what you would be inclined to test out now to see if it clarifies any problems and might help him develop a reasonable anticipation about his success in the future. We will start with Dr. Peal.

PEAL: I had the general picture that this is a man whose important relationships to men have been those of contrast and comparison, and that there seems to be a marked void as far as any relationships with girls are concerned, little girls or older women, and such as they are they seem to be with someone else taking the lead. Something happened in the Navy which was related to him—he began to complain of symptoms—and I am not sure what it was. The possibility of living closely with men and his feelings toward them. He compares himself unfavorably with them and yet his own friendships with people are with boys his age. In his relationship to Dr. Kvarnes, he keeps using words, not knowing what they mean, and when Dr. Kvarnes asks him what he means, he seems to bring up a lot of things, including much of his self-criticism, in an attempt to gain the physician's increasing interest. He uses him and he likes to see him, and so on.

SULLIVAN: I don't quite follow the conclusions that you are driving at in the way of a temporary hypothesis of what ails this man, what requires his becoming psychotic, if you please. I am wondering what you would stress in further work with him now.

PEAL: Of course, one of the things that happened was that while ill he came close to a girl, which apparently made him very much worse, and I think it would be important to find out just what the details of that relationship were. Perhaps it is no more than he said, but I wonder, since he has been covering up many important relationships like that.

SULLIVAN: Do you suppose anybody on the staff, or among the patients, or the employees would profit from confiding in some psychiatrist about their relationship with girls? Do you think there is a notable number of them who feel completely complacent about their operations in the field? What I am driving at is that I am not at all sure that therapeutic expectations could properly be attached to this, shall I say, peculiar emphasis on what is a fairly documented lack of outstanding success in that field. There is a good deal more that might be in a professional hypothesis of what ails the man.

Dr. Witt, let us hear from you.

WITT: First of all there seems to be, from childhood, a very prominent tendency to rate himself in comparison with other people always on the poor side, not looking at any of the things that have been valuable to him or in which he seems to have gotten along as well as other people, particularly in connection with boys. This seems to have been enhanced by the fact that he was able to go ahead a few grades relatively easily. He grades himself with older people and has carried that through all the way. Since he has gotten into more personal relationships, he has continued to judge only the poorer aspects of his character and to do it in an even more far-fetched way than he, with reality, did with older boys. With girls, he always seems to have felt there was not much he could do, that he was pretty much at a loss, that at anything except fantasy he was hopeless. Apparently the only relationship he has had with a girl has been on an intellectual level rather than an emotional one. All of those things seem to point back to the early relationship with his parents, with his family, since he has had these tendencies in all of his history. It seems to me that his mother has always treated him pretty much as a child. For example, exposing herself to him and expecting that he would not be upset by that, and apparently she didn't expect him to show any sexual feelings. Apparently, also, he has had a good deal of feeling that his father was quite superior, that he could not ever hope to live up to that or to his father's expectations, and I think that both fields are important as to what his actions have been with males and females since then. Also, because of his difficulty in sexual fields and because he brings it up, it would be important to find out what the relationship of the father and mother was in various fields.

SULLIVAN: There is no way of assessing what we would discover by further investigation, but in forming a hypothesis it is pretty good usually to be sure one can document each phase of one's structure, and I am inclined to say, whether because I have forgotten the first presentation or because I am right, that you read into the relationship of the boy and the father things that may or may not be correct; that you overlook in this relationship what has certainly been pushed rather strikingly to your attention. I am not saying that to criticize you, but to point out that it is always well to look into the premises that one brings into these hypotheses. We are inclined to build on our own experience, and insofar as the patient is actively schizophrenic, the introduction of something which the patient does not follow can be hard on the relationship. The patient gets into something like this: "Here the doctor understands something and I can't, so I can't follow him at all, so that proves that I am no good"—and for that reason I would say that your statement certainly heads in a very important direction now, gives this the sweep of a life course, but overlooks something which has been stated and stressed, something which may or may not be right.

Dr. Novey, what are your thoughts?

NOVEY: I think this boy is fearful of his own passivity needs. There was one comment in the presentation this morning to the effect that he felt at one with his mother. That is something which might be enlarged. I think this gives an index of some characteristic of the mother also. He seems to feel a great deal of aggression which he cannot give vent to and I would guess that he would come through with a great many hostile feelings toward

Dr. Kvarnes in the treatment relationship—some of it because of his own passivity and through lack of what would represent an outlet for it.

SULLIVAN: I am not at all sure we have a consensus on two things. One is his passivity needs and the other is this aggression. I am never sure of what anybody means by these terms but I am doubly puzzled when I hear about a patient going into the bathroom, being punched in the stomach by another patient who may have hallucinated an unpleasant remark, and, after thinking it over, going back and punching him a few times. Tell me what you mean by these two things. What is his passivity need?

NOVEY: He talked about himself as being at one with his mother. He was unable to live up to the kind of aggressive, outgoing attitude toward the community that his father lived out, and I believe found that a situation in which he did not need to give vent to the same kind of aggressiveness as his father was a particularly attractive one. At the same time he felt his need to emulate his father.

SULLIVAN: What data have you to support this belief that he had a need to emulate his father?

NOVEY: Going to law school, for instance.

SULLIVAN: That was quite a voluntary choice, uninfluenced by anybody in authority.

NOVEY: All I know is that here is his father who is a lawyer, and here is his son starting to attend law school.

SULLIVAN: Then most sons who follow in their father's footsteps would suffer from passivity needs or father fixations? Tell me about the aggressiveness. That is a word that enjoyed enormous popularity before hostility became so popular. Does going out and getting in my car represent an aggressive act, or pushing somebody around, or does success which cost a great many other people something represent aggression? What is this aggressiveness the man has hidden in him?

NOVEY: The kind of thing that interested me was, for instance, the fact that he was struck in the abdomen and instead of responding to it immediately, he went through a whole process of thinking over and then coming back and giving it back to the other patient. Something he thought he ought to do.

SULLIVAN: Count ten before you hit the other fellow. Is that cultural passivity feelings or not? Take my own instance: If somebody hits me, I would be moved to homicide, which impulse would stay with me for an indefinite number of years, waiting for a good chance to discharge it. Does that indicate I have strong aggressive attitudes? What I am harping on, I am trying to discover what, if anything, you mean by something that is important among your terms. I have sometimes discovered that people mean by aggressiveness the tendency to live, and that, of course, makes it rather useless. What is behind all this is that if I talk to a patient about his passivity needs or his aggressiveness, I hope that I can tell him what I mean.

Dr. Cooper, let's hear from you.

COOPER: I have been rather impressed by the lack of show of affection and love by the parents in this patient's early life. I am wondering if he feels very rejected by them, having to turn to other people on the outside, particularly the father of his close friend, for guidance and help. My hunch is that perhaps he has little true love for his family and that this increases a guilt feeling within him because he has from every turn evidence that his family members are rather successful and right people; thus he thinks his approach to them is entirely wrong, therefore increasing his own inadequate and inferior feelings.

SULLIVAN: There is a very close approach to an excellent statement there. That was the thing that I particularly regretted Dr. Peal had not emphasized more. He, being the first one to speak, naturally was the one that I thought of it in connection with. Talk of rejection. If you had torn that down, there seems to be a lot of emphasis in this boy's talk of his past on the unsatisfactory aspects of the family group. It was lacking in organization. He stresses that. I would not want to be too pressing in finding out what he was talking about, but the picture takes on the color that he had remarkable freedom from discipline and was not so pleased with it. That is an obscure way of saying that he was a matter of comparative indifference to his parents. Now I would think that hurts more than rejection. It might be rejection if you have a certain philosophy, but just keeping to what one thinks as a boy sounds like this boy thought he did not matter very much to his parents.

KVARNES: They always considered him a normal boy. He had no trouble so their attention was elsewhere.

SULLIVAN: Run along and do what you please! The contrast almost stands out unmistakably to the relationship of Jim and his father. There is something that gives the thing sense. When somebody says, "Well, I was unusually well treated," I am inclined to say, "As compared with whom?" On the far side of that I will know what he is talking about, and what I am driving at is that it is useful if you can get your tentative hypothesis from what the patient has used, not technical terms borrowed from an analyst in a previous incarnation, but when he says Jim's father and his relationship to Jim pleased him enormously, then I say he has drawn a comparison and it has been unfavorable to his own parents. That is bad news to anybody in the developmental years. It is not that I don't want you to have the conception of maternal overprotection, but I want you to learn what you can say to a patient in terms that the patient will not misinterpret and which will not make the patient feel, "There is something here that I can't grasp."

ROM: Unfortunately, through all this material I don't find a unifying thread. The more I hear, the less schizophrenic coloration I see. He is mainly tense and anxious but not particularly disorganized.

SULLIVAN: Suppose you just rest on the matter of what should be clarified and tell us your theory of what you now want to investigate.

ROM: I would be inclined to think there was some deficiency in the sexual sphere, apparently some obstacle that he just can't establish some meaningful relationship to women. He is always fearful of it, always terrified of it.

SULLIVAN: As you speak about that, I am reminded of an attendant I once had at Sheppard. He had very large external genitalia, and a large number of the female population seemed to discover that in some way or other and made appropriate advances, whereupon this attendant always fell in love. As he was a specimen of personality disorganization which I had not had an opportunity to work with, I was working with him as a therapist, and these love affairs were hot stuff. The fact that they could be crowded into ten days made them interesting as long as they lasted. At something like two-weekly intervals I would ask, in my so-called therapeutic hours, possibly a half-hour before the end, "What about Miss So and So?" He would reply, "Oh, that bitch," which meant that he had had intercourse. That did not seem to prevent his behaving in many ways like a so-called psychopathic personality, but it does suggest a slight possibility that heterosexual success requires certain refinements other than actual genital contact, and there are so many kinds of women in the world and so on that I wonder—you can probably understand almost any patient on the basis of difficulty in his sex life, but it is often difficult to bring about any favorable change in the patient by such understanding. Suppose you were to poke around in this vigorously with this boy. Do you see any way of avoiding his belief that he is homosexual? And when you have accomplished that, what do you do next? Have you something in mind about that?

ROM: That it would be inevitable that he would be convinced that he is a latent homosexual.

SULLIVAN: Then I suppose it is in existence, potentially, and what do we do with it? When it has ceased to be latent and is among us, either as schizophrenia or schizophrenic panic, which will relieve the problem of diagnosis, or as a regrettable accident in the hospital environment, what do we do?

ROM: At this point I am stumped.

SULLIVAN: My whole point there is that that is a piece of insight very markedly to be feared in any psychotherapy, and what one is going to do with one's sex life, no matter how normal it might be, may still depend on whether one can make a living, wear decent clothes—a field in which poking around in a rather tenuous early stage of psychotherapy is much more free from grave risks. We can label the fact that the mother bathed in the nude with the little child sitting on the toilet seat and he thereby cultivated a mother fixation. Sounds almost like heredity. There is not much to be done about it if further progress means that you are actively engaged in sexual desire for men, which carries considerable opprobrium. So, in spite of any emotion one might have about the libido theory, as long as you can entertain a doubt as to whether he is schizophrenic, leave something alone that is liable to make him schizophrenic.

Dr. Styrt, may we hear from you?

STYRT: I wonder why he has to be second best, always has to be no good. For a while I thought that perhaps he had to be sick to get away from always being normal, a person that nobody paid any attention to because he was a good performer, because he skipped grades and was always able to get along well. An illness like this seems to be a drastic way of making up for that, but there seems also to be something he is atoning for. I don't know quite how to put it. He has to be no good. No matter what you give him as evidence of his capabilities, he implies it is not true. It is being misrepresented to show he was better than he was. I wonder if there is some fear of father here that keeps him from competing. I don't know whether trying to get further into it would be more frightening to him. I was impressed with his actions here and what I have seen of him in the hospital, that he has to be useless. In his contacts on the ballfield, for example, if he does well, there is no competition. If one asks him to engage in something else, he is no good at it, and there again he is always good at it, so immediately the competition is no good.

SULLIVAN: You don't suppose he is one of these people who, by belittling his achievement, tends to emphasize it?

STYRT: This is a rather severe way of doing that. If that could be so, he has done it to the extent that he is unable to get along in school in relation to other people.

SULLIVAN: I am not urging that view. I don't think it is relevant. One detail in the data must be viewed before we can pay too much attention to anything in consciousness amounting to actual fear of his father, and that is his getting out of a Naval detail where he had an anti-Semitic, domineering chief officer. There he seems to have done something about it which was—well, without knowing anything, I am inclined to think it was a superior and adequate performance. He didn't know what was going to happen to him but he knew what he wanted and he got it. I don't think I can think of a more classical example of a father image than the chief officer of a ship. I bring this up to suggest you have a pretty strong hunch, and then you look over the data and see what contradicts this. It is always well to go over it and look at it before one closes one's mind.

WHEELER: I have gathered that this boy does not know what he wants to do now or at any point in the past. That instance in the Navy he did know what he wanted to do. Now he may also know what he wants to do and not be able to do it but some way of getting at those things could help.

SULLIVAN: I am very much pleased with what I hear in this. It suggests to me that you would be poking around without too

much discouragement to him to get his eyes turned somewhat to
the future where he might fit in.

WHEELER: To make his own way. I don't think he has done very
much of that.

SULLIVAN: A very helpful goal to be pursued with caution lest
it overload the patient. I would like to comment that in psycho-
therapy we have these opportunities—not to be stressed too much
lest they convince the patient with inadequacy feelings even more
—but always the ideal of what one has wanted to do and what the
hell prevents the realization of such and such aims.

MORRIS: It seems that this young fellow has always been ex-
tremely insecure in any relationship with anyone, that right from
the beginning, from infancy, he has felt this lack of affection, and
tenseness with his parents. The attempts to make relationships
with others have been extremely difficult for him. We have heard
no instance of any intimacy with anyone, even from earliest
time. Many attempts have been made.

SULLIVAN: I can't agree with that. That seems to definitely
violate the data about Jim.

MORRIS: There was a chum relationship there, but I was think-
ing more in terms of being able to talk about himself to this other
person in the form of more intimacy. I think, though, that he has,
in his further relationships, never been able to become at ease with
anyone, been able to relate to anyone, and it has resulted in this
derogatory attitude he has toward himself, his very low self-
esteem. I think that in working with him, it would be good to get
more data on where his relationships have been somewhat more
satisfactory, to perhaps have him realize where he can be more
at ease or find out how much in the relationships has been real and
how much fantasy.

SULLIVAN: You get close to another idea that can be used profit-
ably. I may have mentioned this before. Namely, that there has
been a change, that this pre-adolescent relationship seemed to be
going good, and he does not seem to have been getting near any-
body since, but has been having greater difficulty. How come
that change? This notion that here something unfortunate is
present, it probably began there, especially where you know darn
well there has been a change, then it is helpful, if you can get the
patient to know what you are talking about, to inquire for what

led to the change. It is often the story—there is a tradition almost in the incidents of certain schizophrenics—that somebody got along fine in a restricted home community, then went to a vastly different community or university or something like that and made a fool of himself several times. He gets more and more cautious until he is almost completely isolated from everything but discussions of political science. All I have to work on is the relation with Jim and the other boy, but certainly he did not suffer any such need for superficial generalities of interest at that time. What are the disappointments, mistakes he made in the high school years that led into this?

There is one very dangerous factor here, or several; one has to exercise clinical judgment of a moderately high order because we are already told one thing which is the type of disastrous change which has a good many aspects of hereditary change. He seems to have matured slower than his chums! If you waltz a patient up to something as final as that, and everybody agrees that it happened, what the hell, then I am ruined. In poking around for the change that has made him less and less capable of freedom with members of his own sex, I would always have in mind that I have got to put the good light on the apparent factors of delayed puberty. Otherwise I may be stymied.

MORRIS: Just one more point. Aboard ship there could be more information as to what group he tended to mingle with—the person he roomed with and went ashore with, the type of people and what sort of relationship he may have encountered at that time.

SULLIVAN: Without undue emphasis on the sex element, to get rid of another detail we have to use clinical judgment about, it strikes me that in Panama many of the houses of prostitution are occupied by people of mixed blood and it is most disastrous indeed to lead a patient to confide that he crossed the color line unless you are ready to do something about that immediately. Here is a place where he says he went with another officer. There, if one happens to have the gift for spontaneous inquiry—without being too spontaneous—really considerable interest in this other officer might be a good hunch. With the notion of getting some picture of the other officer by concealing that under one's interest in the actual event. I would hope I could learn quite a bit about the officer, but the patient would seem to think my greatest interest was who proposed the thing and who was happiest about it. I am trying to learn what the real personality factors are under the cloak of other interests. The big thing about an emergency like this is that you don't want it to happen at the end of a session. If you are going to hear that he had relations with a Negro it is better to have it happen about forty minutes before the end of the interview.

SALZMAN: I have been anxious to get clear what is the great underlying anxiety with this fellow, and I have some notion about the one experience when he began to compare his situation, the indifference toward him at home, and the relationship between Jim and his father. Jim gets the feeling in his home of being more significant, more important, and the patient does not have a relationship with his own father of this sort. The first time he saw what went on in other people's homes, I wonder whether this was not one of the early beginnings of his conviction of being a pretty inadequate sort of guy, and whether it would be fruitful to look for more instances of this. Most of the anxiety centers around the fact that he has some conviction of being a pretty worthless individual, of having little respect in his own eyes and the eyes of other people, his parents particularly, in the early years. He certainly set up a chum relationship, but it began to deteriorate and never extended beyond a chum, it never even flowered, and I wonder whether it deteriorated because he didn't feel that he was worth having any real close relationship.

SULLIVAN: You overlooked some data, but there is something that I want to emphasize more in your remarks—this approach is very sympathetic to me. One is always pretty safe in anything except frontal encounters with a person's self-respect. Seems to me an extremely useful term, self-respect, self-esteem, and so on. You develop the importance of the parental indifference, if that be what it is, but you have one technical step that is not in there and that has not been very clearly indicated by Dr. Kvarnes. The failure to take this step to some extent leaves the whole structure resting on an untried foundation. What you say about the comparison of Jim and his father and this boy and his father may be all right, except that to consolidate our reasonable certainty, it is necessary to set up the fact that he could not despise or feel hostile or critical toward his father. If you can blame a parent who is indifferent to you, that is very different indeed from having to maintain an attitude, "Well, Father is a wonderful person and very admirable, but he has no use for me." You don't want to build a structure which can have a conspicuous hole in the lower part lest the drive to escape from understanding his low self-esteem is undermined in the intervals between therapy.

Dr. White, we haven't heard from you yet.

WHITE: I would like to comment that I am surprised so early in the game that he was willing or could talk to you about such dynamite-laden things as the timber falling on a contemporary and killing him and the boy in the Air Force going down in Germany. It means to me that apparently he can begin to deal with that kind of thing and I would like to ask whether it is too soon to go back and find out about those incidents. But my real interest is in the relationship of Jim to his father, where Jim had a goal of becoming an engineer and his father took him on airplane rides. I wonder whether he felt something might happen to Jim, and whether, at the same time, feeling that he could not even take a cold shower adequately, he was not made acutely aware of his anxiety and his resentment that someone could be so tough and he could not. Is it too soon to let him go further with that if he again brings it up?

SULLIVAN: I would want to know all about what was blamable in this timber incident. That brings up a curious slant on this work—if you don't explore something that is apparently very important to a patient, then you are practically required to set it aside. The theory is very simple. If a therapist backs away from something which seems important to the patient, that means the therapist can't stand it or is ashamed of it. Then you have to indicate that we will deal with it later on the assumption that somebody who is low in self-esteem will think it is just too bad, that you are ashamed to know about it.

KVARNES: There was so much other stuff he didn't seem to be upset by it.

SULLIVAN: At the very finish I do want to say a few words about this business of reassuring, which is one of the jobs we have to do a great deal, but I want to hear from others first. Perhaps Dr. Wagner.

WAGNER: I am left with certain questions which my hypothesis does not help. There is a strong need to compare himself unfavorably throughout his life and the most sincere complaint seems to be self-reproach. I fell a lack of information in many of these areas. I do agree that the father who is successful was the example of the good parent, culturally good and successful, and Jim's father was the lovable parent, the one to seek. On the other hand it was not his father. However, subsequently with men, at least with boys, he found his most satisfactory and least anxiety-ridden experiences, and seems to have sought to repeat these except that he had the compulsion to try and do something more heterosexually, which he could not manage. I wonder if, to amplify it, if being a man is being like father, he would rather not. On the other hand, up until the time of puberty, he did have some gratifying experiences, and I would be tempted to direct my question at that particular point. Why didn't he seem to be able to go from there in the usual way?

SULLIVAN: I am afraid of doing it now. That is something I want to defer. I wonder how many see why. The attitude of the patient is, "I am no good." He will attack anything on that basis. "I can't even eat a nut without breaking a tooth."

We know two things about why he did not go on from there. That is, I believe we know it. I believe we know that from all, to him, important considerations of time, he was slow in maturing and we can fill in there with considerable safety the idea that his relationship with Jim deteriorated very strikingly because Jim's interest left him. I don't know about the other boy.

KVARNES: The second boy comes into the picture sometime just before puberty and he continued the friendship all the way through.

SULLIVAN: I am inclined to stress his earlier successes before I am going to apply pressure, lest he wind up, "Sure, I am just no good—what am I to argue about?"

Dr. Will, I don't think you have spoken.

WILL: I haven't very much to add. I am impressed, as everyone is, with this lack of self-esteem or self-respect. Perhaps many of the things that arise at the hospital—activities on the ballfield, with other patients, and so forth, that enable him to constantly illustrate some of his difficulties—might be available for discussion. One question I would like to ask is this, the patient did remark that he felt his contact with you was the type he had not been able to make with other people. I also have been impressed with what I felt the fears of this patient were regarding his own possible homosexual tendencies. You mention the incident of his leaving the room to urinate and I would be wondering a little whether his increasing kindly feeling toward you and his ability to speak more freely with you might tend to precipitate some of his worry about what might be termed latent homosexuality.

KVARNES: Can you think of a technique which might be a safeguard here?

WILL: I can only ask another question. I am wondering whether the therapist would have to be more guarded in his approach to the patient, whether he should be careful not to be quite as friendly.

SULLIVAN: And another element of this general slant on things that is often worthwhile to investigate: if the patient expresses some warm feeling—I have forgotten actually what he did express in the way of a definitely warm feeling toward you—then one can, with safety, in general, inquire, "Well, how do I seem different from other people?" I don't care much what is said, but as long as I am seriously trying to get something said, it is possible that he will begin to draw comparisons which are free from these jittery background feelings and insofar as some of them seem fantastic, there is something for a discussion. One can do a good deal to make clear your relationship to the patient, thereby diminishing the amount of pressure that may be attached to something that can be discussed.

A devil of a lot might be said about how easy it was to talk to Dr. Kvarnes, because he has been a remarkably productive patient. I might learn something about how I am able to bring that about and it takes the pressure off of anything mysterious.

This incident of his going into the toilet: I am glad that was observed and reported, because it is a damn significant contact and I believe that Dr. Kvarnes showed rare clinical judgment in not poking around in it. The highly problematical question is will it do more harm to ignore it utterly than not? But certainly one does not want to inquire too much about that. We know that urgency of urination is very, very commonly associated with a sudden wave of anxiety, but also we know that in certain schizophrenic states at least, the function of urination is dangerously close to the experience of orgasm and with possibly one out of twenty patients with whom that would happen I would have felt quite free to go back when he came back and say, "We were talking about so and so." If he said "Yes," "No," or whatever, I would say, "That is not unpleasant to you, is it?" and that is about all I felt like doing. If he said it had made him anxious, then I would say, "I am sorry I made you anxious, and what is the trouble?" That is a great help. That establishes what I think about the situation and he doesn't have to wonder if I suspect.

KVARNES: That happened in a much more obscure way. This one was associated with a humorous event.

SULLIVAN: Now I remember. You were both laughing. If I had Dr. Rioch here, he might be inspired to comment on one of the aspects of reality—that to laugh is to undergo a reduction in tension. You could speculate that the internal sphincter might have relaxed in the reduction of tension. What actually happened is a tendency to interpret the result of that relaxation. An immediate compulsion to get to the toilet. I base that somewhat on one invaluable piece of data from a perplexed schizophrenic who propounded the riddle to me, "Why do I have to rush to urinate when I see you light a cigarette?" Permutations and combinations from that setting were illuminating, but I do think in this case the mutual good feeling, with a tendency to drop guard, which is the way of experiencing a sudden relaxation of tension—it is not safe to laugh with an enemy, you drop your guard immediately— starts a devious process which I don't want the boy to discuss and I would not, under those circumstances, mention that I made him anxious.

STAVEREN: I had something in mind about this incident that was felt to be humorous. I am not sure it started as humorous; it started out by his talking of his aggression and giving the example of his thought of flicking ashes on the bald head of another patient. If that means an older man, then he is talking about his contempt for his father, and if so it might have been something highly charged and his laughter or smile may have been something highly embarrassing and much more related to anxiety than to the relaxation of tension. In that connection I wonder whether his father is bald.

KVARNES: No. There is the point that he has considerable contempt for the old patients on the ward.

STAVEREN: About the earlier relationship with Jim and Jim's father, what struck me was that he did not bring Jim to his house. Sometime I would like to hear whether he was ashamed of his parents or didn't want Jim to find out what his position in the family was and thereby draw conclusions about how unworthy he was. In other words, what was Jim not supposed to see and notice? Also how much did envy play a part in the breaking up of the relationship with Jim? Jim was going somewhere, was having support, and so on.

I was also puzzled because I don't think he went through the thing that usually precedes pre-adolescent chum relationships— the ability to get along with the group. It seems that this relationship with Jim occurred at the time when most other boys were in group and gang activities, and why was he different in that respect? And when the chum relationship became a general pattern, his seems to disintegrate a bit and become more distant.

Another thing that was important was that he seems to have gotten along better in the Navy. Didn't he get sick shortly after he got home? What was his feeling about getting out of the Navy? Did it mean getting back to some painful set-up lacking in organization? In the Navy he was able to deal with a person in authority rather practically, and did coming home to go to law school mean falling back under the overpowering influence of the father and is that what made him so hopeless?

Also, what insulated his parents against his criticism and his protests? Why couldn't he blame them?

In treatment I had the impression that several points of exchange were incomplete, that he presents things in such a way that it is difficult to keep the door open to the next thing. There are a lot of hints without a chance to go on, and maybe that is responsible for the relative lack of continuity of data. I was wondering whether he puts something in such a way that one could say, "Well, does this make you too uncomfortable to talk about it?" and indicate that you are aware of the anxiety and are not willing to leave the topic unfinished, and get him to continue.

SULLIVAN: You come close to something that I rather wanted to hear about from someone. This man's father and mother were successful politicians. They worked on the job together. I judge that the father's political prominence was such that he would be well known to neighborhood police and so on. I hear no shadowy hint investing this boy as the politician's son. I am willing to poke around and to discover if there might be some factor which led to an attitude among the underprivileged which led to his not being included in gangs.

STAVEREN: His mother's rather masculine professional life must have had quite an influence on him too. He didn't want to be like father, he had apparently considerable problems with father, but mother is also like father and as far as he is concerned women don't seem to be very different from men and if that could get dealt with, this old, obnoxious sexual material would fall by the wayside. Why assume something desirable in girls when the father said mother was a better politician, and God knows what he got out of the exchange between the parents and what his assumptions were about the role of the woman in a man's life, not in a sexual way at all.

KVARNES: He made the comment that mother ran everybody's life, so here is the father who is prominent but mother is the dominating figure.

SULLIVAN: Who could take over when father was laid out? This is hot stuff on the general problem of what ails woman.

I also want to ask about this cold shower business. It is one of those things that my private thinking says we can't leave just yet. Dr. Salzman, what do you think of the panic business?

SALZMAN: The only thing I can make of it is that I dislike them too and I go into the same kind of reaction. I want to get out as soon as possible and I certainly would never go into one if I could help it. I can't take a cold shower and I have no conception why except that it is too damned uncomfortable.

SULLIVAN: When you are taking a cold shower and jumping around and perhaps squealing, what would you expect the other fellow to think of that? You might think he would think you were childish. Is there any more to it, to his feeling about his difficulties with cold showers?

KVARNES: That and the fact that he can't take it, which is supposed to be a sign of weakness.

SULLIVAN: There is something he is ashamed of, that he feels is a childish, immature trait. I don't see any serious danger in making that explicit. That is a place where I am perfectly willing to toss the ball and say: "What the hell are you talking about by panic about cold showers? These feelings that you act childish?" And if the patient says yes, we are disposed of that. There is no compulsion which says we all must take cold showers. That is blown up and I am going to show you that sometimes you can meet things face to face, call them by their true names and be rid of it.

If I were to be critical of Dr. Kvarnes' report, it would be that you have undertaken what I feel is the impossible several times. I will have to talk about this, even though I prefer to have others do the talking. When I say a thing is impossible, I don't mean that I can't get away with it in the treatment situation, but I am firmly convinced that a great deal of psychotherapy is done in the twenty-three hours between the treatment hours. The patient would not necessarily have lucid periods between but they have periods of much greater lucidity when they are alone than when they are with highly significant people. Leave things so that they are apt to get further, or at least survive, and if there is a field in which my experience has indicated I have failed, it is in this direct reassuring gesture.

Under interpersonal pressure, we are likely to leave the patient with the feeling that he is much better than he thought, and he goes away certain of our interest, but soon that begins to be subjected to his lifelong suspicion, and most schizophrenics have been taught that they were taken in easily, and people pulled their leg, and this comes up for review and sometimes is converted into almost the opposite—you must have been making fun of him, you are kidding him and trying to buck him up.

One of the great fields for developing skill is that of indirect reassurance. For example, take Dr. Styrt's comment about the boy doing very well on the baseball diamond and then his saying, "I just spoiled the game." Then I say, "Who knocked the ball further than you did at a certain time?" I make a demand for noticing something that happened. I don't care any more. How can you laugh that off? I have said: "Which matters, the distance the ball went in the right direction or this goddamn claptrap of you being no good?" But I do it almost all by implication and I am through. He will not be able to laugh off that fact.

Time and time again when this bird has done something pretty well—I might even wiggle something out of the incident of getting his transfer and under the circumstances I would say, "What ailed that?" Then you might add, "You got what you wanted without trouble," and again I am through. He can sputter or do whatever he pleases, but he can't get around it.

This business of underwriting practically unquestionable aspects of success by asking the question—for example, I have sometimes cross-examined patients as to their performance in a disagreeable situation and at the end said, "What ailed it?" Damn it, you can't find anything that ailed it, and I am through, I have done my bit. He may think I am a damn fool but that is harmless. That is not going to enfeeble my relationship to him, but I want the reassurance to come almost as if he has to take the next step. It is not a matter of my encouragement. I am distrustful of schizoid and obsessional people's ability to get nothing out of what I would call statements of direct reassurance except in one situation and that can be used only rarely. Sometime, with this boy, oh, possibly two months from now, you can start out practically with his first recollection and chart a course of development in which a notable degree of adequacy has been illustrated. He knew he did pretty much all right here, and you can give the line of success through his life, and then perhaps as if thinking aloud you might say, "From this comes a person convinced that he is no good, not adequate for living. How do we explain that?" That is the one fairly sure way I feel I can again underline certain elements which point in a fairly clear direction; then I make the demand—how come? Again I don't care much what he has to say, in fact the less he has to say the better pleased I am. I sometimes do that at the end of an hour to choke him off. Otherwise he gets it all mixed up.

This notion of developing skill in indirect reassurance is very important and underlies some of my comments about his sexual success. As long as it is a very important, outstanding characteristic, everything proves he is not adequate for life; I cannot work on any of the details in the sense of trying to find out what ails his adequacy, and particularly for the most difficult thing in the world, namely, adjusting to the other sex, before you know how to do it. Why attempt to make a silk purse out of a sow's ear? But after I have gradually built up, by this indirect reassurance, by my wondering what ails him, then I might come in when he says, "You know I can't get to first base with a woman." What difference does it really make? Oh, such things as making a living, being in business is of considerable advantage, compared with most people as to background and influence, but what good is that as long as you can't marry, have children, maintain a harem or what? Drive it into perspective, and if the patient believes my whims of thinking it isn't the most important thing in life, then we can discover what ails him in this but not that that is the only and indispensable business of life.

It is interesting to poke around in sex life but it has been notably unsuccessful with a great many boys and I want to increase the possibility of success. There is not much chance of avoiding dangerous problems until the patient has practically convinced himself that you think he is worth the effort. It has to be done by him. You cannot rub it in.

The question of whether there is a danger getting fairly clear in his relationship to you is, I think, a timely observation, and may I be forgiven for talking like grampa for the moment? I very much dislike having patients find anything in me, even if it were there for the moment, that is not apt to be permanent. I have had some appalling disasters in psychiatry from permitting patients to develop expectations that I had not any intention of realizing when they got better. You pliantly enter into a relationship with them that you would not think of maintaining if they did not need it. Then you see progress wiped out and all therapy by anybody is through. That is the final blow.

When I feel that a patient is developing an appreciation for me, I also think of another aspect of things. Can this patient afford to appreciate me this much? If a person has a tenuous self-esteem, feels quite a bastard, what is the cost of thinking the doctor is wonderful? It is something they can't stand. They have worth only because this wonderful person is interested in them. And there again you make all sorts of horrible mistakes in carrying out such an impossible role, and I am too preoccupied, I have too many things to do to keep such a relationship, and as these indications of high regard and high appreciation come forth, I ask very blunt questions. Sometimes when a patient ventures—and I think you could lead this boy to say he found it easy to talk—I would be inclined to say, "What the hell, it is your first venture." I am not having any miracles, and if he says, "Well, I have never known anybody who could hear all this stuff and still maintain interest," I say, "Look, young man, if you can tell me of instances when you confided in people and they despised you, that will be worth listening to." He thinks I am wonderful because he has not made a fool of himself with me. They will tell you of instances of self-revelation—how it would immediately embarrass the other fellow. The other fellow has laughed at him and then I come along and say, "Don't you suppose he was embarrassed?" Probably the patient never entertained this highly probable explanation of a serious rebuff. I have removed much of the hurt. He thinks I understand life wonderfully. You can't avoid that entirely. There again if I get invested with too much esteem, then I say, "What the hell do you expect from spending twenty years in psychiatry? Do you expect me to know nothing? This is no miracle." I want this person to understand that, of course, I am some good, and mistakes—God, mistakes should be cherished as long as they do not cause anxiety. If a patient can point out one's mistakes, that is something. The last thing—where a patient expresses gratitude for something that has been really very valuable to him: that is a ticklish emergency. Where, for example, you really have helped a patient avoid a serious mistake or aided him to see just what he wants to do that would work, and he is grateful and expresses it. What do you do? Thank him for his kind words, and get on with something else. If somebody makes what I regard as a rather astute compliment which is not a compliment but a commendation, I make it a point to express pleasure only as it furnished clues into the problem. If you do not acknowledge commendation from a patient, you are too big for them. What the hell do you care about what they think? That does not help. The risk which is run more often due to clumsiness is that it goes over so big they think they have to give you plenty. You want to be clear on what you do next, and with me in the old days I had some idea of what I wanted to investigate and I have time and again said to a very kind sentiment, "How are we coming along on so and so to the problem?" Just that simple. The thing I don't dare leave alone.

SALZMAN: I wanted to ask whether the hypothesis of the boy's growing feelings of inadequacy during his relationship with Jim is strengthened by the fact that he did not bring his friends to his own home.

SULLIVAN: I don't exactly coincide in my feeling with the two views expressed on this point. I think we are far enough along in understanding why that was the case so that I would not want to ask the wrong question, but he has rather harped on the disorganization of the home and we know these people were interested in politics, which suggests that the place was a crossroads or that they were always out. In other words, I would probably approach this by saying, "Who was at home during the day at that time?" If he says, "No one except the maid," then I might be interested in whether he had a room to himself and so on. Try to build it up that way. Sometimes patients are quite discouraged by our failure to integrate what they have told us and it is always neat if you can ask questions which introduce new views on what he has told you.

I suspect that there was no home to take Jim to, just a barn that people spent the night in. We know that Jim's father was very much interested in his son. I am intrigued by the absence of Jim's mother. It may be simply that the father was a widower. But there is not the faintest hint, and this is one of the things I put away and watch. In all these relationships in his pre-adolescence and later juvenile period you may never discover any women. There is a curious absence of women. It begins to look as if already this boy was either too distressed to compare his mother with other women, or afraid of all women and tending to erase them from the environment—as if the places would be better if there were no women. That is the thing I watch grow. I am a little afraid of it. I don't want to get into the most difficult area of life until I have him clear and he is beginning to demand that something be done about his sex life.

KVARNES: About the women, there is that lack of mention of them all through. I have to inquire specifically and his mother is seldom brought up. The same goes with the cousins.

SULLIVAN: Even in very mildly problematical people in psychotherapy, one often finds that one side of the sex line, notably let us say mother or father, gets a lot of attention and the other is obviously not appreciated reasonably or just dropped like a hotcake. I think you will all learn as the years roll over you that it is not right to insist immediately on that side. What is there to be produced is a good thing to exhaust as long as it is coming. On the other hand, you must not forget unfinished business and must keep track of these things which were sideswiped. Then you can say, "I guess we better study mother." You can't weave a whole fabric continuously, but you should not forget the hints you get. In fact, mildly problematical people give you wonderfully good hints which you will be well advised not to use for weeks. While they are centered on, let us say, the father, they may toss out a revealing comment about mother. This is a good thing to remember—it is valid because it came without calling—but it is up to you to wait. You exhaust what is pushing for utterance. What is true of psychotherapy with comparatively mild personality problems, insofar as it pertains to your power to control, cover, and direct the process, applies with much greater force to the schizophrenic. He is ready to be discouraged, ready to find evidence that you do not understand him, so that aspect of psychotherapy, the little you hear about mother, you would do well to remember.

About the business of the Navy, I would like to have him asked, "Did you think at all of staying in the Navy?" That would be my approach to the business of the future. He probably didn't. How much was that due to social pressure? Everybody wanted to get out. How much was it due to not liking the type of life? Later I will say, "Did going into law mean you were heading for a political career?" There are more lawyers in politics and this boy, strikingly schizoid for many years, would scarcely look forward to success in politics.

STAVEREN: Do you think it is too early, for instance when he brings up something like the statement about his freedom, to say, "You mean the neglect?"

SULLIVAN: I am glad to have you ask that. I surmise there were a good many elements in the occasional attitude of father and mother to this boy that make it a little difficult to face the idea of his being neglected. That is almost too strong. I try something that is a little less startling and perhaps tinted with humor. When I heard about his freedom I might feel that the situation was such that I could say, "What do you mean, freedom?" I don't want to bring in the ponderous problem of indifference. That is so repugnant, and I don't want to say neglect because that is going to pull strong negation by him, but I am very much in favor of what you are driving at, namely, to question the freedom. Sometimes that can be done slightly humorously without danger of complicating the rapport. That does not mean I never use strong language. I think that neglect is not within his grasp yet. Something about the early illness, in the first presentation, made me think he got a good deal of attention here and there.

KVARNES: He told me of another thing that occurred when he

asked his mother to take him home, something he often does, and her reply was, "If I do, will you behave?"

SULLIVAN: This is the sort of thing where I turn and look at a person with what I trust to be an expression of sympathetic chagrin. You just endorse the rightness of the patient's views. Sometimes under the pressure of things of that kind you can say, "Has she always been that obtuse?" You can clear up a hell of a lot of secretiveness by that simple business. All these very effective things—as I am sure I have said before—everything should be spontaneous except nothing should be spontaneous. You have got to think, "What will this do to the patient?" Even if they are carefully thought out, if they sound spontaneous, it works well. Patients don't want us to be too worried; it suggests they might be in desperate stages.

Comment on Second Session, Twenty-five Years Later, January, 1972

KVARNES: Let's discuss the second session with Sullivan.

RYCKOFF: That's the best, one of the best.

KVARNES: Weren't we going to try to read the whole thing, and then go back and review what we want to do with it—or does anybody remember?

DILLINGHAM: Well, we were going to read the whole thing, then we were going to attempt a line-by-line sort of discussion of it, which I guess includes the option of deciding what to do with it.

RYCKOFF: Going over it carefully was based on some notion about discovering ways of editing it, or using it.

DILLINGHAM: I read the whole thing, expecting to come to some dramatic conclusion, and didn't.

KVARNES: One thing I was thinking about was in terms of evaluation—I don't know what I would have said about this as a learning experience if I had answered a questionnaire within the first week or two at the end of it. Now that I read it, I see the source material and clinical beginnings of all kinds of things that I do. I wonder how we can get the long-term evaluation dimension built in on studies when we are usually evaluating short-term outcomes.

This second session is certainly still rich with clinical inputs and strategies.

DILLINGHAM: I was impressed with the increase in volume of Sullivan's interest in strategy, telling you more and more how to get certain kinds of information, what kind of questions to ask, why you wouldn't ask them this way. I was also impressed by the fact that all the questions he raises as major questions, really vital in terms of necessary information, never come up again. I couldn't tell whether that was because so many other things kept coming up, or whether they did come up in some other form.

KVARNES: Or their significance wasn't understood by us at the moment—couldn't make much use of it.

JACOBSON: That's an interesting observation, because I felt on reading the second one that Bill was very responsive to the requests made in the first one for more information.

DILLINGHAM: For instance, in the first one he talks about the significance of the guy he took the trip with, and that really doesn't resurface very much.

JACOBSON: But Bill does come in with more information about that, the second time, that isn't picked up.

RYCKOFF: With regard to information, is there some question about whether the facts themselves are essential? Is Sullivan trying to compile a complete factual history or is he trying to sketch out the dimensions of awareness that a therapist has to have if he is going to——

DILLINGHAM: I think that he repeats that theme again and again —how you have to listen. I guess he talks about getting information about the trip as a way of figuring out how the guy will relate to you, or to the friend as a man. You know, here's a significant man, and I wonder what that really means. What would he have done, for instance, if he didn't have the trip to talk about?

KVARNES: I'm not sure what your question is, John.

DILLINGHAM: Well, he goes through the whole trip and he says: "I hope you see why the interest in this. I am attempting to explore what I can expect to do as a man with a man, quite aside from the developmental importance of such events." And I am wondering how he would explore that if he didn't have any data on the trip. What kind of thing would he try to elicit? He starts building it up, saying the trip is terribly important, because there were two accidents on the trip——

JACOBSON: Were there other events in his life that might have given him that kind of information? Ask about relationships in the Navy, for example?

KVARNES: I guess my interpretation at this point would be that the trip would be the most recent instance of a situation in which the patient might have told me about himself and another human being, and it might indicate something about the capability for talking about himself—readiness; and also, if you could explore something like that, you get a notion about the naïveté and sophistication of your patient in terms of personal discussion, and you might also get some idea of anxiety areas as compared with strengths. The things that he talked about could be lead-in points for further discussion because they are not endowed with this kind of eerie anxiety. And what didn't get discussed would also point to what you would have to focus on some other time. I think that might be partly what he's after.

Also, I was struck by the hierarchy of sensitivity he was developing in terms of the words "indifference," "neglect," and "freedom." You know, the patient was saying he had so much freedom that he kind of hated it, about which the group used the terms "indifference" and "neglect." Sullivan was indicating that "neglect" is an awful powerful term to use with a real sick patient, and even "indifference" has got a wallop to it, so he was suggesting that he would start this investigation by saying, "What do you mean, *freedom?*," which is a good illustration of the sensitivity that he has in terms of the anxiety that attends to words themselves. And that's certainly something I learned in the course of this: that you pick your language damned carefully because of the affect that you stir up in using inappropriate terms.

JACOBSON: There's a lot in there that's related to being spontaneous or seeming to be spontaneous without being spontaneous—just mouthing whatever comes to you as therapists. I know that kind of concept, but I guess I couldn't put it very succinctly myself and I didn't think that he was putting it very clearly either.

RYCKOFF: I think this question about language and spontaneity is important. If by spontaneity one would mean literally reacting right off the top of your head to something, I don't see that that could very often be therapeutic. I think there is a kind of spontaneity which is based upon some knowledge of the patient and of the relationship. For example, I think there is a big difference between two people who get spontaneous with each other after they know something about each other, and the immediate engagement—you know, two guys walk into a room and start in on each other right off the bat, but they don't really know what they are talking about. What they are talking about under the guise of spontaneity is that which is completely projected from within themselves because they don't know anything about the other person. They are bringing something in with them and supposedly under the guise of interaction it is spontaneous but it is really ignorance.

KVARNES: It's imagination, Irv! You are talking in the frame of reference of encounter groups?

RYCKOFF: I am thinking of a seminar I had last night on family therapy, and we read a long piece by Dr. ———, who's a big wheel in this business. It's an interview, a transcription of an interview, and the tape is stopped and he discusses with an interviewer what he has done and why he thinks he did it. The point is that—I don't know him but others who do sort of agree with this—he's a restless, very'responsive guy, and he can't wait until someone gets into the room to get something going. In the beginning there's a little interaction about how the appointment was set up, and right away it's an argument, and he says to the interviewer, "You know you have to have a fight in order to begin." His need for engagement is such that he has to have a fight or some other intense business, right off the bat. He can't start in some kind of neutral way, saying, "We'll get together, we'll talk, we'll see what happens." I question how valuable that kind of thing is for a patient. As a matter of fact, it turns out that this family had this one interview with him, all kinds of activity going on, and he never heard from them again. I think that's one of the reasons why. Sullivan's the opposite of this type. There's thought about every damn thing that happened, based on some knowledge, some impression, some information, about the other person.

JACOBSON: That's true in his comments about the third party with these guys in the seminar, but that's certainly not true about his interaction with the guys in the seminar. I was struck in the second session, particularly, about how strong he comes on with the members of that group with the exception of you [Kvarnes].

In the second one he was much more supportive of you. But he's asking questions of the seminar participants abruptly, bluntly, sharply, demandingly.

RYCKOFF: He's not being paid to be a therapist there.

KVARNES: It's more than that, though. When I first read these, I thought he had been awfully sharp with some of us. Sam Novey said something about "passivity needs" and I thought Sullivan clobbered him on that, as if to say: "We use terms like that but I still want to know what you mean. I don't assume my association is your connotation."

DILLINGHAM: The whole business seems to be a fascination with particularity—particularity in general. That I think is very obvious in the first session, where he says pick out something that you can understand and "then you have something you can trust." You can't work by inference. You have to find out exactly what he meant by that—for example, that business of freedom. He says, freedom in relation to what? More free than his brother? More free than the people he went to school with? What the hell does it mean? He still wants to know exactly.

I'm still interested in that business of spontaneity. Does he mean that by affecting some kind of spontaneity you are saying to the patient that what the patient is saying to you is not particularly threatening—you can handle it, something doesn't get so immense that it is terrifying? Is he saying more than that, or what? There is another place where he is talking about the Navy. He says:

In developing useful contact with the patient, if one has some of these hunches, it often gives the patient a feeling that you are really making sense, that you are looking for things that matter and that you understand them. Since I have never been in the Navy. . . . [But] it is good to have some hunches about it. . . .

You know, that feels like he is saying you are telling the patient that you think that some kind of rational sense can be made out of what is happening, and not a hell of a lot more than that. But I wonder if there is more to it than that.

RYCKOFF: I think this is all part of a stance he considers important. Certainly I've learned to consider it important. That is, to be always trying to be in a position where you are attempting to get at or help the patient define what he means without making any assumptions. I think it often does involve particular words. In any session you can find this kind of misunderstanding. I had a hilarious one yesterday which I was amazed about. I was seeing a couple, and the woman—this is not unusual for her—says about her husband, "He lets his parents shit all over him, he lets his kids shit all over him," and she goes on like this. Couple of minutes later I said something about contempt. She got furious. She says, "What makes you say there is contempt in it?" and she went on and on and on. She said, "I feel he lets himself be disrespected. I don't respect his doing that, but where did you get the idea that I feel contempt?" Well, I argued with her some, but I thought about it afterwards and I think she has a right to her definition. I think she has more contempt than she is willing to acknowledge, but I also think she honestly did not intend to express contempt. The distinction could escape the ordinary eye but the difference was very important to her, because contempt—I could see it when she got upset—meant to her that they had reached the end of the road. If she had contempt, where the hell were they going to go?

KVARNES: There is also another framework that I think this example fits. To a specific person, some words have a positive value and others have a negative value, and somebody like your patient may make scurrilous comments but still feel they have a positive value.

RYCKOFF: That's pretty much what she said, by the way. That was her point. She accused me of always being negative and cited other instances. It is a tendency of mine. I tend to take what's presented and exaggerate it, move it ahead in the same direction, so that disrespect would become contempt. I sort of poke at people that way.

JACOBSON: But that is part of the process of clarifying.

RYCKOFF: To me it is, but to her it's a reversal from something positive to something negative.

KVARNES: And with lots of patients, particularly schizophrenics, when you get over to that negative value, it's scary as hell. As long as they can put a positive value, even something that comes out so hostile you can scarcely listen to it, they've got it in some kind of framework so it doesn't come out so threatening to them.

JACOBSON: How does the patient's inclination to distort what he's told anyway fit into this? Many times a patient will say, "You know when you told me two weeks ago thus and so—" and when I hear this thing come back to me——

RYCKOFF: You don't recognize it?

JACOBSON: Well, I don't recognize it; I'm appalled that things I said could have become so different in the patient's mind.

RYCKOFF: Well, isn't there always a discrepancy? One of the signs that things are going well is that these discrepancies are getting smaller and smaller; there is a greater and greater congruence in the sense of things.

KVARNES: One other theoretical framework for that is the difference between the autistic and the consensually valid. I always liked that one, because in Ryckoff's instance you are both valid; in effect you each have an autistic meaning to the term *contempt*. That's partially what the distortion process is. You have to work over and over some of those things until there is some consensus, or else—what probably happens much of the time—one of you gives up and moves on to a different terminology.

DILLINGHAM: That's also part of what he is saying about being specific—working over the thing. But also somewhere else he says that the minute you begin to speak paragraphs to your patient you are finished, that if you can't say something in one or two short sentences, then you haven't got it. And I suppose there is some geometric proportion by which when you start speaking in paragraphs you get distortion back.

RYCKOFF: That's a marvelous truism, one that I experience every day of the week. It's true, saying too much. I know for myself if I can't make the point in a compact, succinct way, then it's lost.

DILLINGHAM: He demonstrates that again; he says, "It's the old complaint again," or, instead of going into ten paragraphs about him and his father, just say, "There he goes again," and see what comes up.

JACOBSON: That must have been in a later session. I don't know that.

DILLINGHAM: I can't remember where it is but I was struck by the sense of breaking it down into very small, very digestible units of interaction.

RYCKOFF: I think the compactness of statements not only breaks down into more easily digestible pieces but also forces the other person, the patient—or anyone in conversation, for that matter—to stretch their imagination about their thinking. They've got to take a condensed, pithy, overdetermined kind of remark and begin to think about its implications.

KVARNES: I think sometimes you do talk in paragraphs to patients when you are developing some hypothesis or interpretation, and I think I got out of this experience a realization that, OK, I have to do that sometimes but it's for me; the patient isn't really listening.

RYCKOFF: You are explaining to yourself.

KVARNES: Yes. It gets something put into a framework for me. That's all right, but I shouldn't be fooled about its getting across —that my putting it into a framework really scores with the patient.

JACOBSON: How about the issue of choosing what you say that will enhance the patient's view of himself, or at least not do the opposite? And he was pointing to some pretty subtle kinds of things in this notion of developing reassurance skills indirectly.

KVARNES: Do you know what he means?

JACOBSON: Well, I think he is saying that for this guy you don't treat his sexual problem as the central issue now, and dwell on that, because by treating that as the essence of life you are saying to him that he is a failure at his core. Is that right?

KVARNES: Yes. If you let that be the principal emphasis, the outcome is going to be, *I'm no damn good.*

But let's go back to the early part of the second meeting, where after I presented the material Sullivan asked how they would conceptualize, thus far, about what made the patient get sick.

JACOBSON: Or what ails him.

KVARNES: And it's interesting that the responses are all faulty and faltering, even though there's a good deal of difference in sophistication among the seminar members. The young guys really didn't know how to do it, and at that time I certainly didn't know what would be acceptable to my colleagues, and I think the older fellows also were somewhat uneasy about making a mistake. Yet it's an absolutely legitimate approach, absolutely legitimate question, and that I think should be underscored—how hard it was for this group of inexperienced and experienced people to spontaneously grab hold of that question and do something with it. And really all it amounts to in this seminar is that it's a point of direction. It's a good way to start thinking about the patient's difficulties.

RYCKOFF: There's one problem with that, that people get flustered—I know I do, too—at questions of that sort. For me, it's because I inevitably drop the experiential knowledge that I have about the patient and think that what is called for is some kind of knowledge derived from another reality altogether. So when you used the phrase just now, "respond spontaneously," my thought is, how can you respond spontaneously to the question, "How do you conceptualize so-and-so?" Conceptualization means bringing something out of the literature and having some pre-formed theory of what it's all about, and that's a hard fallacy to deal with.

JACOBSON: In fact, Sullivan doesn't even ask the question that way. He said: "I would like to hear from each of you what you feel you now understand about why this man is sick."

RYCKOFF: That's a wonderful question, put very simply.

JACOBSON: Which is really asking for the experiential level. He couldn't have asked it more simply. I know what happens with me in a situation like that—I assume that he knows.

RYCKOFF: Right. Looking for an answer that he already knows.

JACOBSON: The myth that he knows. He goes on, "I am far from certain that we know why he is sick but I think the picture of developmental history is rather remarkably good," et cetera. ". . . express some view as to your hunch as to what ails this man and I don't mean diagnosis." And yet nobody was really equal to that in the situation.

KVARNES: I must say that that also was a refreshing phrasing for me when I first heard it in that seminar—"What ails this man?" That is so different from saying, "What's wrong with this man?" Previously the question always had been, "What's wrong with this man?," which has a different value load to it.

JACOBSON: Even that's better than, "What's the diagnosis?"

RYCKOFF: It's interesting you used the word *conceptualize*; that's exactly the word he would not use.

KVARNES: Right.

JACOBSON: From your knowledge and experience with him, was that a learned characteristic of his or do you think it was natural to Sullivan to think in ordinary language? You know what I mean?

KVARNES: I don't know if I can answer that, but both in my direct experience with him and in the stuff he has written, I don't know anybody who had higher regard for words—that is, for picking words that fit the situation and so far as possible avoid obscureness and tautology. It's curious that so many people find Sullivan hard to read, and elaborate and involved. I really think that's more related to his struggle, maybe too powerful a struggle, to get the thing said right. In working with him in supervision I thought he was good at using very simple language whereby you move step by step, instead of getting all tangled up with the complicated language.

JACOBSON: It's true that he's not a guy who didn't invent his own terminology. Like his concept *dynamism*, for example; he uses that word for something very specific in his system.

RYCKOFF: He did invent some terrific neologisms, like *parataxic distortions*.

JACOBSON: That's right.

RYCKOFF: Some of those seem to me like no great improvement on other words—the only value they have is that they are fresh, his own definition. He had a great preoccupation with operational language—I'm not sure I know exactly what that is. It's a categorical term. But when his language gets very complicated, the complications do not derive from some intellectualized, obsessive process he goes through in order to arrive at a theory. They derive from his concern about following the experience of the patient, and as that gets more complicated then his language gets more complicated; he insists on trying to reproduce it very carefully.

JACOBSON: Take a single word like *diagnosis*. He doesn't want to depend on that kind of word because there is more complexity in what he means.

RYCKOFF: One of the problems with psychoanalytic theorizers is that they don't do what Sullivan does; they take a concept or a series of concepts which they treat as established units—for example, the concept of the oedipal—and they start building other structures out of them. The more they do that the further they get away from reality.

JACOBSON: And what's more, the patient's experience is being squeezed to fit into the concept.

DILLINGHAM: I wonder how much he moves away from things

like the sexual problem, saying such a discussion ceases to be useful for this patient, because maybe in psychoanalytic treatment circles and culturally the whole area of sexuality has become so overloaded that you'd do well to stay away from it. I wonder if anything is known about how he saw that culture.

RYCKOFF: A good question.

KVARNES: I suppose there is some danger of misunderstanding but this was twenty-five years ago, and God, it was not easy for most people to talk about sex in those days, and certainly the schizophrenic by and large would be dealing with creepy, eerie feelings that he would never put into words, never read about, and that lent a "hands off" feel to it anyway.

DILLINGHAM: I guess what started me thinking along those lines was that he used as a caveat, you know, if we went around the room and talked about our sexual successes none of us would do particularly well. And so that's a demonstration that it's really not that useful to us.

KVARNES: Unless you are really doing it in some way you can make use of. Anybody can find fault with his own sexuality and particularly if he has low self-esteem. There's another dimension to that. I'm not sure Sullivan ever spent enough time developing it, but certainly one of his core ideas was the huge problem in the schizophrenic of gender identity, and the terminology and the concepts weren't developed very well at that point. It is a problem with all kinds of people but particularly with schizophrenics because they've got it backwards much of the time, and the homosexual framework for that is not adequate. It's just simply a scary kind of business where you act out something, but deeper down there is an identification on the part of the male schizophrenic with the female person and that is what they have such an enormous problem dealing with. Then when they get to puberty, they may come apart trying to deal with pubescent sexuality, partly because they now have to assume a masculine role and masculine identity that they are not prepared for. And either he mentioned that in this seminar or I read about it someplace else, but it is something we might keep in mind, particularly with this patient, because he's got a father who is a success but not a very capable model for a kid; he's got a mother he's much closer to but she's crazy. So here's this guy trying to mold himself with these two unusable models. I think that may get somewhat clearer as we go on. As I reflect on it, it certainly seems to be what the problem was for the guy, although I didn't know it at the time, didn't see it that clearly.

I know what I'm trying to get at. The cultural side of this is interesting to me because it's the problem of the integration of the masculine/feminine components of our personalities that each of us individually tries to resolve. I grew up in a mining area where male overassertiveness and hypermasculinity was the usual male attempt at solution and anything which was feminine about one, one tried hard to repress. Those guys who actually couldn't be he-men were seen as sissies or fairies or mommas' boys or worse. Anybody who had some sensitivity was in danger of being ridiculed. But that was a very poor solution; the problem of gender identity is never really solved for anybody if he is stuck with a hypermasculine identity. Culturally in our era the kids have come along, homosexuals have come along, and they have developed this unisex concept which in itself isn't the least bit attractive to me, but I'm impressed with how it detoxifies this whole goddamn gender business. My kids wear long hair and one puts a barrette in the back of his hair, but doesn't have any question about his masculinity. My God, I wouldn't have been caught dead even thinking that at his age. It's interesting to see society attempt to deal with the problem of gender identity and actually do something in the direction of a solution.

DILLINGHAM: I wondered about the incident when the patient was away and wrote to his parents to have them meet the girl he later was engaged to, and then he started developing this rather warm correspondence. And I wondered what cultural context that fit into, whether it was the Russian/Jewish family context or some sort of generation thing that I don't remember reading about or hearing from my family: that you would have your parents carry on this relationship for you. I didn't really know what to make of it. I couldn't tell whether it was a function of the sickness or whether it was something that was culturally reasonable in terms of being an aggressive man after a girl. You send your parents to do it for you.

JACOBSON: Not in my culture.

RYCKOFF: Not in mine—wouldn't have trusted my parents with—I kept everything as far away as possible.

KVARNES: I did that. I had a girlfriend during my internship; I was edging toward marriage; it would have been a disaster. But I brought her to meet my mother and my mother spotted what ailed the relationship; we broke up. I was concerned about her at the time. I thought perhaps I had just fallen into my mother's trap of controlling me, but she was absolutely right. So the process was a good one in that instance.

JACOBSON: But that's different; you brought the girl to meet the mother.

RYCKOFF: Question for you was, were you secure enough to believe your mother?

KVARNES: Or was I using that to get out of something I couldn't handle anyway?

JACOBSON: Well, what are we going to try to do for next time?

III

Case Seminar, January, 1947

The format of this session, again, is like that of the others: an initial presentation by Kvarnes, brief comments by Sullivan, queries directed at the other seminar members by Sullivan, and then a final explication by Sullivan of a crucial conflict or dynamism.

In addition to Kvarnes and Sullivan, the following persons were present at this session: Robert Cohen, Larry Cooper, Edna Dyar, Samuel Novey, Stanley Peal, Joseph Rom, Leon Salzman, Philip Wagner, Charles Wheeler, Mary White, and John Witt.

KVARNES: In the past month, the type of material we have been working on has fallen into two general areas, one related to the home and parents up to puberty or a little later, and the other concerning his more persistent complaints—that is, his current feelings. I thought first I would present the additional historical data and then give some idea of how he is at the moment.

Because he had expressed some feeling of hatred toward his parents—the feeling had been exhibited in rather marked fashion just following his leaving Springhill in August of last year—I felt it might be possible to go into a definition of his position in the home without too much difficulty for him, and he has been quite willing to follow that line of exploration.

In relationship to his father, he seems to feel that from the very beginning he has been in awe of him. In the first nine years of the patient's life, his father was serving in the state legislature, and spent a good deal of time each year in the state capital, coming home for weekends. When his father joined the family for meals, he rather guided the course of events and made frequent comments to the boy about his use of language, objecting to his saying "yeah" and "ain't." He also inquired as to whether Bill had been a good boy. Bill came to feel, as he looked back, that he had probably feared his father from an early period. He mentioned several times that his father was a stranger, and this seems to be in comparison to Jim's father. His father didn't join in his play and, he says, paid little attention to his schoolwork. The mother had given the boy a great deal of attention prior to his entering kindergarten, teaching him to read and write, but when he entered school, the interest of both parents dropped. I asked him if they helped with his school lessons and he said no, never at home.

He has mentioned several times his early interest in reading—often he would isolate himself in his father's library and read for a long time. However, he comments that he did not learn much from the reading, that he seemed to read for something other than the content. When I asked him if it was to gain his father's approval, he remarked, "You've got something there." By concentrating on reading instead of play, he was proving to his father that he was smart and good. His father often brought him presents—toys, and especially books—but they would be doled out following the inquiry as to whether Bill had been a good boy. He did not know what being a good boy meant but thought it was being quiet. He came to see that there was some division in his behavior—that in the home he was very serious, quiet, and well-behaved, and outside or at Jim's home he was different, feeling free to play. He seemed to feel that in the home he was operating in the role of the son of a prominent father, having to live up to what his father expected of him in behavior and grammar.

He also connected this fear of his father with what seems to have been a very early and long-standing fear of authority. He approached all schoolteachers with fear and awe, afraid of being called on and criticized, and was especially fearful of male teachers. On questioning, he remembered only one teacher whom he felt kindly toward—a third-grade teacher who treated him very much as his mother had, kissing and babying him.

For the most part he has mentioned his mother only occasionally and the data on her remains incomplete. He seems to believe that he was always very much in love with his mother, but some of his comments suggest that she treated him very much as the father did—displaying little interest in his schoolwork and his play, and tending to be away from home when he needed her. One day recently he talked about his mother at greater length. He said he felt he had a "mother fixation." When I asked him what he was trying to tell me, he said that from an early age he considered her the most beautiful thing in the world. He liked her blond hair very much and remembers at eight or nine following a young girl with blond hair all the way to school, thinking how much she looked like his mother. He also said in all the little girls he knew at that time, he saw the image of his mother, and therefore liked them.

During that period before puberty, he seems to have spent more time with his mother than his father, both at home and elsewhere, and to have enjoyed her company more. He remembers going to the beauty parlor with her and sitting there in some admiration. He said he can't remember being comfortable with any woman except his mother, and that the idea of his having fear of women from an early age seemed quite definite to him. As evidence of this he talked about his two maternal aunts. One, the mother of the four suburban cousins, was a disciplinarian and different from his mother in that respect. He never felt at ease with that aunt, and was always afraid she would criticize him or in some way instruct him in what to do. He recalls that she took him for an early visit to the dentist, perhaps his first, and that her presence seemed to magnify the terror he already felt about going; he refused to go in until one or two cousins went first. The other aunt was the one who was hospitalized until recently with a paranoid psychosis. He remembers waiting for her in a doctor's outer office while she had a nasal treatment, and being terrified by her moaning and screaming. On his father's side, he lumps his aunts into an undelineated group of figures for whom he had no feeling.

He also mentioned in relation to the idea of mother fixation that he yearned for a sister, perhaps from a few years after the birth of his brother, when he was seven or eight, until puberty. This sister would be a sort of reincarnation of his mother.

At times he also talked at length about the maid. I am not able to get any clear notion of what he thought of her. He remembers he was put to bed by the maid and left lying in the dark, watching the shadows, wanting the light on. He was fearful of going to bed at night, but always the maid put him there, never his mother. The maid was not too severe with him but was rather uninterested. He has recently recognized that she devoted practically all of her attention to his brother David, but I am not sure how clearly he understands the situation. The parents frankly admit to me that the younger boy was the focus of concern in the household. The patient has brought this up many times in an offhand manner, but on direct questioning he still does not seem to accept the fact that part of the difficulty he had in gaining attention resulted from the younger boy's illness and need for care.

He remembers having temper tantrums occasionally, but his only clear recollection is of throwing his shoe at the maid and then feeling guilty about it. He also mentioned that the maid was much less beautiful than his mother and he didn't like her face, but she was a meticulous housekeeper and was the only one in the household who had any idea of cleanliness or order. She remained with the family until the boy was thirteen or fourteen and then returned to her native country. He does not recall whether she was happy or unhappy when she was with them.

We have talked several times about the arguments between the parents. As far as I can discover, the theme of the arguments was the competition between the parents—the father disliked the fact that the mother was out of the house so much and involved in so many enterprises, and the mother insisted on her right to such activities. There were also arguments about financial matters. On several occasions the patient has commented on his great sensitivity to noise, and he tries to seclude himself in an effort to get away from other patients' voices and the radio. When we tried to trace the beginning of this sensitivity, he recalled that his first memory was a family argument when he was about four. After he had gone to bed the parents started an argument that got so noisy that he climbed out of bed in terror and ran to his parents. He threw his arms around his mother, attempting by his action to stop the argument. What he remembers particularly is the noise. During subsequent arguments, which were fairly frequent, the terror returned and he felt like running to his mother. With some difficulty, a couple of days ago he told me of an argument he witnessed when he was fourteen, again apparently over some aspect of the parental competition. At one point his mother screamed at the top of her voice, "I will jump out of the

window," while the father yelled, "No, no, no!" The mother's
words frightened the patient, but he was terrified and disgusted
with the whole performance, and apparently made no attempt to
join in the argument. Since then, there has not been any violence
in the arguments. Over the last ten years or so he has come to
agree with his father more, to feel that his father was more rational in the discussions and arguments and that his mother was
hysterical. He felt that her response to arguments was complete
loss of emotional control. However, more recently the mother
has been less hysterical and the arguments are less meaningful to
him now.

It seems to me that the period from eight to ten was a turbulent
period for him. That was the period when he made a couple of
attempts to run away, obviously with the knowledge of the
parents. He remembered once feeling, "If they don't love me, I'll
show them, I'll run away, and they'll be sorry," and leaving the
house and going around the block. His mother's response was
hysterical, somewhat similar to her response in the arguments.
During the same period there was sufficient difficulty between
the parents that they spoke of "divorce," and he remembers wondering about the word. He had fantasies of a courtroom scene in
which the judge asked him to decide which parent he wanted to
live with and he knew he would choose his mother regardless of
the arguments. Apparently at the same time the mother and the
boy would get together and ridicule the father, laughing about
foolish things he did.

Although both parents took him out, his father had a tendency
not to want to go. When they went to various political meetings
and social affairs, he, as the son of an eminent man, would be
introduced and would feel very uncomfortable. He then mentioned, as he has before, the discomfort he felt when his father
was speaking, although he describes his father as an emotional,
crowd-holding, popular speaker.

Also in these years before puberty it was customary for the
maid to take the boys to a movie on Saturday afternoon. However, sometimes he sneaked off to a movie across the street where
the manager knew his father. He seems to feel now that it was a
protest against his parents and also perhaps a way of gaining attention since at times his father had to inquire of the manager in
order to find him. Several times he came home late; significantly,

on his brother's birthday he came home too late for supper and was sent to his room and told he could have no supper and no birthday cake. However, his father came up later to talk it over with him, and he was then given some cake.

He also complained that during those years on Saturdays or Sundays, he was part of a group of five or six children who were escorted to points of interest by a paid guide. Similarly, he was escorted to the beach with a group of children. Always there is the suggestion that the parents did not have the time or interest to take him on such outings—that he was just pushed off into a group of children to be entertained.

He feels that as a child he was repressed by the necessity of being good, but that occasionally he burst out from his restraints. For example, once when he and his mother were attending a concert by Josef Hofmann, he had yelled out an encore request, "Play the 'Minute Waltz' "—a piece he had been playing repeatedly on his phonograph at home. He seemed ashamed in telling the anecdote, but Hofmann had granted his request and Bill had felt proud of himself.

I tried to get a better notion of his group activities, but it is not clear why he felt he could not join a group as the other boys did. He apparently participated in some scattered group activity on the street. There are a few, very vague accounts of going places with the group of boys at night.

At the age of thirteen he attended a summer camp for boys and girls. He felt it was childish, especially since the name of the camp was Robin Hood and too many of the activities were games for little children, and he would not tell any of his friends on the street that he had been to camp. In the camp he was sometimes not able to join the group activity because he always wanted his own way. If they played softball, he insisted on being the pitcher or he wouldn't play.

He then told of another incident of being excluded, this time from a group of boys who were going to visit some girls. He was certain it was a petting party and that he was excluded because he was one or two years younger than most of the other boys. The boy who was most responsible for his exclusion was two years older than he.

There have only been a couple of comments relating to his naval experience. He told me that during the time he was in the

Navy, he was completely lacking in fear—that he existed without understanding the real danger of the situation. When he joined the APD group, they had had considerable combat and the men talked about the combat experiences, expressing their fear and chiding him for his apparent bravado. He countered that he had been able to weather bad storms in the Aleutians without undue nervous excitement. He said that during the night attack, two torpedoes passed under the APD, and the plane itself narrowly missed the ship. He treated this as an exciting incident to write home about, and prided himself on his feelings about it. However, he was inside the ship at the time and he did say that if he had been on the outside he might have jumped overboard, as another man did.

I attempted to go into the problem of what he wanted to do with his life, but that was unsuccessful. Apparently he at no time considered staying in the Navy. He had had long-standing plans to go to law school and get on with a career. In spite of his great difficulty in talking in front of audiences and his inability to get close to people—handicaps which he recognizes—he was interested enough in political science to make a political career his prime objective. Apparently he had thought of a political career something like his father's. At present all gates are closed for him. Over and over he repeats that he can do nothing, that he has no ability to handle financial affairs, and that his failure makes it obvious that he never learned anything in school. He had no alternative plan that I can discover and perhaps the subject has not been beneficial to talk about. There has been some increase in the feelings that he is doomed, that he must stay here until something else happens to him. My inference is that it would be medical or legal punishment.

He has frequently returned to subjects that reveal the terror he feels in all situations other than the relationship with me. He says he seems always to have categorized people on the basis of facial structure and to have found something menacing in their appearance. Only after he knows a person for a considerable period of time does he lose that feeling. He suggested that he had gotten over looking on me as a menace. Several times when we have talked about our relationship, he has put it on the basis of doctor-patient. He said he realized that he could talk to me quite easily, but felt he would react that way if he had another doctor—in which case he would probably regard me as menacing if I came to see him on the ward. He has many times spoken of his fear of medical situations, and a common thread seems to be running through these and similar situations. For example, getting his hair cut is an uncomfortable experience, primarily because he regards barbers' instruments as fearsome weapons. All during his developing years and up to the present he has been loath to go to the dentist, fearing especially the drill and the burr as weapons of torture or attack. Recently he was sent to the dentist to have his broken tooth repaired. Although there was no unusual overt tenseness at the time, he states that his visits to the dentist have not been very different from such visits in the past. Anytime he saw anybody on the ward getting a routine injection, he became tense and upset. His father used to control his diabetes with diet, but over the past two or three years has been taking insulin, a procedure that has always frightened the patient. Also, on admission, when his blood was taken by vein, he became very agitated and frightened, and said it was the reaction he had shown to each blood-letting in the Navy and in school. He has the feeling that his reaction to shock treatment was similar.

He thinks of the attendants as being threats and has some feeling they are going to jump on him, hold him down, and do something to him. Once when I saw him quite upset on the ward and attempted to let him talk out what was going on, he said the same thing had occurred as before—he had been afraid that the attendants might jump on him; with difficulty he said that it seemed to him that he was toying with the idea of something he might want or desire, and that was disturbing. Nothing more came of that and we talked on about less important things; when later I saw him in the office for an hour and a half, there was no return to the subject.

He talks much about his self-destructive tendencies. When I try to track them down, he says they have been present since an early age, particularly the nail-biting and picking at his toes. He picked up the "self-destructive" terminology in his reading, recognized it as having suicidal implications and hence is disturbed about it. Also during the past month he has talked more openly about suicide, sometimes commenting that he spent a lot of time thinking about suicide, that he should have done something to himself when the opportunity existed, and that he knows he could not go through with it. He admitted that once, before going to Springhill, he had been in the bathroom and had rather impulsively taken a razor blade and scratched it across his wrist; he was so guilty about it that he told no one at the time, and he told me only with difficulty. There is despair in his attitude when he is concentrating on suicide, emerging in questions about why he doesn't do it, or in such questions as, "Why don't they do something to me?" and "Why do they let people like me live?" He has been heard to say, "Shoot me, shoot me."

He said he had some thoughts that were "too horrible" to talk about. I tried to lessen the anxiety by asking how he could attach such a term as "horrible" to them, but he veered away from the subject and has not come back. He has spells of vertigo, a sort of twirling sensation in his head that occurs when he lies down and lets his thoughts ramble. I attempted to have him clarify the thoughts, and he said they just became vaguer and vaguer and at the same time his feelings of terror increased; he would let them go on awhile and then shake his head or get out of bed or do something else to break the train of thought. When he was talking about this, I attempted to have him lie back in the chair, close his eyes, and let things come as they would, but he said no, that there was nothing in there now, nothing going on.

During this past month, he has been concentrating more on "mania." He has a feeling that there is some deep, repressed rage in him which is sometime going to explode. It has not happened in the hospital but it has happened at home. I can't get a clear story of this period of great hostility toward his parents. Apparently he cried out about their mistreatment of him in his youth and blamed them both severely. The outburst led to his mother's going off for a couple of weeks; he stayed home with his father, moved into his parents' room, and slept in his mother's twin bed. He said that he was not able to sleep very well. He seems quite fearful that this "manic reaction," as he labels it, will return.

He then talked about his fascination with violence, saying that throughout his life he had read stories of violence over and over again and has been attracted to it; he says the violence can come directly from him or to him. I have not felt free to go into that more completely as yet. He also said that he has a strong desire to remove his clothing and walk around naked, flailing his arms about aimlessly. That means he is a "catatonic schizophrenic," and he recognizes that he has had a desire to throw off various restrictions throughout his life, but this is psychotic behavior.

Another of his preoccupations has been his feelings of femininity. He first talked about his skin as being softer and thinner than the average man's skin; he is very sensitive to sunburn and mosquito bites and he had some skin difficulty related to feeding in his early years. He described himself as being thin-skinned, and when I tried to pursue that a little he recognized its double meaning—that he was speaking literally and that he was also implying that he was more sensitive than the average person. Another thing which suggests femininity to him is that his hips seem to be wider than they should be. When he looks in the mirror he thinks the conformation of his lower body is something like that of a woman. Both in the hospital and previously, he has stood in front of the mirror and challenged himself as being feminine. He said it occurred to him that his mouth looked like the female genitalia, that the way the beard grew around the lips suggested that. In talking about this, we got into a discussion of secondary sexual characteristics. He began to recognize that chronologically he did not actually develop more slowly than others, but that both prior to and during puberty changes, he felt he would not develop as rapidly as the ordinary person, pre-judged himself, and hence looked for evidence that he was developing more slowly. Another thing that led to his feelings was his high voice before puberty, but his voice certainly changed to the normal range for the adult male.

I think on the same day that we discussed this, which was quite recent, toward the end of the hour we were talking at a pretty easy and comfortable rate, and he got to talking about his brother David; he said that David had a girl now, "There is some hope for him." I talked about what that meant, pointing out that he seemed to have the notion that sex was the whole of life. He said perhaps he did feel that way, that David was pathological in many other ways, but at least he did have a girlfriend and differed from the patient in that way.

Another time he mentioned his tendency to be a loser. In ping-pong and in card games, he would be ahead until the end and would then seem to throw away the last few points, not being able to win the game, to be successful. That seems to have been a persistent pattern in him—he has been adept at some sports and card games, but could not allow himself to win. He suspected that it might be related to many situations in which he was doing things as the son of his father, that he was protesting that role by losing.

During our last hour together he talked in a sexual sphere at quite an easy rate and with some comfort. He started by labeling his masturbation as being perverse and compulsive, and when we examined what he meant by perverse, he said that he had masturbated in the showers or in the bathtub and that during masturbation he had touched his anus, thus heightening the sensation. There is some persistence of masturbation up to the present, always attended by guilt. That led to talk of his relations with girls and he said in all these contacts there was something perverse. I wanted him to describe what he meant by that. The first heterosexual experience had been early in his Navy career; he had picked a girl up in a tavern and then had gone to her room. He had intercourse twice but had become panic-stricken after the second time, had rushed out, and had been unable to look up the girl again. Another time he was in a taxicab with a girl after they had both been drinking considerably and he urged her to play with his genitals. Apparently she did play with his genitals without too much reluctance, yet he felt it was a perverse activity. He continued to talk quite comfortably in spite of the nature of the discussion, and then near the end of the hour he asked, "How can I explain this physical sensitiveness, this feeling of not wanting to be touched by girls?" He added that he remembered feeling that way when he was twelve or thirteen, and associated it with the incident at the camp when the girl invited him into the woods and he pleaded that his hay fever was too severe. He said that when dancing he was unable to hold a girl close. At that same period, at the onset of puberty, he had decided that he would never be able to get along with girls and would have to spend his life as a bachelor.

Twice he has spontaneously brought up some dreams. I would like to read one that he described at the beginning of an hour, following a question on how he had been sleeping, a subject we had been talking about the previous day. He said that he was sleeping pretty well but had had some nightmares, and I asked him what they were about. In this particular dream he was standing in an enclosure with many other prisoners, something like a prisoner-of-war enclosure. He had been on a mission that released prisoners in Korea. There was a fence around them and a large number of people standing outside watching. One of the patients in the hospital was there, Watkins, a man who publicly announced that he wanted to put penises in his mouth and who had been talked about by my patient. This fellow made his escape and was over the fence and making his way through the crowd, when my patient saw a line of policemen coming toward Watkins, running as though he could not possibly escape. Then there was confusion and my patient had made his escape and got on the train. Somewhere before this my patient met Watkins, told him he didn't have money, and Watkins put money into his hand. He said, "He pressed money into my hand." On the train he was uncomfortable and felt people were looking at him, and he went away and got into the bathroom, where it was very dark, and then he woke up. He thought the train was going in the direction of home. He was not able to see anything in the dream and I didn't make any interpretation. Just recently, also at the beginning of an hour, he mentioned that he had had a nightmare in which the attendants got him down and were holding him, and he got up and started to run away.

During the month on the ward there have been days when he has been quite comfortable and has responded pleasantly to the nurses and attendants, and other days when he has been very much upset. The general pattern during this whole time has been that he gets into his room and attempts to seclude himself. He seems to be trying to get away from the voices of the other patients and from the noises and the radio. He goes to bed early, falls asleep without too much difficulty, and averages seven or eight hours. In the dining room he is tense and uneasy, eats very quickly, but maintains adequate food intake. Recently he followed the male nurse around the ward practically the whole day, seeming to want to talk. Just before the nurse left he called him into his room and talked for about ten minutes, giving much the same picture that he has presented to me—revealing the self-derogatory trend of his thoughts, labeling himself as manic and paranoid, speaking of his certainty that he would end up as a catatonic, and suggesting that he was having thoughts that were too horrible to express.

I don't think of anything else just now.

SULLIVAN: I don't know whether you do not know, or whether you omitted for purposes of economy of time, but go back to the first part and the question that occurred to me as you gave this remarkable amount of useful data, when he talked about feeling that he had probably been encouraged to read by his father but he did not think he read for content. What did he read? What books? Then I would ask a question or two to see if he did get content, if he has anything like a coherent idea of the outline of the plot. Why this grows on me is that I am inclined to say I have never heard that statement in my whole life, that one read when very young in what sounded like a compulsive fashion. I don't believe I have ever heard that account, and in any case, since he is so self-disparaging, since his general attitude is, "My whole life has been a total loss," I won't let that go by. I want to find out what books he can remember having read, and if I am lucky enough to know one of them, then his recollection of that. If I don't know them, I say, "One of these books appealed to you and you read it two or three times." The joker is that he was reading compulsively. For all I know he may have read every one of them two or three times. I am seeing what can be here in the way of retrograde falsification, and trying to guess whether it is really true that he was, even at that age, inclined to feel that a quiet, self-absorbed activity was the thing. Did you get anything on what he read?

KVARNES: Not on specific books. During the period he is talking about he read children's books in which he participated greatly in the fantasy part, putting himself in the role of hero.

SULLIVAN: That in itself somewhat wipes out the validity of his statement of not reading for content. I think with this patient there have been a good many instances where his rather surprisingly cooperative attitude with you tends to entrap you into leaving things just that way. I picked up a number of instances as we went along where I don't know that you didn't follow through, but he established a position which might very easily be interpreted pessimistically by his present attitude. The dentist business includes a good bit of it. The account sounds either as if he had acted very much like many people do, but gave it a disparaging slant, or as if he set up a proposition which needs a little more questioning to know whether you have heard what he recalls. I am taking up time talking about it because this is a peculiar fringe of the general area of "no tacit consent." I think I may have mentioned how if you hear a dangerous idea—an idea which will build up into a disabling body of behavior—you register your disagreement with it even if by some very simple operation.* I know that if he were telling me about this dentist business and got on to drills and burrs, I would say, "What is a burr?" I would not be at all surprised to discover he didn't know, but for some reason the word has become important. If I leave it, then here is something somewhat mysteriously called a burr, which is important, but if he does not know what he is talking about, then the thing is impaired as a useful part of his fear of dental work.

About the aunts, we get impressions. They need some more questioning at several points where it is so plausible and fits in so nicely with him, and of all things, this business of the quarreling of the parents.

In the first place, I never get very happy about this patient's extravagant language. Their quarreling "terrified" him. Well, rightly or wrongly with me, each new time I find this boy has been terrified—sometimes I sound a little drier and more sardonic —say, "Meaning you felt what?" I am discouraging this superlative language. It makes him out to be too jittery for words, and as long as the recollections are in this superlative mood, I am not sure he recalls. That can be talked about from what he remembers having happened. A good many times significant material seems to be presented, but not actually recalled as having happened. By my pressure against the literary or rhetorical extravagance, I get a hint that this is not a vivid recollection, and then something worth saying—I ask questions about the setting. For the quarrel when he was fourteen, can he remember the room? Was the furniture the same as it had been for some years? How far away was he from his mother and father? Practically a social geography of the situation. If that fills itself in, I know that his recollection of actual feeling will be valid. The notion of getting people to drop back into recalling the whole situation in which one of these quite significant things happens, often strips off later pathological excrescences of meaning.

I must say this last battle, the battle that more or less ended battles among the parents, that has a good many trends of im-

* Sullivan often registered his disagreement with or nonacceptance of a "dangerous" idea by a grunt or groan or some other nonverbal vocalization.

portance, and I would be, oh, very much disappointed if in my dealing with him about it I had to leave it in this condition where only two very dramatic utterances are reported—mother's speech about throwing herself out of the window, and father's "No, no, no!" What was the fight about? How did it get to this aggravated point? There must have been a lot going on before mother announces dramatically that she will throw herself from the window, and also I am groping for information as to what in the father's expressions required of the mother such a dramatic attack on the peace of mind of all concerned, and I am apt to wind up that account by saying, "Well, afterward did mother express any sorrow for having disturbed you so much?" I am damn sure she didn't, but I am going to get that thought circulating in his mind. I want him to realize how much an innocent bystander he was and I am perfectly free to ask questions which I know damn well are going to produce "No," just so long as they seem the most natural things from the standpoint of polite society, and needless to say I don't want to give any impression of being clever. They are just natural questions which underwrite certain things in the situation.

Those things I had to say now because I was sure I would otherwise forget.

May I say that, as we go around now, I would be glad if you left the dreams alone for the time being. We may look at those later. I would like to hear comment on the whole data we have heard of this patient. In other words, what you begin to think, what you feel still requires inquiry, how you would handle any problems that have come up in this last month. While I prefer to exempt discussion about those dreams, that is not to say you must not speak of them. I will ask Dr. Salzman to lead off.

SALZMAN: What I would like to hear more about, and what I feel has not been substantiated yet, is the early relationship with the friend, this neighbor whose father was such a wonderful fellow. I wonder just what went on with the friend and with the patient in the period of comparison, the home situation of the friend and of his own.

SULLIVAN: And you perhaps wonder a little about why the play with other people continues so very vague? The street play and so on?

SALZMAN: We have not heard anything about that.

SULLIVAN: Dr. Novey, what is in your mind?

NOVEY: I was wondering whether it would be conceivable to deal with any distortions relating to his opinions of his parents. I think they are present. It is quite true they were rejecting of him but his repetitious comments about their rejection is probably something of a distortion, and certainly his tremendous fear of his father, for instance, and his need to try to emulate him, represent something of a more active relationship than the simple rejection about which he talks. I pose the question as to whether it would be of value to try to deal with the distortions in which he says, "I was left out." There was more going on than simply being left out.

SULLIVAN: I am interested in that comment because it shows a certain wisdom. There are always two sides to every story. It is often important to remind a patient that we know there are two sides, but that at present we are discussing only one. It makes it easier to get things clear. Your comment on a superlative hostility to his father is a very good comment and a very tricky topic. When he talks about being afraid of his father, I am greatly interested in the part of the data he gives that his father was always correcting his saying "Yeah," and so on. I have a very good hunch that a boy who just has to say "Yeah" to his father again and again, which disturbs father, is not wholly without motives of discomposing the old man. He doesn't seem to have noticed that at all. Yet I am afraid to do much which he can experience as my seeming to doubt the validity of what he is telling me. If he can only give me a chance, as maybe this "Yeah" business would be, to toss in something to indicate there were two sides—"But you just had to say 'Yeah' to him, eh?" That far I will go. But he is still so deeply disturbed about himself and obviously lacking in grasp of why he is the way he is, that I am not going to say anything that will tend to widen the field of inquiry to a degree that will daze him—bring out that "I am probably wrong about everything," but it is a very good thing to keep in mind always, and certainly with almost all patients—they get so anxious giving a one-sided picture of their parents that one has to reassure them in words to the effect that this is not the whole picture, but as long as we are talking about your side of it, we will talk about it.

Dr. Rom, let's hear from you.

ROM: The father is beginning to loom as the ogre in this case. Dr. Kvarnes and I noted that when the father greets him with a ful kiss on the mouth, the patient responds very much as he does to my greeting on the ward.

SULLIVAN: I know you mentioned that before, but tell me more about it now.

ROM: He recoils. He backs up, and there is almost a look of disgust.

SULLIVAN: And where does the kiss come?

ROM: As they approach each other. His father approaches him and kisses him.

SULLIVAN: Even in the approach there is this sort of defensive bracing of himself? And what happens after that?

ROM: There is some embarrassment and confusion.

SULLIVAN: Does he seem relaxed after that?

ROM: On the contrary, he seems to tighten up.

SULLIVAN: But he loses the attitude of defensiveness?

KVARNES: I might add to that. Subsequently both of them pull away somewhat embarrassed, not knowing how to proceed, and the father will suggest that they go out in the yard, at which time we lose sight of them. At any time I have seen him with his father, there has been an attempt to maintain his distance, and he is more on edge perhaps than he is with me, more defensive.

SULLIVAN: When they go out, do they prowl around or sit down?

KVARNES: The last visit they went for a walk. Prior to that they sat on chairs facing each other, but at some distance.

SULLIVAN: Seems quite possible that father's formula for embarrassing situations is to act in some way or other.

Dr. Wheeler, what have you to say?

WHEELER: I am thinking we should hear more about the younger brother. Also, I can't see why this boy had so little in the way of inner resources for satisfaction to use after he grew up and what kept him from doing something to get his share of attention. Why he saved it all up until now with his sickness.

SULLIVAN: Aren't you impressed by the probability that both father and mother were pretty overwhelmingly busy and important figures who were hard to pin down for this kid? I have a feeling they were just civilized enough to do some lip service to their interest in him and then became preoccupied in their more important affairs. It is hard for a person who has grown up in that to do much about it, short of being quite disturbed.

WHEELER: He is doing something about it now.

SULLIVAN: He is doing something about something now.

WHEELER: Why couldn't he then?

SULLIVAN: I have a hunch you have to get jammed up in problems of masculinity-femininity before you have aptitude for schizophrenia. The last book I read was by a gentleman by the name of Bradley and all that I could get out of it was that he was convinced that there was schizophrenia in childhood. He didn't say why or how he was convinced. If you think this boy is doing this primarily to get attention, that startles me. Is that your view?

WHEELER: I say that now he is getting some attention from the family that the younger brother had and he didn't have.

SULLIVAN: Do you think he appreciates that? Are the parental attitudes to him now the sort of thing he recognizes as being warm appreciation of his merits and needs and so on?

WHEELER: No.

SULLIVAN: No, father doesn't sound much like it.

Dr. Peal, let's hear what you have to say.

PEAL: There are a number of little things. He did mention that his father was forgiving, more so than his mother in the incident of the birthday cake. How to use that for insight is not clear to me. And he quite clearly thought with his mother in a disparaging fashion about his father. There is a lot of meat for unpleasant trends, strong ones for him to digest in a few words, but I would like to feel that something was being discussed that would make it easy to gain insight into his contempt for mother; also he stated he had a contempt for women. Then there was his feeling about baseball, that unless he could be the whole team, he wouldn't play. There might be some elaboration on his baseball experiences to find out what he played and how successfully or unsuccessfully, as a source of reality for him. In the Navy, I felt he made some statements which hint at meaning that he has not expressed —for example, he has spoken about his lack of feeling about dangerous situations, and yet at the same time he says he might jump overboard. It is dangerous to talk about suicide with him but yet it is important to have him talk about fears he undoubtedly did have in the Navy.

SULLIVAN: I have to say something that is not an unmixed compliment, but I have heard you bring up four points, every one of them damn good. Every one needed elaborating and was among those that struck me as things I would like to know about. Then you go on and talk about what your probable interest in these is, which you tend to put in the class of insight, and I can't sympathize with a single one. I am using you to make a point. I am not picking on you.

That sort of thing has impressed me in the development of promising psychiatrists for many years. They know what matters in life. Then they have some goddamn theories about it. If, in their work with the patient, they inquire about what they feel is important, but try very carefully not to prejudice the outcome by developing any of their thoughts about why they feel it is important, it is very apt to be good work.

This incident of the birthday cake provided by father after a court of inquiry: I very much want to know what he can recall of father's position. I surmise, by the way it comes about, that his absenting himself was felt as a slap at little brother. That is a guess. It is not really in any way justified except by the fact that this seems to have been an occasion for discipline. Discipline about what? Father comes up and in some way fixes it with words. What did he seem to be hurt by? What did father complain about? Who knows what will come out? It seemed to be a significant recollection, and I want to know more.

The only other thing that I will mention of the four valuable points is the notion that when the boy said he might have gone overboard, it had something to do with suicide—that I emphatically doubt. There is a special instance where you have not adjusted yourself in your thinking to the probable situation of the patient. For a man to go overboard in peacetime from an ocean liner would probably be suicidal, but for a person to go over in wartime from a tanker which is being torpedoed, that would be the antithesis of a suicidal impulse. To leap over the side of a small naval vessel under attack was probably a frantic life-saving effort. I mention this to suggest that we are quite apt to be right about what is important, what deserves exploration, but I don't think it is important to guess why we think it is important. We are likely to get too much of ourselves in it and it is apt to interfere with our communication with the patient.

DYAR: One thing which impressed me about this boy is the amount of anxiety he has. The question which I would like to ask is what attitude it is possible to use to help him to relieve the anxiety, so that then he can bring out much more valuable information, so that he can see himself what had been going on.

SULLIVAN: Go a little further and give one particular point where you would like to know how to handle the anxiety component. Make it less general.

DYAR: Take for instance any of the situations toward his father or mother—as when he says he thinks he has a "mother fixation." Ask him what he means by a fixation, yes, but then how do you carry it on to enable him to get more understanding of what he means and at the same time to relieve his anxiety? He can't help but have it, he actually tells you he has it.

SULLIVAN: There is a great deal of anxiety connected with a large number of his ideas and that must have been the case in the past, since it is fairly evident that we have no outstanding statement anywhere in this long and remarkable account in which the patient says, "I did that damn well. I am proud of myself. People applauded me." That is conspicuous by its absence, and where there are no such statements we have to assume that low self-esteem has been an habitual attitude or a fantasy of private self-overevaluation, which is somewhat less crushing but equally under the drive of anxiety. This particular thing has not gotten comment so far around the room, but it is an important topic and a very serious technical problem. I am not asking that it be mentioned in the rest of the circle, but as Dr. Dyar pointed out, this patient's statement about his "mother fixation," plus a good deal of data that one vaguely feels adds up that way—whatever he means, where he stresses the fact that father was always a big problem, and mother was wonderful once and always easiest to deal with, there is dynamite there.

WITT: I was wondering about the possibility of preparing the ground along a couple of lines. One is a direct steal from what you said, Dr. Sullivan—the possibility of making it appear, gradually, that the father was not always so right. That he is a person rather than a god, with the idea of not making the patient seem so wrong. Another thing that was brought up was that more seems to be coming out about femininity and the way he looks at himself. My feeling is that it is connected with his father, and the two subjects might be covered together. Perhaps he did not want to be a man if his father was the model, particularly if his father was that rough with his mother, to whom he was so attached. "I don't want to be a man if I have to act like that." It might be easier to act like the woman than to have to be that aggressive.

SULLIVAN: Do you recall his referring to feminine attributes other than the hips and this obscure comment about the mouth? I just ask for information.

WITT: The skin and the voice and the fact that he did not develop as fast as other boys.

SULLIVAN: Yes, which does not seem to be justified. I don't want to give you in any sense the idea that there is not great importance in the things you have expressed. I was trying to refresh my mind on how many attributes he had dealt with which could be definitely regarded as feminine traits.

KVARNES: There was one other thing about that. After I refused to accept all these things as being out-and-out evidence and asked him what he was talking about, he said he supposed it was his submissiveness and that he was thinking primarily of the shock, when he would just lie on the table and not do anything about it.

SULLIVAN: We notice that mother was not painfully submissive.

WHITE: I thought a little along the same line as Dr. Witt. Dr. Witt thought it was a reaction to father, but I felt it was his mother who had failed to give him love and tenderness and as a young child he looked for it in other people with blond hair and then decided he would have to be a bachelor and from then on has been looking for love. Another thing I thought of, he has masturbated, he has an idea his mouth looks like the female genitalia, then he has a dream in which a man gives him money, as though he were saying that he was a failure with women and the only other way was too perverse. He talked about his failure all the way. He is able to talk about his relationship to men, and his father, which would make you think it is the easier thing, but that is where he thinks he is abnormal. He thinks that is perversion. That is, he is not anxious about it on a conscious level. Wouldn't it be easier for him to talk about his mother fixation actually than the other part of it which he feels is so dreadful?

SULLIVAN: Good stuff, and right in the field where I have a feeling there is a big technical problem. I want to ask Dr. Kvarnes one thing. In this agreement which the mother asks him to enter into about the deficiencies of the father, did you get any data of what she complained of?

KVARNES: No. I tried to get what things they were talking about when they were ridiculing the father but he doesn't remember what was said.

SULLIVAN: Sometimes, "What in particular do you recall that she objected to?"—an inquiry as if one detail would be enough—even sometimes with pressure toward free association—is as good as anything. Sometimes one can get particularly good hints. You can't be sure it is good until later, but there may be technically badly needed material in this recollection of what the mother chose to seek confirmation about from her son with regard to the father.

WAGNER: The relationship seems to be going well, so well that I would hesitate to do as you indicated, extend the area of inquiry, and yet the data seem to flow and I wonder what Dr. Kvarnes is doing to keep it that way. I hope next time he will tell us of his own reactions. Since the relationship is good and the man seems integrated and willing enough to give a coherent account, I wonder whether we might not inquire about the reasons for his changed attitude from mother and preference toward father, whether that would frighten him too much. I wonder whether we could go as far as asking him whether he liked the nurse that he followed about, and wasn't it all right to like a person that way, or might we not indicate that we understand what is on his mind and that it bears expression. I don't know whether it would be hurrying things too much. I suppose the data left to flow toward a receptive therapist would eventually bring these things up, and I wonder if the benefit does not diminish in time in that the mere expression of data does not change the patient's attitude, which is what we are attempting to do.

SULLIVAN: This comment of Dr. Wagner's impresses me as too damn doubtful for words in one spot. Namely, he says is not the law of diminishing returns apt to apply if we wait for him to deal with some things. This business of the "horrible thoughts" is a classic example of my feeling that I am not pleased with the extravagant language, and I am not going to give any tacit agreement about things in mind that are just too impossible to say. God, we have enough that won't be in mind without having this patient going about with things that must not be said. The whole doctrine of reservations comes in here. What little I have learned about reservations is this—if there is an agreement between a patient and therapist that the patient has a reservation and keeps it, the damn thing can grind up an incredible amount of time by becoming a recurrent preoccupation. You start to talk about the weather and it brings up thoughts of the reservations and there you block. I have seen patients reduced to brilliant attempts to tell me the same damn story five or six times to kill an hour and to so modify the accounts that I was supposed to overlook the fact that they were telling me the same story. It is not that we give a damn about what the reservations are. Our freedom of communication is such that we don't want to force the patient to relinquish the reservations, but we want to do something which makes its entertainment obviously expensive. We don't have to have the damn thing today but the time is coming when the patient will say it is a good time to discuss it.

COOPER: The first idea that came to me today was about what he read—along the same lines as you expressed—in that I could not see how a child would just hold a book for the effect it might have on anyone. The second thing concerned his feelings about his mother now. He has mentioned that in the past he thought of her as most beautiful and far more benevolent than father. Up to the present the only thing he has said against her was that she was hysterical. I wonder if there is not more against her going on in his mind than he has been able to state. Does she still influence his choice of friends, and does he still compare them to his mother? This came to me particularly when he went into this rage at home and it was his mother who was driven out for two weeks, and he replaced her in her own bed. There must be more going on in his feeling toward her. By the way, I also wondered here about the dream of the other patient—a patient of mine—because that man is blond and very good-looking.

The third thing was his fear of shock, surgical instruments, barber tools and the like. He has expressed many times the idea of self-destruction, even mentioning this gesture toward suicide. I can't understand his fear about these instruments since pain and death are apparently what he wants, even to the point of saying, "Shoot me." He must have some idea that they are there to do the violence that he wishes. That also ties up with the idea of the attendants doing something to him. I wonder what he thinks these instruments are going to do to him.

SULLIVAN: My statistics are complicated forms of humor, but I suppose the people who can and who cannot get used to such relatively unusual things as intravenous needles distribute smoothly on the probability curve and there is no notable correlation between which side they are on and many obvious traits of their so-called psychosexual development. There are other things in that field that would probably bring frank statements of homosexual interests. There is a perfectly good right to question whether they probably would or not. I am afraid they might. What I finally want to talk about, and have everyone else talk about as time goes on, is in that connection.

COHEN: From the standpoint of therapy, I was particularly interested in how you would handle incidents where he made some gestures toward Kvarnes and toward the nurse which fizzled out, in which he wanted to say something and simply ends by talking about how inadequate he is and gets into a panicky state. I wonder whether the panic comes when he gets the idea that he wants to share his real feelings of inadequacy, whatever they may be, or whether it is the panic that is responsible for his being unable to say something, or just what it is that is going on then.

The other question was as to the nature of the approach. Certainly it seems that a direct approach is not going to be very productive except of a lot more material of how inadequate he is, without really telling you the basic reasons for his guilt. When he talked about the rage, I wonder if he was not approaching some of the reasons why he has to feel inadequate, in order to control the resentment.

SULLIVAN: My recollection is that the rage incident was part of his going to Springhill.

KVARNES: It followed the experience at Springhill.

SULLIVAN: Then he denounced his mother and she left the place for a couple of weeks.

KVARNES: That was the time the doctor invited him to live with him.

SULLIVAN: About the dreams: There is the most massive and distinguished work that Freud has produced in his *Interpretation of Dreams*. I trust that everybody who is going into psychotherapy will familiarize themselves with it. I also want to suggest that psychotherapists, in my experience, divide themselves into two classes: those who use the Freud method of utilizing dreams and those who do very different things, and the former, I think, are absolutely disbarred from therapeutic success with schizophrenics so we will leave them out. What is the other thing to do with dreams, instead of a subtle seeking-out of latent content? See if there is some way of making a succinct statement of the manifest dramatic story told in the dream. What is the most succinct and yet clearly relevant statement you can make of the dream? Something like you and Watkins were imprisoned, or rather had been imprisoned. He has already escaped, despite police and so on, and you then escape. You are worried about having no money, he helps you out there, together you get aboard a train and wake up very disturbed in the darkness and privacy of the toilet. You see, I have left out a lot. I have tossed out some and tossed in the Watkins business in a fashion that does not imply anything I am not sure I know about it. Then I want to know if it reminds him of anything. "What occurs to you as to what this is about?" If it works, fine. If it does not, there is still something to say. "Are you right about this business of having awakened in this black privacy of the toilet, because I don't know why you did that? Have you any idea?" Here is the other approach that I think is permissible in this astonishing tale. Here is the aloneness. He would not dream of offering that. You can bank on that but it leads nowhere. If that is what brought the final terror then we would get out of this dream that it is better to be with someone in a disturbing escape from the enemy than it is to be alone. If the intolerable terror is from isolation, that is a good idea for him to get into the record.

What I wanted to say was that with dreams if you are going to do anything, you just want to think twice before you do very much. It is a matter of, so far as I know, a pretty much Freudian approach to try to get free association and ultimately unearth the latent content, which might be disastrous, or if you think there is something in this dream that patient needs to deal with, which is often why patients have dreams when not encouraged to dream. There is a complexity of factors which they cannot get in, that is pushing for expression—then they will have an emotionally marked dream which gets itself reported. Then what do you do with it? I act on the assumption that there is something here that we are not getting at that can be added to. How can I aid the patient in seeing that? Well, being just the reverse of recalling an early memory, I will want the patient to get as much setting as possible, the words, the pattern of action, and probably something of the "dramatis personae." I don't give a damn for the fact that Watkins expects fellatio. Because Watkins is helpful to him and they escape together and it is alone that he has trouble. Watkins is there, so I start out with Watkins and get him in but get him in when there is a minimum prejudice but continuity, and see what happens. The thing has sometimes been fantastically illuminating.

This is no criticism of any other way of dealing with dreams, but it is the way I like to deal with them with people who are going to get well by something other than dreams. The technical problem—Dr. Cooper has come closest—the evidence seems to be becoming very oppressive that this man suffers a lot from something more or less in the field of "Am I, or should I be, homosexual?" At times it seems almost to be on the tip of his tongue. Yet, when he talks about having thoughts too horrible to express we don't know one damn thing about that except that they presumably represent the expressions of force which are extraordinarily alien to his ideation of what one should entertain. They might prove to be thoughts of doing so-called sadistic damage to the environment just as probably as of having homosexual relations with people around there. I hold very little with the doctrine of sadism as entertained, but he has fantasies of being leaped on, and I must say I have never felt the idea of being overwhelmed by a multitude of people as being purely sexual. So, as I say, we are not sure about the horrible thoughts, but we are pretty sure that this man would be relieved if someone were to ask him, "Do you think you are homosexual?" But I think it would be extremely short-lived and followed by ungovernable mental processes which would be tantamount to severe aggravation of his psychosis. Or the question would be taken as a prescription to be carried out in relations with the people in his neighborhood, which in turn would probably provide such an additional load to his low self-esteem the he could never be lifted to recovery.

When it comes to what seems possible, I have to talk to you with great caution. I hope you will take what I say with caution and not suddenly adopt what you think I mean, or leap to this as being useful with many patients. I am talking about something which every now and then becomes more and more probable in my listening to data produced by patients. It is not going to sound very new, but if you follow me, it may sound sort of new.

From certain parental or family groups, a boy finds all attractive merits in the mother. With every living thing in the mammalian class, the mother is the first significant being, and in the development of humans, the mother is the agent of culture, and do it good or do it bad, she is bound to be significant. Sometimes her significance gradually shifts from that which must necessarily inhere in her role or in some mothering one's role to the point where everything that seems to be estimable and good to the boy is an attribute of the mother. That the father may be estimable and successful in the eyes of the world is all right, but so far as dealing with the boy, his virtues are irrelevant or affect the boy so unpleasantly that they are not really esteemed at all, no matter what lip service is paid them. Under those circumstances the pattern of the male is very unattractive. To a certain extent it is something you can't hope to achieve in the way it is embodied, yet you are male. There is all the cultural pressure—clothing, shape of genitals, the way you are treated in school, who you are permitted to associate with—which requires that you be male, although you have no attractive pattern of maleness. Under those circumstances, to a certain extent a boy tends to be a woman. That is, he wants to be what seems to him comfortable and decent and so on, which appears to be personified in the mother, and to that extent there is a development of personality which is a way we can accommodate the traits of the mother without causing much trouble, but requires more and more guarding in the male society lest one is accepted as a sissy, or in some other fashion which is hard on self-esteem, and which you are apt to take precautions to avoid. The later clues to the misfortune in models tend to show as a great interest in and very much thinking about girls. This can easily be taken as some libido development or what not, but the facts are that this has been acceptable to what one really would like to be, not as some goddamned incomprehensible nonsense about castration, but as what one feels suited to be and good at being, yet impossible because of all the cultural pressure and accident of sex.

With the enormous amount of precautions and so on that the school system teaches one to throw about anything like that, one may get so involved in what unhappily is thought of as private life in contrast to public life that one has no opportunity to check up on oneself with anyone else. There is so much that must be kept secret and one hears about all sorts of things, including all sorts of homosexual data in this day and age, and then the fat may easily be in the fire, without, so far as I know, there being any insurmountable barrier to women but with there being a definitely insurmountable barrier to seeking the male role with women.

Do you see something new in this point of view, differing from the somewhat simple statement that homosexuality represents a barrier in the completion of heterosexual interests? I am beginning to think that this boy is nearer that field than he is to the field in which experience has made intimate relations with women intolerable, which is the classical simple formulation for homosexuality.

If you want to know why over the years this formulation has come into being, it is for the following: That I have at one stage had very extensive experience, and recurrently over a good many years, with a few patients under treatment for something including their homosexual way of life. Some of these data I picked up when I was investigating more intimately how these people live anyway, and in treatment situations I found some apparently simple problems absolutely baffling. In other words, all the simple theories about it being a block to developing heterosexual adjustment got nowhere. It could not be documented as to origin and had no particular effect on the patient. It was necessary to look further to discover or get into this category. And as I hear this it occurs to me that it might be well to investigate the earlier years further with an idea of ultimately getting a pretty straightforward formulation of what things about the mother were really estimable to the boy. Not to the world. What things were estimable and noticed in the latter, and they are probably things that this boy has never had any conviction he could manifest. It is in the explanation of these earlier patterns, before they are modified by juvenile society, well before they are recast by preadolescent society, that I believe a safe buttress can be built for what I am certain will presently come out as frank homosexual fears and desires. I don't want them to break out until I have a buttress that is broad enough to hold up the possibility that it is not permanent and perhaps not even real. It may well be an error of judgment—on a pretty good basis but still an error of judgment, and in any case it is only a transitional phase which he finds himself in later than a good many other people have.

I want to throw the group open for discussion. We have a little time left. Dr. Wagner, perhaps you could start us.

WAGNER: Frankly, at the moment I would prefer to ruminate over what has been said. I did like the formulation that one may have a personal and sincere liking for women but not see how one can reach out to them through the role of the male.

SULLIVAN: There must be earlier highly significant details which have strong restricting influence over what I would call the corrective effect of school. We have seen that in this patient. There are pretty strong suggestions that his school life was pretty much concentrated on scholarship and there was no great emphasis on his being a bad or troublesome problem, but he was a good sport. The dearth of data about play on the streets hints that it was more surface participation than any real feeling of being in a team or of strong interest in competitive success. Things which may even be vaguely hinted by this manifest unwillingness to win at games. I have a strong suspicion that he loses these games to avoid hostility. He has a definite feeling that most people are bad losers and it does not do him any harm to lose and then he stands in better. You may think it is a damn funny kind of social interest in a schizophrenic, but think of the kids who steal money to buy friends whom they do not appreciate when they have them. Before you decide that it is a great reversal of early patterns—as when, for instance, the father is the source of tenderness and the mother is an unreasonable disciplinarian, which is a way of getting a kid started straight for homosexual life—consider what I have discussed here, where all reasonable merits that you can develop fall into the pattern of mother's personality, and not the pattern provided by the importance of your own face or hair. Then the father is negligible in character because of routinized performance. He may have said the same things to the boy every time and had a routine of getting done with his parental duties. They are very important, but they are important chiefly insofar as they are part of a pattern which prevents their later remedy.

You don't leap from the family group into adolescent problems, but sometimes the family group has not only given you a bad start in environmental reaction, but has inculcated things that prevent remedial steps in preadolescence. I don't care terribly about the modifying aspects of the home if it has left a person free, or relatively free. That suggests it is interesting and worthy of time but it warns you that you ought not to get absorbed in the position that the patient is now suffering from something which he has gotten rid of long since. In this situation you do find pretty strong suggestions that his intimacy with Jim bordered on visiting a strange world. I don't know what else it included.

Let us hear other comments.

WAGNER: I would like to ask this—in regard to the practical problem of retaining a possibly modifiable element in the patient, is the maintenance of a strained but respectable family situation more devastating than one which is destroyed? Had these parents separated, would the boy have had an easier time?

SULLIVAN: Had there been a good deal of bitterness about it from the mother then the boy would have wound up with catatonic schizophrenia very much earlier. That is based on the fact that while I am pretty sure she was a fair mother until she had a sickly child to center that phase of her interest on, as he got to be well along in childhood, she began to be conspicuous by her absence and put a premium on his being a nice offspring by looking after himself. Then she swings into the role of being the injured woman and taking her child from this horrible man; this change from actual indifference to superheated demands would be the last blow to development. He would be such a mess by the time he reached the adolescent period that his finish would have been inevitable. In some sense, it is because of the partial value of the self-sufficiency forced on him that he did so nicely in the Navy. That is a close situation in which self-sufficiency is not a disadvantage. Any undue dependence is apt to be a nuisance, so that a certain expectation of relatively indifferent tolerance was something he was used to. I am sure that really intimate relationships in which he could express freely to somebody around his own age what he thought was the matter, where he felt deficient and peculiar, will not be uncovered. If it can be, it would be fortunate. But I don't believe it will.

That brings up the topic of what Dr. Kvarnes ought to do that he is not doing. All that is in my mind is that if I had been as exceedingly fortunate as he has been thus far, I would not run a considerable risk by beginning to be unpleasant and demanding about his horrible thoughts and about his terrors. In others words I would now begin to indicate my disrespect for these things. "God help us, why must we have this hokum when we are doing useful work most of the time. I know something bothers you but, God, does it have to be disguised as a catastrophe? These horrible thoughts, do they bring out goose pimples on you?" I might use sarcasm. "If I encounter anything horrible, I expect goose pimples." Obviously things he is exceedingly hesitant to express. Do they have to be cosmic? Distinctly playing down of the—what is, at best, lunatic language. What the hell does he know about schizophrenia, manic, and so on. I would not dignify that stuff by asking what he is talking about. I know he does not know. I would try to play down the whole damn thing, and the unhappy hokum with the attendants, where he indicates all day that he wants to do something with this person, wants presumably to talk something over that is important, finally he leaps into the breach, actually gets into a position of privacy and then get into his belly-wash about manic, schizophrenic, and what not.

Then again, if I was successful, I would say, "Jesus Christ, you could not talk to him." Just say what I think. It is what you do when you can't talk, but because he is schizophrenic, it also brings a little awe with it. "You are talking about these things because you can't talk about what you need to talk about." I am sure he has panicky incidents but I am also sure they can be extremely succinct, and if I can get him to leave the neologistic hoop-la about psychoses and discover when he began to feel frightened, what was in his mind, we will very much more rapidly discover the formulation of his profound insecurities as to a person's worth and fitness for human society.

DYAR: Do you think that by following this technique, you are going to get out of the way some of the basis of the anxiety?

SULLIVAN: I think that insofar as I can prevent a person doing, shall I say, routinely futile things, that even that is an attack on his anxiety. It works something like this, that anxiety prevents you from saying what you need to say. When you look back and cannot be impressed with what you did, it again reflects on self-esteem and in its way means that the level of chronic anxiety is raised; it is for that reason that I set about trying to educate this boy that there is no use of thinking that nonsensical use of speech kids me or serves its purpose. It still leaves his anxiety about what he is trying to express but it does not add continuously failure after failure. It emphasizes that I don't feel it is necessary any longer. The "any longer" in itself is an expression of hope.

With all this business, if I decided to say the first, you ought to be prepared for what may come out. My next venture here is two main points in this patient—and this is wild guessing—some kind of involved business about homosexuality or the sort of abattoir fantasies of slashing and tearing and what not, about which I don't know a terrible lot because one trouble with psychiatry is that if you investigate things you can depend on the patients going to pot. But I surmise these things represent fantasies surviving from an early time when one had to completely inhibit the expressions of rage. Kids find it easy to entertain fantasies of taking the axe to troublesome parents and teachers and making a slaughterhouse. When encountered in people of twenty, you are most likely hearing survived fantasies from pretty early in the school years which express rage that has never been safe to manifest in any clear-cut behavior. I am not sure. I have not been able to investigate too much about it but I would be prepared for it and probably my response would be, "Well, Jesus, you must have felt terribly sore sometimes in the past." That is a heroic venture but still proves that I am not horrified and I don't get in too deep. I have tossed out a lifeline and the awful stuff is before us and we are still there.

I do want to say something about the suicidal element in this patient. I regard a good many schizophrenics as entirely unpredictable as far as suicide is concerned. I trust it will not be entirely forgotten, but I don't regard it as in any sense a long plan that will be built up and realized. It is just one of the things that you can never be sure will erupt but will not be a chronic problem. If it erupts and is a chronic problem it means psychotherapy has overreached or failed. Preoccupation with ending it all and particularly wishing to be dead, they are often very tricky affairs, and I think Kempf showed one of his quite numerous instances of approach to genius in the stress he laid on a good deal of the catatonic operation in a vague sense pertaining to death and rebirth. Now, to die in order to be reborn is a different thing from the type of suicide that depressives think of. God knows when you will ever find this a safe gesture, but I have literally gone so far with some puzzled schizophrenics who got all wound up in the urgent necessity of killing themselves, to say, "That is, you want to begin all over," and I have had them gaze with complete clarity at me and say, "Yes." Whereupon there was an end to the suicidal business.

I am not concerned with suicide in this person except as something utterly unpredictable, unless he gets into an awful jam with his therapist, who is the most significant person in his life now.

One field I can't say a thing on because I don't know Sheppard as it is now, but if I could, after a time in which I hope the patient has forgotten completely my interest in this dream, I might begin to poke around a little to discover who of the people around him he found friendly and interesting. If Watkins happened to be dragged into that, that I would notice quite vividly, and with no emphasis dig up the business of what sort of a person he is. A doctor cannot know every patient on the ward, and it is quite a natural question, and if by any chance he would offer a comment, you would be hearing quite a bit about our patient.

There is always the terrifying job in dealing with psychotics that you do not have the illuminating current events that can be reported and studied with a nonpsychotic, and you do have the same old story, that it is much easier for patients to tell you what is important and unimportant, even about you, if they talk about a third party. With this you begin to see what little sources of interest he finds around him; you may be encouraging a corrective step and get data about what you cannot get otherwise.

Comment on Third Session,
Twenty-five Years Later, February, 1972

KVARNES: This is the third seminar. Irv, are there any points you want——

RYCKOFF: There are some, nothing particularly startling, except that I was very impressed with what a good teacher Sullivan is; particularly, how consistently he teaches the necessity of establishing the grounds on which the therapist and the patient can make some sense. That is, I was thinking about the contrast between this approach of helping establish some meaningful consensus between the patient and the doctor, and—I may not be entirely accurate—the approach of Frieda Fromm-Reichmann, for

instance. The difference is that Sullivan sticks to very simple, veri-
fiable kinds of data between the patient and the doctor. He does
not very easily, at least in these seminars so far, go in for anything resembling a poetic or symbolic kind of response to try to
indicate to the patient that he understands him in some profound
way, some way which transcends the ordinary bounds of language and simple means. I find this refreshing because some of
these other exchanges are presumably full of all kinds of mutual
agreements and so on, that may seem like pure hogwash. The second thing that's interesting to follow is how really delicate and
gentle and sensitive he is with patients and even with you guys,
the degree to which he will try to be aware of all of the possible
sources of anxiety in the patient, and the whole concept of indirect reassurance. It's a very delicate, really a lovely kind of
thing to do for another person.

JACOBSON: I noticed that, especially in this third one—his repeated concern that he be heard by the people in the way he
wanted to be heard, and not be seen as attacking or critical. He's
particularly at his best when asking for information.

RYCKOFF: I also noted down a number of other points. Of
course we talked about his emphasis on objective information on
one level. On another level he also puts a lot of emphasis on sub-
jective information. He'll pick up a remark somebody makes on
sexual inadequacy. He wants to translate that into what it means
to the patient. If the patient uses such a phrase, what does it mean,
what's the experience that goes along with it, what's the subjec-
tive part of that? He also has a concern about getting a fairly
vivid appraisal of the realities that a patient has bumped up against.
Likes to have sharp observations about what it's like to be a student sitting in law school, or to be in the Navy, or to be here, so
that students can imagine what this patient has been up against in
fact. Another nice point was the business of channeling the patient's negative generalization about himself. The patient says, I'm
a flop. Sullivan says, Well, what about so and so and so and so?
How do you account for the fact you got through the Navy, and
you did this? That's part of what he means by indirect reassurance.

KVARNES: Also what he is saying is that for somebody with as
weak an ego as a schizophrenic, direct reassurance doesn't work
because it is not believed.

RYCKOFF: The other thing he makes clear is that in following an organized approach to acquiring information—in Sullivan's terms, following his development scheme—but in any case, the very act of getting acquainted with this person, the doctor conveys to the patient that it is possible to organize, to see the patient's experience and life history in an organized way; the medium becomes the message. I am going to make the effort to think of you in fairly coherent terms, to think of your life experience in those terms.

DILLINGHAM: The other process is the same thing, isn't it, the particularity and the concreteness that you are using to make sure that your hypotheses are not wild, and you are also teaching the patient a method of getting down to organizing his life.

KVARNES: In effect, what you do is in an organized fashion put the data and the patient together so there is some consistency and meaningfulness. Goodness knows, in a disorganized patient there is damned little sense of that.

RYCKOFF: It's really an effort to rewrite the patient's history. The patient always feels it is already written, already there, no question about it.

KVARNES: By a careful reading of this third one I might say some of my early impressions have gotten corrected. I had thought, for instance, that he picked on Sam Novey when Sam had used the terms "aggressive" or "dependency needs." On going over it with some years in between I can see past the apparent criticism to what Sullivan was asking for: "Let's be clear as to what is being 'talked about.'"

RYCKOFF: As a matter of fact, he could have picked on people a hell of a lot more.

KVARNES: No question about it. But, in fact, to put it the other way round, in spite of these stumbling, vague attempts that people made to answer his questions, he didn't jump on the inadequacy, but every once in a while he would say, "You're getting near a point that might make some difference."

RYCKOFF: I thought he was much more positive than he has been painted—all those anecdotes about what a terror he was.

JACOBSON: On the other hand, there must have been some dynamic between him and the people in that group that made them be as fumbling as they were. Because, after all, there is a bunch

of bright guys there and some of these guys are out in left field
—sappy stuff——

RYCKOFF: They are trying to say nothing.

JACOBSON: Right. They are trying to say nothing.

RYCKOFF: Sullivan having established himself as the expert, as
the man who had his own way of saying things, who had his own
system, you were on the spot to see if you were going to answer
right, even without his putting on pressure.

JACOBSON: Wasn't there also, given the actual chronological
time when this was taking place [1947]—which is the time of up-
heaval in the two psychoanalytic institutes, isn't that right?—
wasn't there also a lot of struggle?

KVARNES: The Washington and the Baltimore institutes? It was
going on, but it was pretty subterranean to the younger fellows
at that point, I think.

JACOBSON: But Sullivan already is out and is a theorist in his
own right, and the differences between Sullivan and Freud were
then in the wind somehow. And people like Novey and Wagner
were on the other side of it, weren't they?

KVARNES: They ended up by regarding themselves as psycho-
analysts, not as rigid, orthodox Freudians.

RYCKOFF: You all did.

KVARNES: Yes, but both Sam and Phil would never get classified
as orthodox. Sam practiced in Baltimore but he certainly used a
good deal of Sullivan in his formulations.

The residents from Sheppard were Witt, Cooper, Peal, Rom,
and Styrt, Charlie Wheeler—I'd have to look it over, the makeup
of the group. They were really first- and second-year guys in
psychiatric training.

RYCKOFF: How far along were the rest? Wasn't Otto Will
working at St. E's at that time?

KVARNES: Otto hadn't come to the Lodge yet. Otto and I came
on the same day. He was in on the seminar, I think, by invitation
of Sullivan. Don Jackson, Stan Eldred, Otto Will, and Bob Morris
came to Chestnut Lodge the same day I did so he must have come
in some other way, by invitation. Edna Dyar, of course, was even
then a training analyst and on the staff of the Lodge. Mary White
was in her residency training at the Lodge; Staveren and Bob
Cohen were already staff members at the Lodge.

RYCKOFF: Some of these people had had other experience.

KVARNES: Some had had supervision under Sullivan.

RYCKOFF: I mean other kinds of life experience—professional experience. Otto did and Mary did, I think, before they came. So they were somewhat more mature.

JACOBSON: Did you have supervision during this period?

KVARNES: I don't think so.

JACOBSON: Were you carrying other cases?

KVARNES: Yes.

JACOBSON: Were you being supervised by somebody else?

KVARNES: I don't remember, Stan. I am not sure how well-organized supervision was at that time. I don't think it fitted the psychoanalytic model. I think we did it in case conferences and staff conferences but I don't remember talking on any kind of regular basis about any of my patients.

RYCKOFF: Who was head at Sheppard when you were there?

KVARNES: Ross McClure Chapman was still around as Superintendent, but he was pretty much ensconced in his house. He was an old friend of Sullivan's. Harry Murdock was Medical Director and Will Elgin was second to him. Murdock and Elgin set up this seminar.

JACOBSON: The reason I asked about supervision is that I wondered in reading this today whether there were other influences on you than this seminar in the way you were dealing with this case.

KVARNES: I don't know that I can remember clearly enough, Stan. I don't think there was anything except that the residents would talk about it some. I kept notes on the hours and I did something to cue myself in the presentations, but they weren't written-out presentations.

JACOBSON: But those of you who were in the seminar who were also residents at Sheppard would talk about your cases?

KVARNES: Yes, I'm sure we did.

DILLINGHAM: What were the relationships of those who were at Sheppard to the patient? I mean, you occasionally hear them say, "I see him during thus and so."

KVARNES: Well, they would see him on the ward. He took on some special coloration because they knew a good deal about him from the seminar.

RYCKOFF: Wouldn't different people have contact with the patient while being on duty? Weren't they all doing night duty?

KVARNES: We would have night duty and weekend, and we also saw patients on the ward.

RYCKOFF: Your patient would have been involved with their patients?

KVARNES: Right.

RYCKOFF: Were known to everybody?

KVARNES: Pretty much at that time. I knew most of the patients on all of the wards. Mine and other people's.

RYCKOFF: Such a small hospital.

KVARNES: In reading this last one, I had a real warm feeling about how goddamned decent he was in the attitude toward the patient and toward me and toward the guys and how he really was——

RYCKOFF: He was kind of pleased with your presentation.

KVARNES: Well, I understood that later. I was getting pretty damned anxious at that point. I really wasn't at all sure how this was coming off with Sullivan and I didn't have any sense of measurement of therapeutic progress. I didn't know whether I was doing well or badly at that point. I didn't know whether I was making a fool of myself or saying something very wise. I was having to present and do the best I could and trying to conceal what I didn't know, but I didn't know what I didn't know.

JACOBSON: That fascinates me because it fits so with my reactions. It made me mad because you present the stuff, and this one is so full of so much rich material, it's obvious you were doing beautifully with this guy in this length of time to be getting into that kind of stuff with a schizophrenic, and except for Sullivan, nobody is behaving equal to that. None of the responses are up to the real stuff that is going into this case.

KVARNES: No peer support.

JACOBSON: Or even thinking that is equal to the material. But people like Novey and Wagner could have. They weren't such greenhorns then.

DILLINGHAM: They are awfully cautious; whether that's caution built on experience or caution vis-à-vis Sullivan——

RYCKOFF: Some of this implies another overtone that exists about Sullivan's reputation. That even if he were very gentle with patients, even if he were gentle with residents, the one thing he wasn't going to take was anybody presuming to occupy an equal position to him—that someone would presume to have a definitive opinion or make a judgment. Reputedly he couldn't stand competition, he had to be the unquestioned leader.

KVARNES: Are you saying this is his reputation, or do you read it in here?

RYCKOFF: Of course nobody tries in the seminar. Everybody keeps himself in a novice position in relation to him. The anecdotes—I don't remember any specific ones, but the stories I've heard are to the effect that as soon as somebody raised his head and presumed to spell something out on a more definitive level he would immediately counterattack.

KVARNES: Well, I saw that happen a number of times later, but it seemed to be entirely justified because guys would overstate or pontificate.

JACOBSON: There is a place in this one where he speaks to something related to that—about how psychiatrists have the ruinous habit of overgeneralizing, being too definitive. I liked that.

KVARNES: That goes along with what you're trying to pick out here, too, John, the tension between the particularization and the generalization.

DILLINGHAM: To get it down to some kind of form. How did he puncture other analysts' overstatements? Was he just annoyed at them?

KVARNES: He might be annoyed, might ask them some question. "Doctor, please fill me in on how you arrived at that decision." Something like that.

DILLINGHAM: Because he is so sensitive about not putting patients in that position of leader and follower, I wondered if this extreme sensitivity relates somehow to his position outside that atmosphere, where he was probably comfortable being the leader and making sure people didn't overassume.

KVARNES: My experience isn't broad on this but I think where he would come in sarcastically was with someone who was being somewhat smart-alecky or pompous or overknowing. I think Sullivan doesn't come across as an authoritarian figure in this seminar; he comes across as having a genuine respect for relationships and the language and the process and so on.

DILLINGHAM: That's what I'm getting at, whether that stuff with other psychiatrists is born out of an insistence that that kind of overgeneralization is ruinous both to human relationships and to getting some information that you really need.

JACOBSON: Well, don't you think this thing I am referring to seems to fit that, that it was really deeply part of his professional philosophy? He says:

That sort of thing has impressed me in the development of promising psychiatrists for many years. . . . Then they have some goddamn theories about it. If, in their work with the patient, they inquire about what they feel is important, but try very carefully not to prejudice the outcome by developing any of their thoughts about why they feel it important, it is very apt to be good work.

KVARNES: I certainly am having a stronger and stronger conviction that a good deal can be done to make this into a highly readable thing; it will take some editing and some rephrasing, but hell, it flows. This business about reservations:

God, we have enough that won't be in mind without having this patient going about with things that must not be said. The whole doctrine of reservations comes in here. What little I have learned about reservations is this—if there is an agreement between a patient and therapist that the patient has a reservation and keeps it, the damn thing can grind up an incredible amount of time by becoming a recurrent preoccupation. You start to talk about the weather and it brings up thoughts of the reservations and there you block. I have seen patients reduced to brilliant attempts to tell me the same damn story five or six times to kill an hour and so modify the accounts that I was supposed to overlook the fact that they were telling me the same story. It is not that we give a damn about what the reservations are. Our freedom of communication is such that we don't want to force the patient to relinquish the reservations, but we want to do something which makes its entertainment obviously expensive.

That one has stood me in good stead many times. Also, another thing I want to call our attention to: "My statistics are complicated forms of humor." He just doesn't have all that great reverence for them.

JACOBSON: I wasn't sure what that meant. As a matter of fact, I wasn't even sure what he was ultimately saying in the passage that follows that. About people being stuck with a needle.

KVARNES: He said: "My statistics are complicated forms of humor, but I suppose the people who can and who cannot get used to such relatively unusual things as intravenous needles distribute smoothly on the probability curve and there is no notable correlation between which side they are on and many obvious traits of their so-called psychosexual development." That needs to be translated. I guess I don't know what he is saying there.

JACOBSON: Don't know whether he is saying it is or probably isn't related to psychosexual development.

RYCKOFF: He is saying it probably isn't. He says, "There is a perfectly good right to question whether they probably would or not." Homosexual or whatever.

JACOBSON: It's very interesting to me to see how important it is to him to tell all you guys and himself and patients that sometimes a cigar is only a cigar. That symbolic reality is not the only reality.

RYCKOFF: What's crazy about that kind of situation is that even when it is an important reality it never is the only reality. Even if the cigar is a phallic symbol it also is a cigar—the actual thing has another connotation for everybody.

KVARNES: I remember now that I wanted to underscore a particular exposition. There's a long piece in here in which he develops this concept about heterosexual failure coming from the kind of family situation in which the mother has all the estimable qualities and the father is pretty much of a cipher as an acceptable model. At the time I really didn't understand enough about the theories of homosexuality to see this one in place, but what he was doing here was actually presenting another theoretical explanation of a predisposition to homosexuality. One configuration is the severely disciplinary kind of mother, with the father as the only one who offers the boy affection; this sets it up so that the boy sees the affectionate relationships along the male lines, and the female, a power figure whom he may model himself after somewhat, still is threatening. Now, this hypothesis is a much gentler notion—that the male may pattern himself after the mother if she's got enough estimable qualities to allow him to do that and if the father doesn't come on the scene enough to afford a counterinfluence. What Sullivan is proposing, as I see it, is that in some instances, through the early years of personality formation, the mother is the only parent evidencing attractive qualities that the boy can emulate or incorporate into his personality. This is relatively safe until he arrives at adolescence. At this point the boy's feminine qualities could give him trouble with the male role now expected of him, and his feeble efforts at forming heterosexual relations may get shipwrecked. Presumably there could be several outcomes to this—pulling away from relationships with females and turning to male sexual companions, or avoiding heterosexual genital relationships without turning toward sexual activities with males, or an extended adolescence during which male traits and behaviors are slowly developed in low-keyed heterosexual relationships where there isn't too much demand for full-blown masculinity. Some men don't assemble their final masculine traits until fairly far along in life—after a successful analysis, for example.

RYCKOFF: It puts the emphasis on a rather positive identification, identifying with the more admirable of the two parents.

JACOBSON: It seems to me he was distinguishing that kind of pattern from a pattern that would develop into homosexuality; that is, he was saying that one can discriminate between early influences leading to a failure to achieve heterosexuality and those that can lead to an unrelenting lifelong kind of homosexuality.

KVARNES: He says that in the schizophrenic male particularly, they always have difficulty about male/female identity; they have a real problem with it. What this formulation talks about is the process of the development of a feminine quality modeled after the mother and not integrated later into a more confident masculine pattern because there wasn't the male model to subsume it. Now, if that's the development, that kind of guy is extremely vulnerable to the self-accusation of homosexuality; even though he may have made no moves in that direction at all, the vulnerability comes from this feeling about his feminine component.

RYCKOFF: Of course that's the basis for the common feeling of vulnerability, the accusation of homosexuality, this component that we ought not to have.

KVARNES: And it's one of the huge dilemmas in life, I think, when one meditates about it a little bit, because if you're growing up in the company of a mother who has qualities that you like and you model yourself after her, then you arrive at puberty with an unacceptable component. You're sandbagged in a way; you really thought you were doing something that you felt was right, then all of a sudden you've got to be a man and, goddamn it, this doesn't fit at all. And I think the other thing it highlights is that we tend to see this mother as a bit of a monster, an anxious, controlling neglectful mother, when what Sullivan is saying here is a little bit more decent than that; that actually this woman did have some kind of relationship with the kid, and the patient does say later, in terms of separation, "They're all I've got." And it's a very poignant statement at the point where he now has got to separate himself off from his parents. Because he is a man and there's nobody else. And even though she's a mess she's somebody.

DILLINGHAM: She's a mess from the very beginning, where you get the information that he and the mother used to go aside and make jokes about the father.

JACOBSON: There is something about the real identification of this kid with the mother. It came through in their getting together and ridiculing the father; of her taking him to the beauty shop. And it surprised me that the group didn't pick that up at all, that somehow their characterization of the mother didn't yield the whole issue of the closeness of the relationship; they kept talking about the kid not having any relationship. Well, it was pathological but it damn well was there and it was profound.

RYCKOFF: That's the kind of generalization made when something is of less than perfect quality or maybe is very bad in actuality; it gets dismissed as being nothing. He had no mother and no father, which doesn't make any sense.

KVARNES: I would like to add a piece of personal history here. The seminar started about the same time I started my own personal analysis, so I wasn't too savvy about many aspects of myself. The patient's background had many elements that were similar to my own. My mother was an ambitious, driven woman who for many years regretted her marriage. I'm certain her pregnancy with me was resented. My hunch is that the ambivalence of love-hate toward me in the first year contributed to my spending my whole life proving I have a right to existence. Somehow around the end of the first year—I've pieced this together from various sources, including strong hunches—she began to see me as "smart" or "precocious" and from then on I became "her" child. She seemed to form a stronger bond with me than with my father or sister, and I was heavily influenced by her "estimable qualities." Fortunately I had formed some identification with my father which came much more into awareness during later adolescence. My evolution from a marked disposition toward my mother's attributes to a more acceptable masculinity was a slow process—the last male figure who strongly affected my achieving a comfortable masculine identity I had met only three years before the start of the seminar. So in presenting this patient, with his gender quandary, I was also presenting myself. I didn't know then I was also talking about myself, and happily nobody else offered that interpretation. Because I couldn't have handled it—it would have blown the whole seminar.

RYCKOFF: As a matter of fact, if anybody discerned the point that was raising its head they would not make it. That's the kind of point Sullivan might discern and never say.

KVARNES: It's also the kind of point that some smart aleck might pick up and jump on with some new insight, and I think in that instance Sullivan would have torn the guy to bits, and with maybe nobody ever quite knowing why. But I was interested, now as I read it over for the umpteenth time, in what the selection process was. I thought I was presenting an interesting case to Sullivan—in part, I was presenting myself. Some of the real problems I myself had this guy brought out, and fortunately in the process I learned a great deal without at that time having put it together at all.

JACOBSON: Sullivan says something about this toward the end, about how much easier it is to talk about a third party. Therapists as well as patients, as a matter of fact. I wonder if he did know.

KVARNES: In addition to that, I suspect you'd find that Sullivan's makeup or family configuration had something of this in it too, because he had a very strong mother and a quiet, reserved, retiring, farmer father. Some of the myths about Sullivan obviously came from his mother, that he's the child of the West Wind and that kind of thing. Hadn't thought of that until this moment, but maybe here we have the patient and the presenter and the supervisor all having a similar family configuration.

JACOBSON: Whether one has that particular family configuration, dealing with one's femininity is something all of us have to suffer with, and what's impressive is that Sullivan knows that and he is sensitive enough to that in all you guys around that table. He knows that all of you have to deal with that in yourselves and he knows that as young residents you have not resolved this. He knows that he cannot push them, this is something everybody has to work on in his own way. He explores the Navy experiences of the guys around the table; well, he could also very easily explore universal male experience but he doesn't.

KVARNES: That's right, Stan. I do know personally that several of the fellows were struggling with this problem. There was lots of drama going on that wasn't talked about.

RYCKOFF: What's always so refreshing about Sullivan is that he is free of—guess I'm repeating the same point—free of any preformed generalization that he has to stick to. Really tries to think out what it has been like for somebody.

KVARNES: And also how free of the jargonisms. He even goes to the term "self-esteem" in a delicate fashion, like he's talking about something that especially applies to the patient and is not a generalization.

JACOBSON: I must say I was startled after reading the long history you had given, the first thing Sullivan picks up is this thing about reading but not for content; all this rich material—father, mother, homosexuality—and he picks up this little thing about the kid says he's read early but not for content. And I wonder what the hell that means.

KVARNES: Why do you think he is doing that?

JACOBSON: He is cozying into the thing.

KVARNES: Giving all of us some time——

JACOBSON: Of course——

KVARNES: To deal with it.

DILLINGHAM: I was struck by that when I read it—about the reading. I'd just read an article about an early childhood psychosis having to do with reading—and I was just wondering if he had really never heard of—some hairy, scary sort of thing they picked up lately.

RYCKOFF: I'm interested in this because I have a patient, a girl who has a master's and almost her Ph.D. She has an important job, she speaks Chinese, she's an expert, she's only twenty-five. She says she can't read and she says she doesn't read. She has a whole elaborate system for picking up enough information, getting by without reading. She describes how she dishes out all kinds of smart-alecky generalizations and people are favorably impressed. But she insists that she has gotten by all along without absorbing anything, even in college when she was getting A's.

KVARNES: Wonder what her concept of reading is. Maybe somebody who is able to sit down and concentrate for four straight hours. There are all kinds of reading styles.

RYCKOFF: By next week I will have finished all of mine.

KVARNES: We'll read the next part and the typist will have the last part ready for the week after.

IV

Case Seminar, February, 1947

Here, Kvarnes begins to describe changes in the patient, and also reads substantial portions of his interviews with the patient. The usual Sullivan inquiries follow Kvarnes' presentation.

In addition to Kvarnes and Sullivan, the following persons were present at this session: Larry Cooper, Robert Morris, Samuel Novey, Stanley Peal, Leon Salzman, Herbert Staveren, Jerome Styrt, Charles Wheeler, Mary White, and Otto Will.

KVARNES: The main thing during the past month is that there has been a change in the patient—not a prominent change, and yet obvious both in the office setting and on the ward. It occurred largely during the past two weeks, with the patient being more at ease in the office, talking without jumping up from the chair when he gets on an anxious subject, without rolling paper into a ball and chewing it, or tearing up my matchbooks. The initial approach to each interview has changed in tone; he does not always start out with such a self-derogatory attitude.

During the past two weeks he has been complaining that he has a void in his mind—says he feels at ease and seems to believe there is nothing going on to talk about. Within a minute or two of the start, however, he is talking quite readily and still bringing up some fresh material.

On the ward he has been somewhat more outgoing. He still does not participate in hydrotherapy or occupational therapy, but he has tried to have social conversations with a couple of people, principally the male nurse that I spoke of before, and a student nurse.

I have tried to go into some of the things we talked about last time in an effort to clarify some of the questions. I got very little extra data on the birthday cake incident. He is not willing to clarify what was called the "social geography" of these various situations. My asking questions generally evokes an "I don't know" response after perhaps one comment. It does seem that it was obviously an attempt on his part to insult his brother by his absence. It was his expression of dislike for the show that was put on for the brother. He maintains that during his whole first ten years he was quite the center of attraction in the family. He refers to being taken out by his grandparents, to the attention shown him by his "Uncle Joe," the family doctor, and to the display made over him by the father's political friends, but brings up very little evidence that he was the center of attraction in the home. One of the things he mentioned, with an attitude of "look how they treated me," was that in his very early years he was dressed in a patriotic costume and put in a baby parade which was related to one of his father's election campaigns. He has pictures but does not remember the incident.

The dental situation has also come up several times since and I did get around to asking your question of what a burr is. He did know what it was, but that particular train of complaints has subsided recently. He still complains of uneasiness in medical situations, but does not clarify that too well. He speaks of "treatments" that would be painful to him, and I have suggested that they are painful to anyone, that there are people who dislike any kind of injections and yet otherwise have nothing particularly wrong with them. It seems he associates the medical situation, for one thing, with lying on his back, and the discomfort he feels. He spoke of this in connection with the shock treatment—the anxiety he feels when he is on his back, and relates that, in turn, to other earlier experiences all the way back to an incident at three or four when he had a cut over his eye. He refused to have the cut sutured, and Uncle Joe was involved again—the fellow who took him on his calls around the hospitals, and offered him cigars. The boy remembers him as unkempt, and recalls that his mother always felt that this doctor was a gossip. I tried to point out that some of his anxieties relating to the medical situation may have arisen there—that a kid of five or six would be likely to play with the idea of becoming a doctor, and that actually his feelings toward Uncle Joe were very pleasant; he has to some extent accepted this interpretation.

The idea of discerning what he felt to be estimable in his parents I have not been able to work with. I do not have a clear grasp of how to approach it. I made an attempt to find out what in particular he liked about his mother but he was resistive and I got nothing from the approach. He has mentioned that he seemed to derive a fear of authority from his father. The father's aloofness and tendency to correct him are things he remembers with some vividness from the early days. Earlier, he had reiterated the idea that his father never played with him as a boy, in contrast to Jim's father. The father's attitudes undoubtedly vacillated, but now the patient believes that his father did play with him in his early youth. He said that perhaps one of the reasons his father was unable to play with the boys on a companionable basis was an injury the father sustained when the boy was two. The father had been struck by an auto and suffered a fracture and subsequently never showed any interest in athletics. Bill said also that he had never been able to boast, "My father can lick your father." He talks about his father's ability as a public speaker, of his emotional and colorful speeches, and said he was as moved by his father's speeches as by any others he had ever heard.

He also expressed the notion recently that from an early age his parents had been pushing him into a career as a lawyer, and from college on he thought that he would enter law practice with his father.

I went over the argument between the parents, and he was loath to give me more details. He remembered his mother's position in the room, but he could not remember where his father and he were.

On Saturday he got around to talking about swear words and he said he never found it easy to utter them and even in the Navy he was less likely to use them than the other fellows. There was no use of such terminology around the house. He remembers that in an argument, again during puberty, the mother became upset and called somebody a "whore," and he added that she seemed to lose her awareness that he was in the room.

He continues to use psychiatric jargon. He has settled on paranoid schizophrenia, and I am not too successful in breaking through that. I have tried to deride his use of the language. I don't use it in our talks, I try to stay away from terms that are purely psychiatric. He is the one who uses them, and we have gone on in the subject of diagnosis somewhat on the basis of his pushing and questions. I have stated that diagnosis was not the important thing, that we had not arrived at any conclusive diagnosis, and certainly we had not called him paranoid schizophrenia, as he seemed anxious to label himself. During the past two weeks there has been less of that but some use of the words in relation to others, which I will bring up later.

He has dwelt, particularly in the early two or three weeks of this month, on his lack of ability in many spheres, his inability to learn, his inability to grasp anything he read, inability to perform anything mechanical, his lack of any kind of skill. In reference to that, he brought up that during his high school years he considered anything related to manual training as being in the province of the less bright boys. If they did not do too well in school it was suggested that they spend more time in vocational subjects, and he veered away from that. Through it all there seems to be a questioning of why he did not learn, why this and that did not make sense to him. I tried to use that as a place to suggest that his own feelings and his own goals and desires were not considered too much, that in some of his previous schooling and patterns of living there was a lack of a thread of personal orientation to it all.

SULLIVAN: Tell me what you meant by this "thread of personal orientation."

KVARNES: What I was thinking about was his feeling that he has never learned anything in his subjects, that he would study only the last two weeks of a course to cram through for the examination, his point being the examination rather than any fundamental knowledge of the subjects. He says that occasionally he chose a subject because it was easier. Related to this is his following a law education without any real desire for it. He brings out all this as if everything he has done in the past has not had too much meaning for him, and he now has to throw it all over. As an illustration of this, he condemns himself for being unable to do anything in OT, not being able to handle the work tools, or to do any simple task down there, and being unwilling to try; he relates that to his having derided such things in high school and college when his interest seemed to be primarily intellectual. He seems to feel that all he had learned had been so useless that he must have lacked fundamental abilities.

In the past month it has become clear in many ways that at all periods in his life there has been pressure, environmental pressure, pressure within himself, to act as an older person. He skipped grades and was one of the youngest boys in his class, and the association with his parents always brought out in him a sober, quiet sort of behavior, a feeling that anything he did would be labeled childish. I have emphasized with him that he always had a tendency to try to behave older than he was, to label ordinary things that other kids did as childish or juvenile—that he never seems to have expected himself to live through some of these ordinary experiences.

Somewhere in the middle of the month, he had been talking about his failure to ever talk freely with anyone about himself, how this experience with me seems to have been the first time, and also about his feelings of loneliness and melancholy through-out the developing years. The patient mentioned to somebody, but not to me, that his friend Barney was also a roommate during his college years, and that is something I have to investigate, the idea that he roomed away from home during part of his college career. In a couple of days there it became clear that he had been rather lonely and distant all his life, and at that time I used that dream that he had had of escaping with the other patient and winding up in the toilet on the train feeling very frightened, to illustrate what seems to be a pattern of loneliness. This he accepted quite well. I have the feeling that the clarification of his feelings of loneliness has contributed to the change in the patient.

About ten days ago I realized something I had been doing that I suppose is related to this seminar. I felt obligated to get a lot of data and I had been pushing him—starting his interviews if he had nothing to say, pushing him if there was a lengthy pause, and also trying to pull him back to situations that I wanted clarified. He allows me to do that generally, but I think I have perceived some resistance to that approach. I have also had great difficulty in forming any kind of idea of what sort of goals he has had for him-self—both prior to his illness and now. I think that going into it without a clear notion of what to present to him as a possibility has had some detrimental effect. It has led to a lot of talk about doom and this being the end of the road and inability on his part to formulate any plans about his leaving the hospital.

One day about two weeks ago I questioned him about his aims and goals, this time relating it much more to the situation between us. What was he trying to achieve in our relationship and what were the goals in what we were trying to do. Again I got very little; he was reluctant to define his goals and yet he did not question me. I felt I might help him to develop an answer about the aims of what we were striving to do and about some of the prospects, perhaps not too specific, as to occupation or way of life. I felt I could point out that in our talks we could explore his feelings about what he might do to feel more comfortable, both now and later. I think I changed a little bit in my approach. I think I was less pushing and, for some reason, I was feeling more comfortable myself in relation to him and some of the pressure came off. That again is related to this period of change.

One thing he does is rather amusing, and I was a little uneasy about how to handle it. He talked one day about his "gullibility" —how he believed anything that people told him or that he read. One day on board ship one of the sailors had an epileptic fit. When he saw the fellow writhing and asked what was going on, someone replied that the fellow had "lost his marbles." Immediately Bill went into a fantasy about this fellow rolling around on the floor trying to find his marbles. I was not able to control my smiles and finally laughed outright, and then he laughed and looked at me in a sort of "look-how-ridiculous" approach. Initially he looked at it as something pretty shameful. He looked at me suspiciously for a moment and then we laughed again and from then on the situation was quite comfortable.

In a similar instance when he was in training on board ship, he was at the helm and became very anxious and upset when another ship approached and he didn't know what orders to give. He was told to "go below" by the instructor, and, never having heard the term before, he started to turn away and walk down the steps. The instructor asked him where he was going and the crew laughed, and he felt ridiculous for not knowing that that order meant to surrender the helm.

In the last two weeks his father has visited twice and he has been much more at ease with him. Prior to this he has used his father as an outlet for all his self-derogatory comments. But during the last two weeks he said that he was calm throughout the interview and was questioning about some things but not upset.

I thought I might read part of a couple of interviews to show you something of what way the questions and answers went.

SULLIVAN: Where are these interviews located in the month?

KVARNES: One was on the twentieth of January, which I think is a little before I recognized that he was getting calmer in interviews. He came in, sat down, and seemed to be getting weaker and weaker and unable to move, and so I asked him if he had had visitors. Of course I knew of their recent visit and guessed that his "weakness" might be an expression of despair because of the visit. He said: "Yes, my parents were down. Same kind of visit. I was calmer, I guess. Same sort of talk. I mentioned my fears of barber instruments. My mother said that was not true, that I liked to go to a barber shop when I was a kid—always asking to go. Told me I went in once and asked to have a haircut like my uncle's." Q. "Uncle Joe?" A. "No, this was another uncle, who was bald. I see something in that. No conception of reality as a child. I see myself as schizophrenic from an early age." Q. "Back to schizophrenia again!" A. "Well, I was. I'm sure if some sort of psychological tests had been done, Rorschach, etc., they would have disclosed that. All they did was the IQ." Q. "Are you equating any kind of developmental problem and schizophrenia? There is only uselessness in trying to pin a label on such things. I don't see where our labeling something as pathological, schizophrenic, abnormal, helps one bit in understanding. We want to know what these various things that you remember mean to you, not whether they are 'normal' or not. What do you see in this haircut incident?" A. "I don't know." Q. "Well, do you mean that you had made the horrible mistake of thinking of baldness as some kind of haircut, or because your mother brings it up now, or what?" A. "Mostly that I didn't see the reality in the situation and thought that baldness was some sort of a haircut." Q. "You were five or six?" A. "Yes." Q. "Isn't that a likely thing for a kid to think? Hair is mostly a nuisance that one is told to keep combed and I guess most of us want to get it cut off at that age. Don't you suppose that's what you were after?" A. "I suppose so. That's another thing—I'd never let anyone comb my hair. Insisted that I wash myself, button my own clothes—sort of an exagger-

ated sense of self-sufficiency—wanting to do everything myself."
In talking about his parents the patient said: "They mentioned
that they could get me all kinds of jobs. They see this as if I were
going to stay two or three weeks and they said they'd take me out
anytime I asked them. I don't know whether it is good that they
visit or not." Q. "How do you feel about it?" A. "I don't know.
[pause] They're all I've got—if I've got them." Patient became
tearful for a short time. Q. "You said 'if I've got them'?" "I'm
just alone—I guess everybody's pretty much alone. I just see this
as the end, that's all." Q. "That's part of a pessimistic approach to
everything that you have, isn't it?" A. "What do you mean?" Q.
"You aren't in the habit of looking optimistically at things, are
you?" A. "No, I've been pessimistic all my life."

The patient then said that his mother brought up the time he
had his tonsillectomy. "She said she went to the hospital with me,
and even to the operating room. Said they called me 'the professor' after that—I'd go around visiting all the people in their
hospital rooms." Q. "Why 'the professor'—serious?" A. "No, I
was talkative. Guess I was regarded as a smart kid, that's why."

SULLIVAN: What hospital was it, a teaching hospital?

KVARNES: I don't know. I didn't inquire.

The next day we had the following interview: Patient said, "I
feel the same, quiet. Went to OT but couldn't stay there. The
noise——" Q. "Is it only the noise?" A. "No, I have no interest in
anything—when I went there when I was more agitated, I saw
everything as a weapon with which to hurt myself." Q. "Always
to use against yourself?" A. "Yes, some sort of violence against
myself. I don't think I thought of using it against someone else—
maybe I did, I don't know. I know I do like wandering away from
the group until I'm called back." Q. "Where?" A. "OT or outside
hydro waiting for the others." Q. "There is a certain repetitive-
ness to that—wandering away until someone calls you back?" A.
"I guess so. I don't get the feeling of the ward as a group—so
seclusive—trying to get away from the noise—resentment of the
attendants and so on." Q. "But those things aside, there is this
repetition of wandering away from the group—do you recall
anything similar to that?" A. "What do you mean?" Q. "I mean
the repetition of something where you expect a response from
someone telling you not to do it?" A. "I don't recall anything. It is
a sort of attention-getting maneuver—I always tried to get

attention—like at a beer party where someone spilled beer on me and I took my shirt off and waved it around." Q. "I don't mean something like that." A. "No, I don't recall anything else—I always got things distorted, couldn't learn anything. Took a course, neglect the studies, then cram for a couple of weeks for an exam, and not remember anything about the subject afterwards." Q. "Well, I just refuse to believe you didn't learn anything." A. "Well, I didn't. I didn't learn anything. [smile] Isn't it likely that a twenty-five-year-old schizophrenic wouldn't learn anything? [smile]" Q. "No, I don't think it is likely."

At another part of the interview I asked him: "Have you felt resentment of things I say or of others on the ward or in the hospital? You mention resenting attendants but we never go into that. I think it would be useful to go into some of your feelings, don't you?" A. "Well, I have resented some things you said. I notice I resent your challenging my using 'schizophrenia' or when I tell you something about what I've done or what I've said you always remark, 'That's normal,' or 'What's unusual about that?' " Q. "Are you thinking that perhaps I approach all this as unrealistically as your parents do? I do recognize that you are ill, but we are attempting to go into these various things in terms of appropriateness of feelings. There is a necessity for comparing views on things and events and I try to tell you something of my feelings about what you say. I don't think I approach your illness unrealistically. I wonder if your resentment here isn't a carry-over from your feelings about your parents' remarks." A. "I guess there's some of that, all right."

In the past two days, several interesting things have happened. On Friday he started talking about sex. He talked about his girlfriend at greater length, generally with a condemnatory attitude toward it all, but said during the month they were together they got to be quite intimate sexually. In reply to my inquiry about what he meant, he said that they did not have intercourse but they were around his home naked and there was some mutual sex play. He had not known whether he could go ahead with it, whether he wanted to, and then he said he had premature ejaculations and he felt this was lack of control. In trying to relate this to his experiences in the Navy, he said he never felt the same at home, feeling that it was more difficult to operate there, feeling the idea of his father's prestige and his own prestige. I inquired whether he and the girl had any easy talk about it at such a time and there had not been any. I pointed out that she apparently was somewhat uneasy about it herself, just as he was, and that it was not a situation that anyone was likely to find easy at their stage of development. At that time I mentioned something about his moral rigidity but we did not go into it any further.

On that day, prior to my seeing him, one of the doctors from the Veterans Administration had been out. The father had prepared a request for aid from the Veterans Administration because he considered this illness service-connected. The patient signed the paper and then condemned himself for doing it because he did not feel his military service had anything to do with it. The VA physician asked him some simple questions—for example, "Do you like the hospital?" To that he had answered affirmatively, saying it was a good hospital. He seemed rather chagrined about saying it was a good hospital, and I suppose that since he had talked about his feelings that the attendants were pushing him around and that there was pressure for him to do things in the hospital, he felt he was being inconsistent.

He also mentioned that he had acquired some fear of authority from his father and disdain for authority from his mother. He did not go into that any more other than that her disdain for authority seemed to be shown in a lack of conventionality.

That evening, after our talk about his relationship to his girl, about 6:30 he was heard in the bathroom saying: "I should die. I should kill myself. I should not be allowed to live." That is not uncommon on the ward. He remained quite restless, went into his room and asked to have his light turned off at 7:00, which was done, and about 7:30 a student nurse heard him shouting and went into his room. He looked very calm and said, "I just had a nightmare. I have them frequently and it's nothing to get upset about. Would you mind talking to me for a while?" She agreed and they talked for about an hour and a half. He asked about nurses' training, then wanted to know if she were interested in pediatrics, said that his friend Barney had been interested in pediatrics, and asked if she liked children, to which she replied, "Yes." He then got around to talking about himself, mentioned the diagnosis that he makes himself, wanted to know more about how we did shock treatment here, and described how it was done at Springhill. He felt there must have been something wrong with it because he could remember everything but the actual shock. He also inquired about insulin shock. The nurse handled the situation well and was as honest as she could be.

SULLIVAN: Did he ask whether she thought it did any good?

KVARNES: The nurse didn't say. He feels that it obviously did him harm and has never inquired whether it was useful to other people. When he talked about her being a nurse, he said, "My illness had something to do with a nurse, too." He had had a nurse at an early age but this is something he has not discussed with me at all. I only know at the time of his father's illness there was a nurse in the house. I have inquired about her but he denies remembering anything.

When they were discussing insulin shock he said, "That takes needles and I have a fear of needles." Then he added that he used to fear talking to his doctor, but recently he has not been afraid, since he has realized that there was not going to be any special form of treatment which was going to hurt him.

About halfway through this talk, he said, "Gee whiz, look at me, talking to a woman just like a normal person," and he continued in a calm and interested manner. Then he said, "Thanks a lot. Being able to talk to a woman gives me some hope that I can get well." This is his first comment in any setting referring to the idea that he might get well, that there might be some change in his course. After this he went to sleep quite easily.

Saturday he started the interview by saying that his mind was a void, that he feels calm with no more vertigo. Then he talked about having a high singing voice, and he said that as a kid he had a soprano voice and sang in choirs before puberty. At thirteen he was in a stage production which required his being painted up with rouge, lipstick, and eyebrow pencil, and at that time he thought he looked very feminine. I said, "Did you like the way you looked?" and he denied that. I said: "Were you considered a handsome kid? Were you frequently given compliments?" He said yes, he had been singled out because of his healthy look and being a pretty child. After that he mentioned that he always seemed to be approached by men on subways. At thirteen or fourteen he remembers a man in the subway offering him a piece of candy and asking him to go with him. At the age of ten a man in the subway exposed himself to him. I inquired whether it was specifically to him, did the man smile and gesture to him in some way, and he said yes. He said he was so frightened he "froze stiff." During that part of the conversation it was my feeling that it was a safe time to introduce the term that had never been used in our talks—that it could seem to be not too disturbing—and I asked him in a questioning tone, "Did you think it was possible that you might be homosexual?" He paused, and then said no. He was not upset by the question and I merely said that it was the age when kids learned about such things and were very alert to them.

At the end of this there was another specific incident. We walked out, and as he went ahead with the attendant, he noticed that one of my other patients, a sicker patient, was sitting with two children in his lap, smiling. As I stopped and talked to the fellow, inquiring about the children, the patient came over, stood beside me, and seemed very comfortable. As we walked away he said that was something he could never do, and I said, "Have you ever tried?" He said he had played with kids before and had a good time.

Last night the nurse again went in to talk to him.

SULLIVAN: She did that spontaneously, or did he ask her?

KVARNES: She just went in to inquire about nourishment, and he picked up the conversation again. He talked about his childhood, said his parents always wanted him to be a lawyer and that he didn't think it was good for parents to push a child. He asked when she was leaving, and unfortunately she is leaving tomorrow. He inquired about what she thought of psychiatric nursing and told her that she should consider it, because she had a very good relationship with the patients. He was reading a book that the nurse thought related to feelings people had at various seasons of the year, and he was trying to talk to her about the possibility that general feelings in relation to various seasons had something to do with one's personality. He asked if she liked winter or summer and then said, "You have a very well-adjusted and well-rounded personality." They got onto the subject of shock again, and then he said he certainly felt better about talking to his doctor now, that he was certain nothing bad was going to happen in the way of treatment.

Another thing which is rather different for him is that during the conversation he heard a popular song on the radio and sang a few lines of the song without too much timidity. I asked her if he seemed to be singing to her, and she said yes.

That is what I have for this month.

SULLIVAN: This is really immense, from the standpoint of the seminar. I would like to hear everybody discuss two topics. The first, what they have in mind about the patient and the therapy, and the second rather astonishing thing of what would you like to advise Dr. Kvarnes about his interviews. There are a number of things that each of us is almost certain to wonder about in what anyone else does. They usually reflect an element of our own personality in such work, and as we are really most concerned with our own work in such situations. I would like very much to hear any ideas that might be expressed. This is the first time we have had quite illuminating excerpts of the therapeutic interchange—incidentally they are very illuminating excerpts on the therapeutic relationship—and this interchange with the nurse, so that I wonder if I should not take time toward the end of the session to deal with certain elements in it, but in any case I would like to hear you talk both of the therapy and the immediate future and any questions on the differences in your views as to how things should be done. Remembering my oversight of last time, let me see what Dr. Cooper thinks.

KVARNES: Let me just mention my attitudes toward him. I don't know how clearly I can judge my own feelings but from the very beginning I have maintained an air of optimism throughout. My general attitude has been one of trying to recognize the fact that he is ill, but not irrecoverably ill. I think there are things that can be done which will aid him. I accept it as a matter of course that he will ultimately get; well, not in the naïve way that his parents do, but as a kind of a feeling that I have in myself. I don't feel frightened by the situation with the patient, not particularly defensive, and I have noticed, too, there are many times in which I can get to be quite pushing in the relationship. I am finally becoming aware that it is not too fruitful, but it has never worked great havoc. He is still anxious to talk on each occasion. My general attitude is one of, I might say, cool friendliness. It is not a back-slapping, easy comradeship level, but I don't try to be too serious whenever I meet him. I try to greet him in much the way I might greet some of the hospital personnel. When I have occasionally tried to be a little humorous, he has generally laughed. It has not been too harmful to him, too close to him in its approach. Also, I have not tried to do any interpreting to any degree; I have occasionally related things as I see them, but generally the whole period to date has been one in which I have been trying to find out data rather than letting it be on an easy speaking level. I think it is important that I learn something about that, because as I have said, during the last two weeks, I've had the feeling that I had been pushing quite hard, and I would like to know something about how to proceed from now on.

COOPER: Early in this hour, Dr. Kvarnes mentioned that he thought during this past month the patient for the first time spoke of loneliness, of being lonely during much of his life. That is something that could be gone into with the idea of finding out from the patient just what he had to contribute to his own loneliness—whether outsiders were to blame or himself.

I was a little critical of Dr. Kvarnes' approach when he mentioned the fact that men had often tried to contact him in subways or had exposed themselves to him. When Dr. Kvarnes said, "My God, did you entertain the idea that you were homosexual?" I think the patient could only answer no, to please Dr. Kvarnes. I think he should have been more accepting maybe, along the line of "Well, were you interested?" "Were you frightened?" "If frightened, why?" More with the idea that everyone goes through some of those feelings at one time or another. I believe the patient now believes it is distasteful to Dr. Kvarnes and perhaps will not mention it again.

WHEELER: I noticed that Dr. Kvarnes mentioned that the patient had seemed to improve lately, and also that he had changed his approach in not so much trying to ferret out answers to various questions that had come up here and was letting things go more at their own pace. I think that is good and probably has something to do with the favorable turn.

SULLIVAN: Anything that you feel different about in Dr. Kvarnes' questions to the patient?

WHEELER: Well, when the patient speaks of himself as being a paranoid schizophrenic, I would not be so anxious to deny it; in other words, I would let him use whatever words he wanted to with the idea that it was no great obstacle.

PEAL: I have been thinking of a number of things that went on before. I thought at first that Dr. Kvarnes was very accepting of everything the patient had done, was interested in everything he said, and it seemed that next the patient began becoming quite—annoying is the word that occurs to me—it is not a very good one—in his persistent contradictions and repetition of statements that obviously had no meaning. That was followed by Dr. Kvarnes being more questioning and more demanding concerning these statements, and now it seems that a third period is occurring in which he is less pushing, as he puts it, and it seems to me that the opinions have changed concerning people. In the past, the patient was pushing and Dr. Kvarnes was pushing in the direction of self-criticism and criticism of father. Now, as Dr. Kvarnes relaxes, the father becomes more friendly and also the patient makes friends with a nurse and is more friendly to his father in his visits.

SULLIVAN: Which precedes which? In the sense of change in Dr. Kvarnes' attitude or change preceding his attitude?

SALZMAN: It seems to me that in the last month what is happening to the patient is related very much to the problem of loneliness which has come out in the open and which the patient seems to be handling in a very overt way. He has relaxed considerably in his relationship to Dr. Kvarnes. That does seem to be related to the removal of some of Dr. Kvarnes' pressure on the patient. I had a feeling all along that some of his approach is like father. "You have to live up to some expectations that I have of you." "You have to get well and you have to do it and approach it the way I want you to." Apparently some of that has relaxed and the patient has been able to deal with Dr. Kvarnes on a more open and friendly basis.

The last month seems to have gone very well, particularly leading up to the interview where the patient is able to speak of his loneliness. It is in that interview that I would like to make some comment about Dr. Kvarnes' handling. It seemed to me that was a favorable opportunity to discuss, at least to a slight degree, the implications of loneliness. Dr. Kvarnes did not do that. He rather moved away from it and proceeded on another tack, an intellectual approach that stimulated in the patient only the response—and I think this is probably the only response that has been stimulated for some time—that I have to give some information and I have to think out all the answers to the questions. It seemed to me the way the questions were asked stimulated only some intellectual preoccupation rather than any examination of his emotions. At this point, where he mentioned his loneliness, there might have been some real expression of his feeling about loneliness if it had been followed up.

My other comment on Dr. Kvarnes' relationship to the patient is that it seems to be a little too friendly in that there is some hesitation on the part of Dr. Kvarnes to stir this fellow up. I think it is a good idea to toss aside the preoccupation of being a paranoid schizophrenic. I think that has been handled well since it is merely a device, an obsessive device to avoid dealing with some of the conflicts in this fellow's mind, but while Dr. Kvarnes tosses it aside, it seems to me there is little stirring up in other directions.

NOVEY: I have been wondering, as far as Dr. Kvarnes' relationship is concerned, whether there is not something more going on than the taking off of pressure. There was some discussion about Dr. Kvarnes relating some of the patient's feelings to the reality of his situation, to his relationship to Dr. Kvarnes. What I wonder is how much more of that might safely be done. When he talked about his contact with other doctors and his fear of them, whether it would be safe to relate that to this situation, which is the reality one.

KVARNES: I have asked him specifically about feelings toward me and also tried to get out some expression of what he feels toward some specific person. To date, the only relationship which has been mentioned is that he had some trouble with the recreational director, and he recognizes that he is too much like his uncle. The uncle is bald and has the same easy manner and physical development.

NOVEY: At some point there was a comment about his feelings related to you. What I wondered about was whether more of that was good stuff or not.

KVARNES: His resentment about my not accepting schizophrenia and such.

MORRIS: It seems that this fellow has had so much difficulty making any contact with anyone, any sort of intimacy, that it has taken a long time for him to see that he can approach Dr. Kvarnes in such a way that he is not going to be hurt. I think perhaps this discussion with the nurse and becoming aware of the fact that he is not going to get shock may indicate to him that he can become more intimate and not be hurt. This is indicated by his being less anxious in talking about something which he probably has not talked about with anyone, his homosexual fears. The situation of talking with the nurse, where he is able to talk with some woman, reminds me of a patient I have been seeing for some time in which the same situation came up—he talked to the social worker about some of his problems which he did not talk about with me, and we wondered, too, if she should continue coming to see him. This same patient also was in the service for a couple of years and there was a period where he felt he had confidence; I wonder if this patient ever felt he had confidence in the service and whether something could come out of a situation where he felt he had confidence.

KVARNES: To date, with me, there has been no comment about his ever having felt good or having done a good job and I know of no comment about his relationship to people.

SULLIVAN: In talking to the nurse, he expressed delight that he was talking to a woman. He did not mention that to you?

KVARNES: No.

STYRT: The patient has also been able to talk a little more recently with the male nurse on the ward, and I wonder whether he said something about that. Most of the patients on the ward have been able to talk to this male nurse. He seems to be a helpful figure on the ward. He has been explaining some of their anxieties to them. One of the other patients on the ward was coming off sleep treatment and was quite shaky and attributed a good deal of his shakiness to the oppressive atmosphere of the hospital and this nurse attempted to show him that some of it might be a physiological reaction to the sodium amytal.

SULLIVAN: Has this man been psychoanalyzed?

WHEELER: He told somebody that he had been treated by Schilder.

STYRT: He was with the OSS during the war and has done no nursing except on specific assignments.

WHITE: In thinking of the therapy, it seems to me that Dr. Kvarnes gives the direct reassurance about content, and that he might give greater reassurance if he thought about what the patient was trying to tell him. With regard to this preoccupation with paranoid schizophrenia, that doesn't mean anything as such, but isn't he saying, "I am a hell of a sick person"? In that case he doesn't want a pat on the back, but he wants sympathy. In other words, acknowledge the severity of the illness and his stake in the outcome, and I think it would relieve him of his anxiety. I think, too, in the episode of the hair-cutting, that one wonders what that bald-headed relationship was in his mind. Dr. Kvarnes jumped to the idea that a boy of six would want to get rid of his hair. Well, perhaps so, and also perhaps some reassurance and interpretation might lead to the fact that he might have meant that bald-headed men are less virile. It is more a matter, I think, of actually what he means by what he says; a lot of what he says covers up something else. There is the episode of talking about his gullibility. When one is caught like that, one is terribly humiliated. In the case of the boy with the seizure, fits mean that you are out of your head, to the average person, and the remark of the other sailor to the patient that this man has "lost his marbles" might have meant that he had lost his wits, or his brains. Dr. Kvarnes laughed when the patient told him this painful thing. That must have been very humiliating. I think you are reacting with some anxiety, instead of putting yourself into the position of trying to feel what this boy suffers. Then he tells of another experience and he gets, "My God, do you think you are homosexual?" instead of, "My God, what of it?" Then he says to a female nurse, "Maybe I can get well because I have been able to talk to a woman," but doesn't that perhaps mean actually, "I can't talk to a man. Even though the hours are going better, it means the only hope I have of getting well is to talk to a woman"? If Dr. Kvarnes could only say, "It seems to me on the ward and with me you have been more relaxed and it is going better, but actually I wonder how much of it I have missed."

KVARNES: I think I should clarify that homosexual thing, because the idea or implication that I had some air of disgust is not what was meant. My attitude at the time was that it would be possible in this connection to introduce the word, and I introduced it. I am sure my comment was not disparaging. It was more of a questioning one, but at the same time, I was trying to imply that it was not something I have been entertaining all the time.

WHITE: He has told you it was his preoccupation and can't you assume it?

KVARNES: No, I don't think I can, yet. I wouldn't feel comfortable doing it in this situation.

WHITE: I would think it would reassure him to know that everybody has that preoccupation.

KVARNES: It is difficult for me to describe how it went, but I did not have the feeling of disgust and I don't think my tone implied that. It was more of an inquiry in a situation where there would not be much anxiety about introducing the term.

WILL: One little item that has been worked out rather well impressed me and that was the remarks that were made about this young man's disparaging attitude toward his previous scholastic work. He feels he selected some courses to protect his prestige, and goes ahead to make some remarks about his inability to handle mechanical things and this is a civilization in which respect is paid toward that ability. Of particular interest was the next point, which was that he always felt he would be more comfortable with older people and always thought of himself as being older and not a contemporary of his own age group. That interested me because I was wondering if this attitude expresses the fact that he never was comfortable with anyone, either of his own age or anyone else, but has come to look into another age group where he can fantasy himself being more comfortable. Just as some people look forward to adulthood or maturity or later years, feeling that they will be more comfortable then. That is close to the type of loneliness that Dr. Salzman talked about. It would seem something that could be developed with the patient without too much pain to him.

SULLIVAN: I think this attitude toward the vocational business— the explanation he gave was rather impressive, that as he saw the school management, it looked as if the scholastic inferiors were headed toward manual training. I am afraid that happens. Apparently he has never been able to discover that might not always follow.

STAVEREN: I was thinking somewhat along the line of Dr. White. Gullibility is not gullibility at all. The patient interprets it that way and feels that way about it and adds another derogatory element in his thinking about himself. It is much more literalness, and that would bring in the factor of anxiety as one possibility and a sort of malevolent misunderstanding on the other side. One does not know which it is in various instances. I think it might help, if there is an opportunity, to sort of refer back to this and say, "Well, was it really gullibility? What was gullible about it?" Maybe the patient was so frightened by what he had seen that he took the first interpretation and preoccupied himself with it, with the fact of the marbles, rather than the extremely frightening experience of seeing something he did not know anything about and did not understand. The same would apply to the order to "go below." If he had not been so concerned about making a mistake or not knowing—in other words, if his prestige had not been at stake—would he have interpreted it that way? I think that might be something that should be discussed.

The other thing is the way he uses schizophrenia. In the first place, one might try to find out more about what schizophrenia means to him. It is not at all warranted to assume that he even remotely refers to the textbook description of schizophrenia. In the second place, a more long-term point of view might be taken and maybe Dr. Kvarnes would observe at what times he drags in schizophrenia and see how it is being used and what purpose it serves. What particular feeling about himself—a realization of failure perhaps—is being avoided that way.

About the contact with the student nurse, I imagine he was aware that the student was going to leave in three days and this would be perhaps more in the nature of an experiment with somebody he is not likely to see again. Therefore it is not necessarily a matter of difference in ease with men and women but more a difference in ease with a person he is not likely to see again, like a shipboard acquaintance.

About Dr. Kvarnes' comments to him, I have a feeling that some of them might have a tendency to shut the door on what he is dealing with at the time, and I thought maybe that some sort of statement would indicate that Dr. Kvarnes does not quite understand yet, and could the patient go on.

Inasmuch as something happened about two weeks ago, and Dr. Kvarnes did not remove the pressure until about that time, and inasmuch as it seems not too likely that a person as sick as this patient is going to respond immediately, I think the change in the patient has very little to do with the change in attitude that Dr. Kvarnes was talking about. Probably the pressure is quite useful. That does not have to mean that there is anything in common with the father's attitude. The pressure—if it means asking questions, trying to help the patient to stick to a subject and avoid evasions, and studying why evasions occurred at a particular point—is a respectful attitude toward the patient which has not occurred before. I don't see that it does any harm.

Also I was wondering whether it was not time for Dr. Kvarnes to discuss with the patient what getting well means. It may mean something terrifying to the patient, something like becoming a person that his father and mother and Uncle Joe and various other people would not appreciate and approve of, and that may be a completely unfavorable combination of things beside having damn little to do with what the patient wants for himself. Maybe if Dr. Kvarnes put his own ideas in opposition to that—merely that the patient could look forward to a life of his own choosing, even if it disagreed with the aims and goals of people in the past, that perhaps his own aims and goals would assume a greater significance than those of his past environment—maybe that would do something. Also perhaps Dr. Kvarnes should communicate to the patient that he derives his satisfaction more from the way he does his work, not from the results achieved—that his satisfaction does not depend on whether or not the patient gets well. That would relieve the pressure of expectation and obligation for the patient.

SULLIVAN: I am moved to say that I think nearly everyone who has spoken has shown rather remarkable alertness to matters that might well engage thought. Curiously enough, it is like the story of the old judge who advised one to "give your opinion but don't tell why it is your opinion." I am commenting on this because I am pleased, not displeased. It strikes me that a good many of you don't know how good a feeling you have for psychiatry, and a good many of you suffer from a need of serious discourse one with another to clarify what you feel toward psychiatry.

The report has so many important things in it that I have an intense feeling of irritation that I did not take notes. I would like most to talk with Dr. Kvarnes about certain aspects of this, but before I get to that, I want to mention two things in the collateral information through the nurse. I, too, have a strong suspicion, which I would like to have verified, that the patient was aware that the nurse's term at the hospital was near a close. That was common knowledge. I am not at all displeased by that, but it is somewhat relevant if he is taking a chance on success or failure of establishing a relationship with someone who is going to be around for a short time. It seems to me that the patient has practically proven that for a time in his work he was under considerable tension as to whether this work would lead to more shock therapy, something of that kind. Now, it might very well serve to point out to all of you the pretty serious effect on a therapeutic relationship of unknown anticipation on the part of the patient. If he was always feeling on his mettle that he had to do something—he did not know what—or he would get more shock therapy. What I suggest to you is that if you could get skillfulness sufficient to see an appropriate opening to ask a question of the patient as to what his idea is of what we could do. Asked at the wrong time that can be discouraging, but to assess what the patient feels might be the outcome of an interview.

Another thing that is sort of free-floating in my mind is this report on a visit from the father in which the father is reported to have told the patient, "We will take you out anytime you say." I don't know how Dr. Kvarnes handled that but the suggestion is that it was regarded as an unrealistic attitude which the parents have toward the patient. I am willing to regard it that way, but there is something of very much more importance if you look at it my way. This is a move by his parents to show their devotion and interest in the patient, telling him that anytime he feels driven to be a damned, unutterable fool, that because of their great love for him they will be entirely unable to resist him. That sort of thing is a savage disparagement of the good sense of the patient and a statement of complete irresponsibility by the parents toward the patient. I hate to have such really desolating things passed off as unrealistic. That would probably have provoked me to say, "Wasn't that helpful?" Something like that. A succinct gesture by which I shake that off my hands. If the patient gets what I am doing, that is good. If I do anything more complicated, he may think I am telling him he ought to ask to be discharged.

That brings me to the major comment from the therapeutic excerpts. Rightly or wrongly, it seems to me, in dealing with schizophrenics, some schizophrenics at least, you cannot trust the communicative situation to carry very much strain and therefore again, as I say, rightly or wrongly, I have exercised myself over the years to produce the effect I want with a minimum of attention on the part of the patient. If I am going to take as much as four or five complex sentences to communicate, I have to feel considerable faith that the patient is following me with single-track attention and alertness. That consideration often means you can't undertake things that might seem desirable because you can't see how to reach your destination in a simple series of moves. To make this more communicative, you have to say four or five sentences to make your point. Particularly with a puzzled schizophrenic. This man is not by any means clearly in that class, although all schizophrenics are apt to be puzzled at times, but with the ones that are puzzled most of the time, there is very little telling whether language has any singularly varied meaning from minute to minute. They can drift off with great speed, show signs of falling asleep at times, and their understanding becomes more woozy and dreamlike. If you have to keep their attention and get them to follow you four or five steps, you have to get them up and rouse them from time to time to be sure they are getting it. One form of skill of development is to move quickly to communicate successfully. That, however, can be a menace, because it can degenerate into the wisecracking kind of communication that can be exceedingly unfortunate with schizophrenics. That is, you pay no attention to the fact that what you say might be misinterpreted. The natural result is that the patient feels he is nowhere near up to you, can't understand you, isn't bright enough, and has had a profound rebuff and quits. Quits all attempts at communication. The way to achieve this quick success or failure that I am driving at is a particular function of great alertness to be in the place of the patient as you can best imagine it.

A classical instance of failure in that particular, if you will forgive me, is one of the incidents that has been commented on both by Dr. White and Dr. Staveren, and that is the sailor with the epileptic fit. From the two remarks, everything that I have in mind can be readily inferred, but let me talk about this. The allegation more or less is that this man had never seen anyone in a fit. They are, as has been said, unutterably disturbing phenomena—simply unutterably disturbing! I have seen a good many. I still think they are pretty—oh—something in the nature of a loathsome variant of human behavior. A great many people have a tendency to practically withdraw all their receptors so that they are not there. Feeling myself in this man's position, that he has the almost uniform reaction of—oh—something in the neighborhood of horror and loathing, as well as astonishment and complete puzzlement as to just what has happened, somebody says something which is a fresh piece of slang, and the boy says he immediately began to think of this patient in a tonic phase of the convulsion as looking around for marbles on the deck near him.

Dr. Staveren's point is entirely correct that this is a frantic seizing of a preoccupation to get rid of the uncanny feeling connected with the experience, but in this effort to be where the patient is, instead of where I, as the therapist am, I am still vividly aware that this whole thing has come to mind to show me how gullible he is. When a personality, having stated the cue, then produces something as shocking as this business, it is essential for me to notice that his hurried preoccupation with developing this wisecrack, this slang statement, stands in his mind as an instance of incredible gullibility. Under those circumstances it is extraordinarily unfortunate to feel humorous about it. Why in hell should this thing be one of his classical instances of gullibility? Apparently he has not caught on to the fact of how useful it is to preoccupy himself with trivia in times of great stress. I am trying to keep in mind, "What is this patient telling me that I could follow if I were there, if I were in the situation?" Then I immediately say, "Hell, he thinks because he seizes all sorts of things that are said, that that proves he is gullible and unfit as a human being." Being gullible is obviously a strongly self-depreciatory judgment and so I have to watch for instances where he can develop his social incompetence because of obsessional preoccupations, to avoid severe anxiety or even uncanny feelings. I have learned a great deal from this. I have got a big job.

I am not sure I have made this clear to you but I think as I continue it will get clearer. Why should this patient make considerable use of what he thinks are trivial obsessional preoccupations where the allegedly ideal person would immediately face reality and be sensible? This is a special aspect of the great problem of loneliness, and I am going to digress.

I wonder how many of you recognize the importance of loneliness. It has been an astonishing feature of the history of psychiatry in the last fifteen or twenty years, after it occurred that loneliness was important. We know that this boy was reared to be older than his age, to be no trouble and so on. We know that he was boosted over several classes so that he did not have the very helpful experience of growing up with a group of people in his juvenile era, and since it is a generally known fact that boys show deficiency in their automatic skills in all areas where they have been denied the conventional opportunity for acquiring them, we expect this boy, from a very early age, to have had to live a good many of his juvenile motivations in fantasy which could be communicated to no one. He had to be more nearly an adult than he was, ever since he can remember. Unhappily, you cannot short-circuit the course of maturation of your ability, which we see in everyone, but you can learn from human example how to act as if you were more mature, and, if you are not under great pressure, to get away with it. But it still leaves you with unsatisfied longings and needs for development and experience which your sudden maturation has denied you. You have to discharge this in fantasy and sleep because what you are doing in fantasy and sleep is not what is done or talked about by more mature people with whom you are associated. It makes for your avoiding any intimate exchange with others. As if what you would like to talk about is childish, and if you don't have an automatic grasp of what other people like to talk about, you don't talk about yourself and your natural interests. Is that fairly self-evident? So that so far as being really close, confidential, frank, and outspoken with anyone, we can see that before he left the home and went into school, he was already considerably handicapped by that. Really profound inferiority. You are so childish you don't dare talk to anybody.

I am going into all this to emphasize to you how a person can become very markedly schizoid in his relationships with others. He is very careful, so careful to keep under cover, that he cannot have the benefits of pre-adolescence, and he arrives far in life on the basis of things that—although they haven't a ghostly connection with sexual matters, so far as the cause of the situation is concerned—are bound to have disastrous effects on sexual development because someone has to be skillful in adjusting his deception to others.

All this is an effort on my part to stress two things: (1) What an enormous forest you can get into looking for a tree when you gallop on sexual preoccupations with schizophrenics, and (2) what a great deal is to be done about this loneliness business.

Coming back to the interview, which unhappily I can't remember—I am not saying that Dr. Kvarnes did anything wrong—I am trying to discuss certain things that I have to say about what he did so that you can take what you can out of it.

Dr. Kvarnes, I wish you would read me parts of the interview again, and I will stop you when you come to the part I want.

KVARNES: [Repeats portions of the interviews that he read before.]

SULLIVAN: This business he brings in—this "alone" topic, and before that where he says of his parents, "They're all I've got"— I see an excellent thing to operate on there, but no sooner do I look at it than I realize I am getting in damn deep water. Suppose I were to say what I really feel like saying—"and they aren't very much, actually, are they?"—which is what I might say to some people under similar circumstances. What have I done? I have opened a huge field. It may have so much anxiety that I will never be able to close it. Suppose he is thoroughly upset? Then I can't go on and say, "And in fact they are not in any sense all you have," because if he can't hear me, then I have kicked a prop out. With an excellent chance to attack, I see I can't safely reach a desirable destination, so that dies. Then he comes and says something about how alone he is, and there, in view of what I have already thought of, he has practically done it for me. Now that is quite another matter. Then if I say, "Well, you are still thinking of your parents," notice what happens. There is no trick to this. It is just that I see what can be done, then decide it is dangerous to do, and he gives me a magnificent opportunity with no prejudices. If I say, "You mean as to your parents?"—if he means that then he knows I understand and sympathize. No danger of anxiety and I have done all I want to do. If you will notice, you present a question about his general attitude to all reality *—with no inclination to express the least disparagement of your work. That is an order for a schizophrenic to take, and if he takes it, where are you? In the world of philosophy. The schizophrenics are glad to get into that. You are in no danger of getting anxious there. You can see what I mean by the closeness with which you follow the patient's performance. It is an instance where Dr. Kvarnes is being very diligently a helpful physician, but is unfortunately so busy and interested in how he can do that that he misses a golden opportunity to do something for the

* Pessimism.

patient, and is moved to attempt something which I would assume is nearly foredoomed.

Were I to try to stress to this boy how pessimistic he is about everything, I would say, "Huh, the gloom again, eh?" Something like that. It is some time before I get to that. By the time I really got to that, he would realize that I had not gotten to thinking of him as a person always no good.

I hope we are not getting lost as to what I am trying to do. Because when I tell you this, I wish you would follow patients with extraordinary alertness of what it means to them and how it can be used.

KVARNES: [Reads again from the verbatim interviews.]

SULLIVAN: There the business of schizophrenia comes up and he said what, so far as I know, is an excellent statement of opinion widely held by psychiatrists and Rorschach testers and so on. Had they tested anything but his IQ years and years ago, they would have discovered something. Because this has been a remarkably sensible statement as judged by prevailing opinion among comparatively sensible people—I don't know whether it is so or not—this is the time when I am not going to attack his use of schizophrenia. If I am going to do anything, I am going to say, "Yeah, tests show lots of things." I would probably leave it alone. It is not at all promising.

Pretty soon we come to the alleged homosexual topic. Go on into that interview.

KVARNES: [Reads the part where the patient was called "the professor" in a hospital where he had a tonsillectomy.]

SULLIVAN: In teaching hospitals the chief of service is frequently called "the professor," and in certain hospitals dealing with immigrant stock, all people are professors, and this is an instance of remarkable success by this boy. Those things I like awfully well to substantiate and document if I can. Think first how completely lacking in understanding about the professor title this boy may still be, and second, note that after what is almost certain to have been a bloody operation and one probably that left a damn sore throat, this kid seems to have been a success talking with other patients. He gets himself called "the professor." I don't think they would have given that title to somebody who gassed them about the weather or how funny they looked, and I wonder if there are not elements of Uncle Joe, the doctor, in this thing. I am apt to develop with the idea that I may be kicking the underpinning of the schizophrenic idea moderately successfully. Maybe he impressed people even at a time when he did not feel so hot, and I may get something good out of this. This looks fairly good and worth some effort.

Let me talk about the other, now, because I do want to hear some comment. We come in the next interview to the matter of his experiences in the subway. As I heard this story, and the discussion of it, I found myself keenly curious as to how many of you have ever been on a New York subway. Is it possible that half of you haven't, or that there are people who haven't? What occurred to me was that even in discussing Dr. Kvarnes' comment, it seemed to me that you were as remote from the reality concerned as you well could be. If you were discussing Bengal it would not sound less immediately there. I can't blame anybody for not knowing a lot about local history, but I don't like, in dealing with a schizophrenic, to be content with learning that something happened in Africa. So far as I know it is fairly important when he is talking about men approaching him to know, first, whether it happened in the toilets. One of the most notorious things in any subway is the toilets. Subway toilets, for psychological and other reasons, are rather highly infested with homosexuals. On the other hand, certain people feel out attractive young men in crowded subway trains, and incidents of exhibitionism on the train or the platform, or in the privacy of the subway washroom, are diametrically different things.

Why am I harping on this? The best way on earth to communicate to a schizophrenic that something very dangerous has not happened is to discover what the hell is being discussed in a fashion that cannot precipitate violent anxiety. So I feel all of you are so far from the subway situation, so far from thinking what this boy may be thinking, that I don't think any of you would have done very well with this. I want to know which it is—in the train or in the washroom? If I discover the exhibitionism happened in the washroom, did the advances take place when there were very few people in the washroom? Or was it on the platform? Then I can say, "Jesus, don't you know that happens to damn near everyone?" It does. I might add it never happened to me, but then I also discourage spiritualists, mediums, and so on, and they are common events. But find out what I am discussing.

Apparently most of your confreres did not establish what was being inquired into and so you could run risk. You did not do too badly when you did inquire if he wondered if he were homosexual, but I condemn the whole procedure as if looking like you and all your colleagues get too anxious to do anything, to come anywhere near the right thing.

I would like to know if no other boy has ever reported such incidents to him. And that brings me back to a thing which I would say is literally very dangerous, and that was the discussion of the school theatrical which preceded this. If you look it over you will see why it was risky. How he looked and so on. That is so dangerous and I wish I could express why. The way that Dr. Kvarnes reported the discussion of when he was painted up for the show could, I think, to a good many schizophrenics, suggest, as the whole development of things would suggest, that the doctor might think that he was an awfully good-looking person for a man, if actually he did not look feminine. The patient can tell us those things but we must always be extremely careful that our operation does not permit them to think we infer such things. You may actually kick out several props from under a person in that way. He was a kid and this was evidently something. When I had got all he had to say, then, "I don't follow this feminine business—everybody is made up for theatricals." Everybody knows, and he knows that too. Then I would say, "What was the feminine business? Were you playing a girl's part?"—but not how he looked. That is rough stuff.

What do I think has happened? I have not the foggiest idea, but I am inclined to think that the getting of this lonely business into the field has been extremely useful. Discussion of loneliness of this kind, particularly in a one-sex situation, where a man is dealing with a man, is both of some significance in the developmental history and something that is safe. It is up to the doctor to see that it is not worked just because it is safe. Loneliness is rather in a class with anxiety and fear. It is such a driving force you are not going to notice that it can be overworked. It is another instance of preoccupation with sex that characterizes certain analysts. That is for you to notice. It is an important part of the history of all of us. It is so important that people suffer extremely in talking about and remembering having been lonely. It is a thing you don't like to remember and you talk about it rather than talking about what you remember about it. It has the same driving force as lust. It takes people out of their houses at all hours.

Since I am anxious to discuss this point brought out by Dr. Morris—I know the questions brought up by several people about the patient talking with the nurse—I wish that you would state that again, Dr. Morris, clearly and concisely.

MORRIS: My question with regard to my own patient was whether this social worker should continue to see him since he was talking with her about things that he had not brought up to me.

SULLIVAN: In our own case there is also this business of the male nurse who sometimes does Schilderian therapy, or did one time. One of the miracles of institutional intensive psychotherapy is the difficulty that is said to characterize the transference. I don't put much stock in that. What about events that you are informed of by others but not by the patient?

I believe the first great critical judgment to be made, and one for some people very difficult, is: Is this good or bad? Is it more probably a contribution to the patient's progress or more probably the source of a lot of trouble in treatment? As we hear this conversation with the nurse, I think that it was quite an astonishing and useful event. I see nothing in this that menaces this boy or his therapy in any way. Maybe there is, but my clinical judgment is that this is all to the good. Since I am fortunately advised as to what went on, I have useful collateral information. It does not teach me anything about the greater ease of relating himself to a woman than to me, which I would be inclined to swear could not be the case. It is, as I say, all to the good. If I don't hear anything about it, it is all right by me. Suppose something of crucial importance had come up there. One thing did, namely, his chronic fear that he would cease to see you and go on shock therapy. There is something so ominous about this that soon I would attempt an elaborate clinical judgment. Is there a way that he can engineer me into a position where he has got to discuss what he discussed with the nurse? Quite often you can, but if I feel I can't—this is too urgent—his difficulties with me are too great—then I do my damnedest to think of some way that I can indicate knowledge of this performance with a minimum of damage to everything else concerned. I don't want to deteriorate his confidence in the woman's interest in the conversation. I don't want to give him the idea that he is surrounded by spies, that everything he says is told to me. Why I don't want to damage the relationship is that he is perhaps going to get to tell somebody something of critical and dangerous importance that he can't tell me and that is a psychotherapeutic aid I cannot be without. For God's sake, use a little judgment yourself before you adopt this technique. The best I have been able to do is to say, "Mr. Jones, do you know how deeply interested Miss So-and-So is in your welfare?" That sends up a Roman candle but it fixes attention and creates expectation. Then I say, "Miss So-and-So came to me and said she was greatly worried about you, that as she understood it"—here I deny anybody being to blame —"as she understood it you are having difficulty telling me about so and so. Is that right?" That comes with such force that by those maneuvers I get, "Yes." Right away then I am busy with, "What in the world made it so hard to talk to me about it?" but I must also remember to say, "I don't quite know how the nurse got the idea, but I am terribly glad she was interested enough to make mention of it." With that finished, then he can go ahead and think, "What the hell happened?" I demonstrate to him first how helpful this has been. It is only after that that I can toss it off and try to direct what he will think of it.

On the other hand, sometimes I think something dangerous in the way of a relationship is growing up, as in my days at Sheppard. And in these marvelous modern communities where there are millions of analysts and analysands, all operating on each other day and night, certain relationships do appear which seem to me to threaten trouble for the patient and his work with me. I don't believe I need to tell any of you who have had parents that direct prohibitive intervention is something you don't attempt if you have any ingenuity. Sometimes I have to say No, it has to stop—but it is essential that I know how to do it before I do. Otherwise I stir rebelliousness. I attempt to get the thing under discussion and get some data that seems to give me something to talk about and then I quite visibly, like a ham actor, get disturbed about this. I frown, and I worry, and I give the patient time to realize this. According to all we know about personality, that means that the boy gets anxious about what I was worried about,

I don't want it too much so he can't hear me, but then I say, "Look, I am not sure that I know what is going on, and I am not sure you are right about what is going on. Is this an important relationship to you? Can't you let it rest awhile?" Do you catch on to the steps in this? I have not said anything. I don't know what a direct statement would do. Hell, I might precipitate panic or disastrous action, but what with mixing in bum dramatics, and my questions which practically shout my uncertainty and feeling that this is not advisable now, I hope the patient will realize that I have been concerned, but not in any sense mandatory or given to disparaging anybody concerned. This indicates something striking me as pretty important since I don't usually look at patients, but it is easy to know when their attention has been centered on me, when they show physiological signs of it. In this business of my dealing with comparatively healthy people, I say "Time out" or even get up and leave the room, to consider something. I don't have to tell them what ran in my mind. It is none of their business, but it is part of my business to be an expert and it is unkind to the insecure to drop things flat. I usually try to lay the thing down, but say it puzzles me, "Is it important to go on with it now?" If they want to know what puzzled me, depending on the situation, I might mention several things for them to glance at. Quite frequently say, "Let's put it this way. I don't know this other person. I am not impressed with your knowing him, and what do you get out of it?" The sort of drifting off to a question that can't be answered but it communicates my feeling that it is not so hot.

With regard to Dr. Morris' social worker, here is a situation where I gather the patient is quite sick and is expressing significant material to the social worker. I don't know, unless she is a little het-up as to her possibilities for being a psychiatrist, why it does not occur to her to wonder now and then what does the doctor think of that. What they are apt to do is unhappily not very clever. "Have you told it to the doctor?" You see why that is stupid. It shows that you at least entertain the idea that you have the patient's confidence. But if you change it and say, "What does the doctor think of this?"—assume it has been discussed with the therapist—then the patient says, "Oh, I haven't told the doctor," and the worker can be astonished and say, "I think he might make something of it." Build up the idea of the therapeutic relationship with the physician. If he is very sick, I would not want to cut out any channel through which he was expressing important material. I have no way of knowing whether he will be able to express it to me but as long as he is expressing it, it is better than being mute. I don't want to cut it off until it has ceased to be the exclusively useful contact. I don't know why it can't be used to build up the idea—it would be such a mistake to say all this to the patient, but the realistic aspects of the thing are this—the patient is more able to communicate to the woman than to the physician. The woman's training is not actually in line with making the best out of it. Insofar as it is good for him to have a confidante, she is very happy to carry the role. But to get maximum returns in the way of benefit in understanding certain present and past difficulties that should actually come to the attention of a skilled psychiatrist, as I say, that should be the principle from which you and she build your operations. There is no sense in expecting a schizophrenic to take this lofty, abstract view.

The other question was about the male nurse, and I don't know that I could do very much about that. He is probably more useful than troublesome. It is a very complex business to say what useful people ought to do. I think twice before I suggest revisions. The fact that he established some kind of contact with this patient, as well as others, suggests that he has some lay value for being in his position, and in the old days when I had energy, if I thought he had liabilities I would try to get clearer on the assets and gradually discourage the liabilities.

If anyone has anything in mind, let's hear it.

KVARNES: I would like to know what to do with the situation that came up about the recreational therapist who has physical similarity and some personality similarity to his uncle.

SULLIVAN: One simple answer as I hear anything about that, I immediately ignore the physical resemblance, which you know is relatively baseless for thought where the uncle comes in, and I am interested in asking questions about his relationship with the uncle. I have forgotten just how the physical therapy director compared——

KVARNES: He is glib and talkative——

SULLIVAN: If you could, in your stride, say, "This uncle was always handing out advice to you." Something like that, just drop off immediately to the uncle, you are serving the proper cause insofar as this boy is suffering from an intense identification of the director and the uncle and it is the uncle who set the pattern. Drop to the significant figure in the past, try always to ask easy, good questions that are relevant. Remember also that any target figure in convalescing schizophrenics is apt to have two sides to him. Never bother the patient with that, but always keep in mind that somebody seems to be wonderful, too, in some way. "He seems to be damn friendly, but I suppose——" and then discuss the other side. Don't take this too seriously, but always it is well to remember that schizophrenics are not going to find the perfect person and it is rather expensive to them to find themselves coloring a picture intensely favorably, and yet they are glad to have anything, and they are always in danger of having a moment of insight in which they see it is largely fantastic, and so I provide the drainage. A classic example being the father taking him out any time he wants. I hit it hard. It is hard to believe, I think, this his parents are all he has. No danger of my being misled.

Our time is up and I think we will have to stop.

Comment on Fourth Session, Twenty-five Years Later, March, 1972

JACOBSON: The thing that struck me about this session—and I'd like to ask you about it—was that you come on with much more authority than in the previous one, like a guy who's more sure of himself. In the previous seminars Sullivan very rarely directed any questions to you. You gave your report and everybody else talked about it. You were kind of silent. Anyway, in this one, I was struck by a kind of greater critical quality in everybody, and wondered whether that was in response to your coming on more confidently so they could say stronger things in return. I wonder if any of you saw any difference in this regard between this session and the other ones.

RYCKOFF: I think there was a more vigorous going-on. One feeling I had about that was that by this time there had been more jelling of the group around Sullivan; people knew the dimensions of Sullivan's interests and likes and dislikes and his whole approach, and there was a more sure sense that the class was working with him as Kvarnes was.

KVARNES: That apparently says that I was getting some sense of direction out of the seminars. As my memory has it, I was getting more anxious as time went on and less certain, more scared, and yet this account doesn't come out that way at all. I think there were probably a couple of related elements in this. One of them was that I was getting into my own therapy, and I suspect that I could say a little bit more about what was going on with me than before that; I was about three or four months into my own analysis at that point, and noticed I could pay more attention to what was going on between me and the patient. One of the things that impressed me was that Sullivan came on with very substantial support and compliments to me, particularly in terms of the rich material, but I felt he made very poor use of it as compared to the previous seminar, which is near brilliant in exposition. This was so scattered, and it's hard to figure out what he is saying. Perhaps he got lost in too much material and couldn't get his thoughts together rapidly enough, but it just doesn't have the quality of the previous one. Did you feel that?

DILLINGHAM: I thought he was very hard on you, that whole thing about gullibility and so forth——

RYCKOFF: This whole thing about criticizing you for the homosexual thing—it came across clearly that the others had done very well in that area, but what the hell was Sullivan talking about?

KVARNES: That was startling to me on rereading. Might be worth it to try to pick out those things for the hell of it.

RYCKOFF: One thing you had not been was insensitive or destructive.

JACOBSON: That translation of it was really something.

RYCKOFF: I must say that one of the things that kind of busts things up, where I felt Sullivan began to go off, is in response to your presentation. It starts off, "This is really immense, from the standpoint of the seminar." Then he goes on, "I would like to hear everybody discuss two topics"—patient and therapy. And then says: "There are a number of things that each of us is almost certain to wonder about in what anyone else does. They usually reflect an element of our own personality. . . ." But he is also opening up to question some interpretation of your needs as they get into the situation. It's kind of ambiguous and I think that accounts for some of what happened later on.

JACOBSON: I read that as being his encouragement for the guys to be critical of Bob's therapeutic approach, given this opportunity to have excerpts of interviews and so on.

RYCKOFF: Well, that's a little disjunctive here because the seminar had been moving on pretty well, trying to understand this patient, along with the medium through which they were getting a look. Bill was the camera, and he's been a damn good—not a camera but a good participant observer, and he produced much more of the same for this seminar. Then they don't continue to talk about or enlarge or refine their notion of the patient, but go off on something else.

JACOBSON: Sullivan's questions in other seminar sessions would be like, "What do you think is wrong with this guy?"

RYCKOFF: "What ails this guy?"

JACOBSON: And here he drops——

RYCKOFF: He sort of almost says, "What ails somebody else?" —Kvarnes or the hospital.

KVARNES: This remark of mine followed the description of his being painted up when he was thirteen with rouge, lipstick, and eyebrow pencil, and then the subway incidents, and "it was my feeling that it was a safe time to introduce the term that had never been used in our talks—that it would seem to be not too disturbing, and I asked him in a questioning tone, 'Did you think it was possible that you might be a homosexual?'" Then a few pages later Larry Cooper says: "I was a little critical in my own mind of Dr. Kvarnes' approach when he mentioned the fact that men had often tried to contact him in subways or had exposed themselves to him. When Dr. Kvarnes said, 'My God, did you entertain the idea that you were homosexual?'" and then Mary White a little later.

JACOBSON: At some point you got in and said it wasn't like that.

RYCKOFF: Cooper invented that statement.

KVARNES: It was a misquote. Mary White says: "Then he tells of another experience and he gets, 'My God, do you think you are homosexual?' Instead of, 'My God, what of it?'" That is a beautiful example of an anxiety-based phenomenon because this is what they expected to hear and they heard it.

DILLINGHAM: This thing where she says: "In thinking of the therapy, it seems to me that Dr. Kvarnes gives the direct reassurance about content, and that he might give greater reassurance if he thought about what the patient was trying to tell him." Sort of gratuitous, isn't it?

KVARNES: Well, what she was driving at, however, was a pretty good theme—that is, instead of immediately responding to the manifest content, figure out what was being said. At that time I was too anxious to think very far.

RYCKOFF: Bob, do you think that all of this is really a response to Sullivan? Because I think a lot of it, most of it, has really nothing to do with you. These people are anxious about Sullivan and here's a way in which they can demonstrate they're on the right track.

KVARNES: I see it as having three different dimensions to it. Maybe the most important is Sullivan's presence—that is, the teacher who has the greater awareness and insight and can expose you as being kind of stupid in your remarks or you don't get what's important, something like that. Second, I think a lot of anxiety was generated by the material because it was pretty ripe material and nobody was very comfortable about it. There was the homosexual business, the schizophrenic level, the developing relationship between me and the guy, without anybody's quite knowing what was going on, whether it was good or bad. Sullivan's obviously being pleased with the material would add some anxiety, too, because they couldn't be sure what that meant. And I think the third thing was the fact that I was the presenter and a peer and needed to be cut down sometimes either because I was showing off or looking too good, or because Sullivan was saying pretty good things about me. I think all three of those things showed through—especially the material itself.

JACOBSON: I was thinking that after the session when we talked about one's feminine component being a universal male problem, and got to the point of talking about the people around the table and their own concerns in this area, that it was really a very good illustration of the relationship between anxiety and learning, what you are turned on to in the seminar, what you are ready to hear and learn.

KVARNES: That's very true, Stan. This is a teaching/learning experience and you have some straightforward data on whether people learn anything or even hear what's being said. That's the dramatic aspect of this homosexual business.

JACOBSON: It really is.

KVARNES: There's even a contagion in there, you know.

RYCKOFF: I noticed the incorrectness of the words.

KVARNES: I also noticed nobody said, "Hey, Cooper, that isn't what he said." Everybody let it go and I don't know whether Sullivan even corrected it very clearly. I started to——

RYCKOFF: Seemed defensive.

DILLINGHAM: Do you think it came partly because the group had jelled more and could take more risks in jumping in? Maybe even the fact that you were getting compliments sort of legitimized other people taking chances.

KVARNES: Do you feel they did take more chances?

DILLINGHAM: Yes, I think they are much more direct. They are coming out and saying, "Kvarnes did a dumb thing"—which implies that they have a correct diagnosis.

RYCKOFF: That's true. What they did, in effect, was to mishear Kvarnes in a certain way that would enable them to say the right thing if he had said what they attributed to him. So they set it up that he made an error, in Sullivan's terms, and then they could be the right pupil, saying he did the wrong thing.

JACOBSON: Also, I had the feeling after reading this that there was some resistance to what Sullivan had been pushing for. Sullivan had been pushing for getting the facts and being clear about the facts, making the guys substantiate what they meant and so on. There was a lot of resistance to that kind of thing in your work here—people are saying, "Start listening to what the guy wants to tell you," and, "You are pushing him." Maybe that's anger at Sullivan over their own failure to do this, and maybe they're trying to say to him that he's wrong.

DILLINGHAM: Seems to me there is another level to that, too. The anger might be that they see the logic of getting the facts but are so anxious about getting them that they push and then don't feel comfortable doing that. So getting angry seems the only possibility, but if you do you get led into a trap.

RYCKOFF: You began today by saying Sullivan somehow seemed to be not working as well this time, and I think it has to do with precisely this area. I think that as his role in this seminar, Sullivan had been pressing for the facts. I had the feeling he was continuing to press for them after he got them, and that he failed to move from this particular level to the somewhat more general level. I think Bob gave him all the material he needed to move, and that he failed to do that. Everybody then anxiously gets stuck on picking on particular facts or more facts or on your saying the wrong thing. Sullivan failed somehow to move on to a more useful level of generalization at this point, and this throws this seminar off a bit.

JACOBSON: In view of what we have been saying about Sullivan's motives and methods, what do you think about his compliments to everybody about what they are doing in this session:

I am moved to say that I think nearly everyone who has spoken has shown rather remarkable alertness to matters that might well engage thought. Curiously enough, it is like the story of the old judge who advised one to "give your opinion but don't tell why it is your opinion." I am commenting on this because I am pleased, not displeased. It strikes me that a good many of you don't know how good a feeling you have for psychiatry, a good many of you suffer from a need of serious discourse one with another to clarify what you feel toward psychiatry.

KVARNES: You have trouble with that?

JACOBSON: Yes. I thought I understood it the first time I read it, but I don't even understand it now, to tell you the truth. What's he saying? That they are carrying on too much? Laboring things?

KVARNES: I heard Sullivan comment on this in other settings, so I think I have some idea of what that's about. First of all, it was a group primarily of first- and second-year residents at Sheppard, and I think he was really trying to tell the group, "You're doing all right," because it was a very uncertain group. I think in seeing them in action you could pick that up—they needed that reassurance. And also it would encourage them to be somewhat freer in talking. The other thing is that I think Sullivan came to feel that probably the greatest learning experience was peer exchange in psychiatry, that there was not enough of it, and that it was particularly worsened at that time by the psychoanalytic model. You go and talk to your therapist and presumably you learn about psychoanalysis from your own analysis, but you and your analyst maintain a certain secrecy about your analysis, so there was a tendency not to have a free exchange of what you and psychiatry are about. I think he was pointing at that. I think time has borne him out. I would hope that there is a lot more learning from each other going on now. I think Sullivan once said something about over the years he had probably studied two hundred and fifty people intimately, extensively. That sounded like a lot to me at the time, but when I got to thinking about this as a series of cases on which to base your judgments about human behavior, that's awfully damn small. If you are going to do a statistical study of compound fractures of the femur in which you put in prontosil or sulfanilamide you want about five hundred cases to make a comparison study. So that it's from the exchange of experience that we broaden our base. I think that is part of what he was getting at.

DILLINGHAM: I think that, too, you have to take that in the context of other remarks he has made, such as "Some psychiatrists I know label and do so and so"—and here everybody is sort of sneaking out little theories, but probably never talking to anybody else about them—just sneaking them out so Sullivan looks at them before they jerk them back. And he's sort of saying that they ought to come out and really confront each other with what they feel about it.

RYCKOFF: I'm curious about this phrase of his, "good feeling you have for psychiatry," which I think is an important issue. That is, psychiatrists as a group don't tend automatically to feel good about psychiatry. Obstetricians feel good about obstetrics—there is no doubt that you are in a good field, you're going to make money, and so on. Psychiatrists don't start with that. There is enough doubt and uncertainty and lack of clarity about what the hell it's all about, what am I going to do—about possible failure—and that's what he is referring to. He feels the group is generating some kind of positive sense about what they are doing.

JACOBSON: Part of what you're saying seems to fit in with this first comment of Sullivan's that you wondered about, where he says one wonders about what other people are doing.

KVARNES: You know, I didn't really think his charge was very good in that—it didn't really set the discussion.

JACOBSON: Isn't he saying that Dr. Kvarnes has revealed some pretty intimate stuff about the way he works with patients?

KVARNES: Yes, that's right.

JACOBSON: You know, we all have questions about things like that.

RYCKOFF: It almost sounds as if your presentation of a sort of verbatim account of two interviews was in itself quite a revelatory experience—people didn't do that.

JACOBSON: That was pretty strong of you, kind of brazen in fact.

KVARNES: I suppose I was riding some kind of crest of confidence, because I had gotten into therapy at that point and knew you could talk about some things. I wasn't far enough in to know much about the implications of it. I'm not impressed by what that material is when I read it now, but I think it's true that——

RYCKOFF: You're impressed by your having read it to the group.

KVARNES: And also that it was a way of bringing in another dimension.

DILLINGHAM: I was struck by the fact that without being solicited you suddenly produced the transcript, saying, in effect, "I want you to hear this." Do you know why that happened?

KVARNES: I couldn't tell you now why I did, except I guess I was feeling that, hell, this is something that you should do if you are really going to do something with it. I was braver then than I was five years later.

JACOBSON: I'll bet you didn't expect to get the kind of flap that you got on the gullibility thing.

KVARNES: No, I didn't.

DILLINGHAM: Probably another factor that you have to take into account is that instead of giving them a kind of precis of what had happened, all of a sudden you gave them this kind of exchange, and they had something they could get into, which was very different from just a summary.

KVARNES: I thought Herb Staveren's dealing with the gullibility was beautiful—in which he was able in an expository way to talk about how the anxious person picks up one little piece of data and dwells on that as if that were the whole thing; he can't deal with a phenomenon, and so he deals with this thing—"He lost his marbles." I didn't understand that process, and the others all got trapped in the humor business. The fact is that the light humor was just a pretty good way of dealing with the patient, if I was on the same wave length as he was.

RYCKOFF: It came across as very good, the two of you laughing about it. There was no question but that it was genuine.

KVARNES: I wasn't laughing at him. It was kind of a funny phenomenon for him to think of it that way.

JACOBSON: A schizophrenic patient gained some perspective on life.

RYCKOFF: Even if you had laughed at him a little bit, it seems to me that there was enough friendliness in it—quite reassuring, if what he does can be responded to.

KVARNES: I haven't felt too hostile about Sullivan's comments on it, because I think he took it to dwell on the damaging effect that can come when you deal with something as if it were humorous when it is dead serious. And I've made that mistake with schizophrenics and lost them. Because I didn't know how to deal with it, it came out as some kind of superiority about how stupid they were, and that's devastating. I find humor anyway goddamn hard to deal with in treatment. I try to use it, and it backfires most of the time with quite ill patients.

RYCKOFF: I remember a strong article in which the author practically says never be humorous, it's always bound to be seen as hostile. Even if at the time it comes across as okay, the repercussions will always be a hostile implication, which will dawn later on. I personally feel that some humor can do a lot of good and I lapse into it. Or I'm even sarcastic; humor is not always gentle. And if I had to not be that way, I'm not sure I'd want to go on.

KVARNES: We can't deal with this work in dead seriousness all the time.

RYCKOFF: If you can't shift gears at all, and if the patient can't tolerate that——

KVARNES: Partly that depends on how strong the ego is in the patient.

JACOBSON: I'd like to bring up a different kind of issue if we have time for it, and that's the kinds of interaction we see that are covert in the Sullivan seminar material. That is, somebody distorts what you say to the patient about being a homosexual. Okay. You don't come back and say anything about the distortion and nobody else in the group picks up the distortion. Sullivan doesn't do it. We assume that a lot of the comments here are made not in relation to you but in relation to Sullivan—there is that dynamic going on. There are people in the room who have their own problems about homosexuality but that never gets mentioned—all these kinds of dynamics are going on. Okay? Now, I am struck by the difference in the norms of the seminar and those of sensitivity training, for example, in which you develop a climate, a set of norms, making it appropriate for people, necessary for people——

RYCKOFF: To give vent to all——

JACOBSON: Right. To come out with that. To say, "Hey, wait a minute, he didn't say, 'My God, do you think you are a homosexual?' At least I didn't hear him say that."

KVARNES: You are obliged to come up with that?

JACOBSON: Right. That how you are dealing with the inputs is as important as the inputs themselves.

RYCKOFF: So that you could see a way of shifting away from what Kvarnes was presenting about the patient to focusing on what was going on in the group itself. Isn't that what you are saying?

JACOBSON: Well, a big question in this whole thing is, Can a task-oriented group also become a group-oriented group in order to enhance the effectiveness of working on the task? Would there ultimately be more learning for the people in this seminar if a norm of the group was that you did get into how this material strikes me—whether or not I can hear this, and so on.

RYCKOFF: Well, of course, nowadays I think people would be more sensitive to that. But isn't there always a question of how far you go with that? At some point the orientation toward the group, as you indicated, would swallow up the whole——

JACOBSON: Right. No question of it.

RYCKOFF: Would be the end of it as far as the seminar was concerned.

KVARNES: Before we break up there's a piece in here I think I'd like to read with you, and I think we might go over it later.

I wonder how many of you recognize the importance of loneliness. It has been an astonishing feature of the history of psychiatry in the last fifteen or twenty years, after it occurred that loneliness was important. We know that this boy was reared to be older than his age, to be no trouble and so on. We know that he was boosted over several classes so that he did not have the very helpful experience of growing up with a group of people in his juvenile era, and since it is a generally known fact that boys show deficiency in their automatic skills in all areas where they have been denied the conventional opportunity for acquiring them, we expect this boy, from a very early age, to have had to live a good many of his juvenile motivations in fantasy which could be communicated to no one. He had to be more nearly an adult than he was, ever since he can remember. Unhappily you cannot short-circuit the course of maturation of your ability, which we see in everyone, but you can learn from human example how to act as if you were more mature, and, if you are not under great pressure, to get away with it. But it still leaves you with unsatisfied longings and needs for development and experience which your sudden maturation has denied you. You have to discharge this in fantasy and sleep because what you are doing in fantasy and sleep is not what is done or talked about by more mature people with whom you are associated. It makes for your avoiding any intimate exchange with others. As if what you would like to talk about is childish, and if you don't have an automatic grasp of what other people like to talk about, you don't talk about yourself and your natural interests. Is that fairly self-evident? So that so far as being really close, confidential, frank and outspoken with anyone, we can see that before he left the home and went into school, he was already considerably handicapped by that. Real profound inferiority. You are so childish you don't dare talk to anybody.

KVARNES: This is—Christ!

RYCKOFF: You know why he is so good at that?

KVARNES: Yes, he knows exactly a lot of it.

RYCKOFF: Because this is Sullivan.

KVARNES: Because it is a beautiful exposition——

RYCKOFF: He is right about himself and he is right about this fellow.

JACOBSON: When I read that I got so depressed because it is the story of my life—I think it's the story of my life——

RYCKOFF: There are people who've got you beat—look at me. [Laughter]

JACOBSON: He probably says it all fully in some exposition of the juvenile era that I've never really read adequately.

KVARNES: I don't know if it is as well put in anything else.

JACOBSON: I have a patient, a girl in her twenties, who regards herself as having had three traumas in her life. The first is that her mother forged her birth date on her birth certificate so that she could enter school early, and so she had to live the lie of being older than she was for a number of years. What a profound effect the whole experience had on this kid in just this way—she always has felt out of it, that she missed a piece of life because she was put in advance of herself and wasn't with *that* group or the *other* group.

KVARNES: And there's so nice an illustration in this of the

difference between "seeming" and "being," concepts that Buber used. If you grow naturally, it's *being*, and if you grow in this fashion, it's *seeming*. You have to make it look like it's real and goddamn it, it isn't. And it's an enormous dilemma.

JACOBSON: Good spot to end on.

V

Case Seminar, May, 1947 *

Because of the unexpected transfer of the patient from Sheppard Pratt to a Veterans Administration hospital prior to this final session, the seminar discussion is somewhat limited, focusing in part on the problem of abrupt, unanticipated treatment termination. A report on the patient from his new treatment setting is given by W. Deaver Kehne, at that time a staff psychiatrist at the Veterans Administration hospital, and is followed by the usual exchanges. At the end of the session, Sullivan answers a series of questions in the area of treatment of psychotic patients; the questions had been submitted to him a few days earlier by the participants from Sheppard Pratt.

In addition to Kvarnes, Sullivan, and Kehne, the following persons were present at this session: Larry Cooper, Robert Morris, Samuel Novey, Stanley Peal, Joseph Rom, Leon Salzman, Herbert Staveren, Jerome Styrt, Philip Wagner, Charles Wheeler, Mary White, and John Witt.

KVARNES: This covers the period from the first of February until the patient left the hospital, on the eleventh of April, 1947. I am only going to try to bring out some significant new material and some new understanding. In an effort to clarify the parental personalities, I thought I would break the material down and present it that way.

There is no new material about the father. It became evident that the pattern as illustrated earlier was the way the boy regarded his father: busy, active, successful, with no time for his

---

* Snowstorms on the Sundays scheduled for March and April forced cancellation of those seminars.

son, engaged in a multitude of activities and a member of "eighty or ninety" clubs, according to the patient. He would go to movies or to ball games with the patient occasionally and usually fell asleep. All of this the boy ridiculed.

About the mother there was some new material. One day as we were discussing the medical and dental situations, I asked him what it all meant to him, and he said it was neglect by his mother. The infrequent appointments and irregularities, the fact that she did not pay special attention to his decaying teeth, all this signified that he was being neglected.

His approach was that he had been terribly pampered in the first three or four years and then thrown out on the streets (to go to school).

The mother's pregnancy with the patient occurred during a time when her father had scheduled a trip to Europe. The mother was supposed to go along, but the pregnancy interrupted these plans. I am not sure when the patient became aware of this, but he said that he had been guilty about it as a child. It had not been brought up recurrently in the family, however.

Also, during the period of difficulty around the age of eight or nine, his mother got involved in an auto accident. She was a notoriously careless driver, and bumped into a fireplug. His attitude was that everybody expected her to do that. He also said that if anything had happened to them at that time, he would have been "a goner for sure." Apparently that is one of the most turbulent periods.

The patient could remember little about the accident, the father's appendectomy, and other traumatic events in the home, and was unclear as to how he felt about them.

I might also describe the events that accompanied his leaving the hospital. The father had come in several times, talked to me, reassured me that the patient would not leave the hospital, and said that he considered me the key to the patient's possible recovery. One Thursday he assured me of this again, and on the following Tuesday, the hospital received a letter saying that arrangements had been made to transfer the patient to a VA hospital on the coming Thursday. It was a whirlwind affair that nobody at Sheppard knew anything about. The mother came down when the patient was being transferred and said she did not know where all this hurry came from, but I suspect it was from the father. When I told the patient about the letter, he blanched, became anxious and frightened, and had difficulty talking for a couple of minutes. He asked a few questions—"What does this mean?" "What is going to happen to me?" "When am I going?" —and then settled down into the typical self-depreciatory pattern. It was all his fault, he had signed the original paper requesting veterans' aid. Ultimately he asked me what I thought about it, and I only replied that I disliked his father's breach of faith very much; I had been reassured that the patient would stay, and then this happened without my knowledge. His only comment was that this was the craziest mess he had ever heard of.

On the next interview he talked about his parents again, about their giving him everything he wanted, and his pattern became quite clear. His father had been solicitous, but the patient had always made requests to the mother. He thought the reason for this might be his fear of his father, but that did not seem to be at all clear. When the father came home, he was friendly to the boy, and if a request was made to him, it was granted. But if a request was made to the mother, she would invariably discuss it with the father in the evening, and the fact that both parents were involved was important. It was not the request itself, but the fact that he could interest both parents in him at least for a short time.

He mentioned his teachers, describing the kindergarten and first- and second-grade teachers as friendly, but indicating that the third-grade teacher was stern, uncompromising, and punitive. One day the boy across the row accidentally dropped something, and the teacher came over and rapped him on the knuckles with a ruler. This upset the patient because the punishment was not merited. He said that the boy had ended up in a reform school, and he attached a good deal of significance to the teacher's punishment of him.

A couple of other events suggested that the boy had been regarded quite highly by people in college and in the Navy. For example, while he was in training, a lieutenant commander made a special trip to the superior officer and requested that the patient be assigned to his ship.

I might mention also some statements that were in the Nurses' Notes. The nurse that he had talked to left a couple of days after the last seminar, and he immediately picked up with the next student on the ward and continued the conversation. Some of the comments were, "It's funny my talking to you. I have only been able to talk to Miss M and Mr. B. Sometimes I think I might be getting better, but other times it is all so horrible. I can seem to sleep better now—but that is no indication that I am getting better. The tension is just a little less. I wish I could get well, but there isn't much hope, I guess." A few days after that he talked about the panic he had in the tub, mentioning only that he got so panicky that he tore a hole in his cheek. The last note in February said: "Every time I see my doctor we have quite a time. I'm trying to convince him I'm crazy, and he's trying to convince me I'm not."

It became necessary to follow up some of his ideas of schizophrenia and paranoia and several other psychiatric terms which he used recurrently. I suppose I showed my dislike for the use of such language throughout, and so when the patient got into a self-depreciatory trend he ended up by labeling himself as a paranoid or a schizophrenic. Before he left, the use of these terms was almost routine when he got on the subject of what the future meant to him. I suggested that he might conceivably want to set up a pattern independent of his parents, but no matter how the subject was approached, it invariably ended with his labeling himself a schizophrenic. On three different occasions, when attempting to describe what he meant by "paranoia," he brought out three different ideas. The first was "a delusive pattern which took the place of some other interest." At another time he told me that when he was playing a record, he would be thrilled by some phrase in the music and would play this over and over, and this in some way meant "paranoid" to him—that the way the theme got stuck in his mind meant "fixed delusion." On another occasion he said he felt elated in roller skating or flying, and this good feeling, this elation, was carried into "delusions of grandeur."

I have, I think, a beginning notion of how he constructed his illness. The term "visual misperceptions" came up frequently, and by that he meant that he saw things differently than other people. He saw them as masses or as whole objects. He would look at an automobile and only see the form of it, and have no understanding that there was an engine and a top and so on. Another thing was the littleness with which he saw things, or the bigness, the littleness usually being on his side and the bigness being the world. Everything he saw—halls, buildings, people—all appeared massive to him. When he had a physical examination for flying, diplopia was discovered, apparently on a phorometer, and he was disqualified. He hid this fact, repeated the examination, and passed, but the awareness of the diplopia remained and seemed to explain the visual misperceptions—the diplopia was a constitutional inadequacy which accounted for his seeing things differently, for what he labeled "delusions" or "misperceptions." This led to the use of "schizophrenia," in the meaning of "split personality"—in some way the misperceptions led to incorrect evaluations, and therefore a large part of himself was constructed on these misperceptions, developing into the split personality. He also tried to define "Oedipus complex," but dropped that. One Freudian term which he repeated was "anal erotic"; when masturbating he would stimulate himself further by touching his anus, which to him proved that he had an "anal erotic character."

Over a period of time it became evident to me that he was getting me involved in a sort of an argument. It was pointed up by his remarks to the nurse that I objected to certain terms and he objected to my not liking them. One day we were able to talk out some of that and ultimately he said, "I seem to want you to get tough with me, get stern and demanding." We were able to investigate that a little, suggesting that this sort of arrangement, especially if I fell into the pattern, was perhaps a way of relating himself to people, but a pretty inefficient one in the long run.

Among the things we talked about at some length was the panic he felt after he had the first sedative tub. He said that in some way he put shock treatment and tub baths in the same category, that he had been very frightened that whole weekend about the possibility of having more tubs, and that his panic reaction arose in relation to that. He saw a little more clearly, as time went on, that they were different, but his reaction was as if he had been again subjected to shock treatment.

One day he talked about physical aloofness and wanted to go into some of the reasons for his being aloof. His parents constantly warned him to avoid strangers, not to take candy from them or to talk to them. Nevertheless, he did talk to them a couple of times, and he remembered that at twelve or thirteen, a man had offered him candy and he refused. He was beginning to become aware of homosexuality at that period. He felt it was an intriguing subject, looked it up in the dictionary, tried to read about it, but talked to no one about it. He concluded that talk about homosexuality, which he had brought up himself, with the statement that he had never noticed anything in himself, but was quite aware of it in other people around him. This was the period when he started to avoid physical contact, with boys as well as with girls. Prior to this he was able to play in street or camp games without thought of avoiding physical contact, but after that he looked on it with suspicion and as something to be scrupulously avoided.

SULLIVAN: Was there any actual incident to which he related this avoidance?

KVARNES: It was not as clear as that. It came up when he was talking about the offer of candy from an older man and how he refused it; that led to some talk about homosexuality and how he avoided physical contact.

SULLIVAN: But he claimed a definite change in his attitude?

KVARNES: I thought that his talk about the discovery of homosexuality might imply that from that time on he was much more cautious in physical contact. He tried, as we brought out before, a few contacts with girls but was always full of anxiety and consciously avoided any physical contact with men or boys.

SULLIVAN: When did the puberty change occur?

KVARNES: As far as I can tell it was about that time. It was not delayed. He always considered himself slower in maturing but each time I went into it, it seems that it occurred at about thirteen.

Dr. Kehne is here today from the hospital at Perry Point where the patient was transferred, and I think it would be interesting to hear his comments.

SULLIVAN: Did you admit this patient, Dr. Kehne?

KEHNE: Yes, he was admitted to the hospital on April 11 and taken out of the hospital on April 15. We had no idea he would be moved. He did not know why he had been removed from Sheppard. He said his father had done it, but he seemed to blame himself, saying it was his fault, that he had signed the original papers without thinking what he was doing.

The reason the father gave was that he thought the amount of improvement the boy had shown was not commensurate with the money he had been putting out. I talked to the mother and father for about twenty minutes, and their relationship was quite unusual. I was at my desk, the father was in front of me, and the mother was just slightly behind him. If she was talking and I looked as if I wanted to ask a question, or if he wished to say something, he would snap his fingers at her and she would drop the conversation in the middle of a word. Then when he had said his say, he would wave his hand at her and she would begin to speak again. Apparently there was no protest from her, she just stopped and started with the fingers.

As far as his stay at Sheppard is concerned, the patient had nothing good or bad to say about it. He did say that he did not seem as nervous as he had been before admission. The family gave almost no reason for removing the patient from Perry Point. They just showed up one morning, out of the blue, and the patient was very surprised. He just said, "Here I go again." This was just another thing that was happening to him beyond his control. They said they felt he would be better off nearer home and nearer friends, and to my way of thinking, this is exactly what the patient feared, because he told me on several occasions that some of his friends were doctors and he had a great fear of ever having to face one of them in his present condition.

When I asked him what difficulties had caused his hospitalization, he replied, "My present state is one which is the result of a long series of complicated circumstances which had their beginning somewhere in childhood and continued to the time of hospitalization. I am a paranoid schizophrenic and you know that the chances are fifty percent recovery." I ask him why he felt that, and he said, "I dissociated from reality, I show regressive impulsive behavior, and I am the victim of deep-seated terrors and fears, and I have frequently had suicidal ideas. This failing to materialize, I am now up against a blank wall. I have identified with my parents, I resort to neurotic acts to avoid uncomfortable situations, I lead a fantasy life, and I have never had a really satisfactory life. The real blow came when I found I could not make a normal heterosexual adjustment." By "normal" he meant both parties being satisfied. He said that he had tried before but now he knew it was impossible. He then said, "It was at that time that I developed all sorts of strange neurotic feelings. I could not be still and I tried to do a million things at once. A lecture in college loomed before me as horribly threatening. The professor did not seem like a normal man, I was always terrified lest he call on me, at which time I felt something terrible would happen to me. One day this became so bad that I had to leave the class and call my father to take me home." He said he hated to do this because he always called his father when he got in a tight spot. I asked him if his fear developed before or after he was aware of the difficulty with his sexual adjustment, and he said it began before, but it was in connection with thoughts of a heterosexual relationship. Whenever he became disturbed by these he resorted to fantasies in which everything was just the way he wanted it to be. He said, "I tried to force myself to have intercourse but a great fear overcame me. I broke everything off and began to get panicky. Everything disintegrated. They took me to a hospital. At Springhill they gave me shock and it only made me more afraid—quieter, but more afraid. Everything made me more afraid. I would shudder if anyone touched me."

I asked him about his stay at Sheppard Pratt and he replied, "Well, I am not as frightened as I was when I went there, but I am still disorganized. There is no way back. I have completely wasted my life, never learned anything." I asked him if his doctor understood him, and he said, "He did and he didn't." What do you mean? "He could never have been so calm if he had really understood what was wrong." I then suggested that maybe the doctor didn't think that what he was saying was really so bad as the patient thought. I asked if that had occurred to him and he said no. Then I said that if he understood what was wrong with you, and was not upset, did you ever wonder why you felt the way you do? How did these ideas arise in your mind? He said, "We talked about a lot of things but I always felt like a guinea pig, felt I was being pushed." "What do you mean?" "Well, you have seen them in psychology class, where you put a rat in a maze and watch him run—well, that's how I felt." I asked if he felt the doctor was interested in helping him and he said yes, but that it took him a long time to get over the fear that shock gave him. I asked him how he felt before he left and he said, "I felt the doctor was my friend and was interested, but I doubt if he could cure a paranoid schizophrenic. Only fifty percent recovery, you know. In some ways he was like my parents." "How?" "Never punished me when I did something bad. When I was a child I did many things and expected to be punished. I never was and I always felt guilty. I guess I thought they didn't care. Sometimes I would have fantasies in which I would punish my parents."

I wondered if he had fantasies about the doctor and he said no, and I asked why and he said that he would take time to talk. He further said he liked the doctor and felt he could trust him. I asked what symptom was most relieved by this contact and he said the terror reaction.

Throughout the short time I spent with him, he was always tense and usually would tear up anything he could get his fingers on—papers and matches would be in shreds. He was always co-operative and anxious to talk. It was difficult to get him out of the office and back to the ward. He was almost clinging. One time I let him stay, just to see how long he would stay, and after two and a half hours I gave up.

SULLIVAN: Did either of you ask the father if he was acting under anybody's advice?

KVARNES: The father did not come down when the patient left, but I think perhaps two weeks earlier the patient was visited by Dr. G on the father's request, and he told Dr. G much the same story, using the psychiatric terminology. Dr. G thought perhaps some insulin therapy might be indicated but did not say much to us about it.

COOPER: His mother came down the day he was transferred. At that time she was very friendly, did not have any complaint against the hospital or what we had done. She seemed to place the whole thing on a financial basis. Her husband had to undergo surgery, and being a diabetic he had to stay in the hospital about three weeks before the operation, and they could not afford to keep up the expenses at Sheppard. However, she was amazed at the speed of the transfer. In most cases they investigated, and it usually took two weeks or more for the Veterans Hospital to receive the patient. They had depended on that delay in order to get down and warn the patient of the transfer, but suddenly they got word that the VA was ready for the transfer.

During that time I was acting as chief of service and took care of the correspondence with the patient's father. All of his letters were of this very reassuring quality, "I will not take the boy out of the hospital!" He had sent us word that a representative from the Veterans Administration would be out to see his son, but it merely meant financial aid and he would not consider taking the boy away from us. If they tried to make him do that, he would drop the request for financial help.

KVARNES: The father had been working as the executor of some estate and had worked himself out of a job. There was apparently a real financial problem, but Sheppard would have reduced the rates in an effort to keep the patient.

STAVEREN: In the Veterans Hospital what is the status? Can the family take the patient out of the hospital if the patient refuses to leave?

KEHNE: Yes. He is declared incompetent and so he would have to do whatever they wanted.

SULLIVAN: The most interesting technical point, and one I think we ought to have discussed, is what do you do when some disastrous intervention like this occurs? I used to think when I was in institutional work that if a schizophrenic started pretty well on the way out of his illness, one of two things was probable: that the patient would contract pneumonia and die, or that the family would take him out. It is such an impressive business that I think misanthropic psychiatrists are justified in wondering if improvement of the patient is not worrying the family. The thing is, how can one deal with the emergency so that if possible the evil aspect can be minimized? Rather than say anything of my own impression of Dr. Kvarnes' comments to the patient, I would like to hear each of you express something of what, in being confronted by such an emergency, you might feel inclined to say to the patient, ask the patient, if suddenly you learned that the patient is to be removed from your care. Let's start with Dr. Witt.

WITT: I'm damned if I know. I had the same thing happen to me and found there was not too much I could say, or that I knew to say. I think in scrambling around, what I finally came up with was that if it was possible that the patient had been able to talk to me at all—and she had—and found that it was a little easier to talk to somebody than it had been before, then it was also probable that there might be somebody else to whom she could talk. That I was not the only one. In the next hospital there was some chance at least that somebody would be available that she could talk to who would have a good deal less of the parental reaction, perhaps, than most of the people she had known before she came to the hospital. That this was not something completely final.

ROM: Something did happen between the patient and me when

the time came to leave. I knew there was a crisis and that day or the next, I approached him and he was much more outgoing and responsive. That had not been the case with me, as I have reported here. Shortly after that, on another visit, I indicated to him that, well, probably a change of environment may be beneficial, and that was all. When the time came for his departure, I approached him and told him that we would probably meet again some day on some happier shore, and he was the best that I have ever seen him.

SULLIVAN: What did you hope to accomplish by the comment that maybe a change of environment would help?

ROM: I thought that was the most graceful way to end the thing.

NOVEY: I would be tempted to move in the direction that Dr. Kvarnes did, and express something of what I believe I would be feeling myself, namely, some sense of regret at what had happened, and not attempt to offer reassurance as such. It seems that it is the sort of thing that might be successfully shared with the patient. It is an unfortunate incident in his life and we should recognize it as such.

STYRT: I think that one of the things I would try to do, if the patient were receptive, would be to go over some of the things that had occurred in the hospital that had been accepted by the patient as indications of improvement. Or try to get him to accept the fact that in this hospital he had been helped, and it was possible for him to continue elsewhere. That there would be people who would try to understand him and help him. I can't help but express my own feelings, sometimes regret and sometimes anger, but what I have done is concentrate on the fact that the patient had been able to get help with us, and that he could try with somebody else.

PEAL: I don't know what I would say to this man. I would want to know how he felt about it and what it meant to him to go to another hospital. As to what I would tell him in the way of encouragement or non-encouragement, I would have to tell him what I know and would like to use it as a real situation and hope that the patient would be objective and gain something by it without any influence—or forming opinion by me.

SULLIVAN: Needless to say, I was not there, and I don't know the patient except from these meetings, but I find myself somewhat lost by your reference to what the real situation was. You feel there are lots of things you don't know about this situation that you would need to know in order to meet it, or what?

PEAL: I would have to know more about what he thought of me and what he thought of hospitalization, and I feel particularly convinced that it is necessary because of what the patient said at the other hospital.

SULLIVAN: In general you would expect the best thing you can do, in any emergency, is to keep quiet—because I am afraid you will always be in need of this data.

COOPER: In this specific case, if I knew something about the hospital that the patient was going to, I would feel a little more at ease as to how to approach him. If I felt he was going into an understanding environment, I would decide to project a little hostile reaction toward his father over moving him. If I did not know about the other institution, I would be afraid of suddenly throwing the patient into a state that I could not help him with and that might not help him on his admission, and I might be more likely to avoid any statements like those Dr. Kvarnes made because the patient has been so unwilling to place blame on his family. I think I would try to assure him that he would no doubt receive very good care and have contact with someone who would be understanding.

WHEELER: I would probably try to prepare the patient for further, perhaps endless repetitions of the same thing, and find some way to open his eyes to the fact that sometimes when the patient is getting well, his parents actually are disturbed. Not that that happened in his case, but that such things could happen.

MORRIS: I think you don't have to ask the patient—I would know he would want to stay. He wants help and it seems obvious this is the best way of getting it. And soon as I got wind of the transfer I would try to get his cooperation to stop it. I would point out to him what his parents are doing and, if possible, get the patient to make it clear to them that he did not want a transfer. I would make every effort to talk to the parents to get them to keep him there.

SALZMAN: There would be several objectives I would like to achieve in such a situation. One would be the recognition that there is a good bit of helplessness in the patient and therapist in facing something they have no control over. At the same time I might want to use this as an example of what is certainly a tendency on the part of the parents to be really malevolent while trying to be so helpful. That, I suppose, would have to come in terms of rounding up the work that was done with the patient. I think it is not a good idea to let the work drop without any evaluation of what has been done. The patient could very well feel that a lot happened, but he can't make any sense of it at all except that the doctor was a pretty nice fellow and he has gotten something out of the contact. I would feel that would be a very important thing, and would attempt to discuss with the patient the possible ways of continuing the work in the new situation.

I would like to ask a question here. Is it good, at such a moment, to create new anxiety in the patient, as Dr. Kvarnes might have done with his provoking attitude toward the parents?

WHITE: When Dr. Kvarnes told me of the way he did it, I liked it. It seems to me that the patient must have been very hurt and angry about this further failure so characteristic of his whole situation and his life, and Dr. Kvarnes' reaction—"I am mad at this because it interrupts my work"—tells the patient that he is free to be angry, too. I don't think it would make him anxious. He is anxious already. I would go one step further, regretting that there was not more time to find out whether they had a really serious reason for this move. If it was financial collapse, try to get him to see that it is beyond our control. Then the business of telling him that possibly he could go ahead with another individual, and then still another step: "If you ever feel that help can be achieved through Sheppard Pratt or through me, I would be glad to take you on, either there or somewhere else. This has nothing to do with your parents except for the financial arrangements. Come back if you want. Work might progress even better if you want to come, and urge it." Then I would try to carry that over to the new situation and say: "Now you are going to another hospital, not because you want it or I want it, but if you go having faith in what has gone on here, then you will have a better chance than if you go just mad because your parents took you out of here. This is your life and you should try to live it."

STAVEREN: My thoughts are along the same lines as Dr. Morris' and Dr. Salzman's. I would like to establish with the patient that some benefit has come out of the contact and therefore the thing is not a disaster. That should be clearly mentioned. And then give it a turn by saying, "Let's get the best out of it while we are still together." I think I would review with the patient the father's letters and visits and this move, and see if we could find out that similar things have gone before. It is not likely that this has occurred because the father has suddenly developed spots or lost them—it must have been done before in many different ways. The other thing I would try to do something with is this: Here is a fine demonstration of what is probably the explanation of the derogatory attitudes he has toward himself. It seems inevitable that he is enraged, and instead we see him running himself down, and that implies a vast amount of anxiety. Some of that might be relieved by legitimizing the rage against the father. Any kind of reassurance about a happy future and things like that would be practically wiping out anything that had been achieved before. A person at that time is not in a mood for anything like that and could not use it, but if one could sum up what has been done, and the outstanding positive points that have been achieved, and ask him whether he did not think he could work with another person along that line, that I think would be valuable.

WAGNER: My remarks are somewhat of a summary of what has been said. I think one should consider with the patient the facts that brought the transfer about and the repetitive pattern; to project oneself with the patient into the new situation as to what might be anticipated about real or fantastic dreads, and what the patient can do about forestalling some of these dreads; to reassure, as others have suggested, perhaps by indicating that the experience with the therapist is one that is available elsewhere, the therapy not being unique, and perhaps, as Dr. White suggested, some sustained contact, perhaps by suggesting that you would like to hear from the patient.

SULLIVAN: It seems to me that all of you will perhaps profit from doing some further thinking about this business because I actually have some data to indicate that the handling of these emergencies is sometimes very valuable. Myself, profanity coming with the greatest of ease to me, in these situations I do, or have done, one of two things: In one case I gave a poor demonstration of my variant of wringing my hands—that is, trying to share with the patient a feeling of furious desperation; and in the other simply staging more or less of a vocal tantrum of rage. I have always insisted that a great deal of psychiatry has to seem spontaneous, *and* to be carefully thought out. I do this because it seems a golden opportunity for the ordinary protection of awareness to be broken down and I attempt to set an example for what I hope will come into the patient's awareness. I try to make some use of this for expanding the patient's awareness of certain of his attitudes which are intolerable to him. I am sure this patient had a better chance of becoming quite furious at the impersonal way he is being treated as a chattel. He is shoved around. It is reasonable to assume that the father is behind that, and I am going to give him a working diagram of how I feel about his father— hoping his consciousness will be overwhelmed with the same emotion. Then I will try to do as several of you suggested, want to know how much experience he has had with this business of suddenly being boosted from what he was interested in into something *papa* thinks is wonderful, getting as much into awareness as possible. I do this with reasonable safety because I know that the next thing I am going to do, once the dust has settled, and I have capitalized on this, in terms of expanding his awareness of his feelings toward his interfering parent, then I will say, "Well, but damn it, the situation boils down to the sooner you are over this damn disability and unquestionably able to run your own life, the sooner you will get rid of this person." With that as a key to my further efforts, I try to first indicate that I know a good many people at this hospital. That happens to be the case with me because I know some thousand or more psychiatrists. It does not entail any difficulty because I can likely find somebody at least that knows me, and I wish to spread the network of fellow feeling. Try to accomplish that on the basis of knowledge and esteem for other people. What I have actually often done— perhaps partly because in the old days the convenient thing to save money was to transfer patients from Sheppard to St. Elizabeths, as is now done to Perry Point—is to say that I would like to sort of pass on some of the profits from our work, that the patient might not be perfectly clear on, and that I would look in in a day or so and talk with his physician if that suited him, the patient before me. I let him fizz awhile because I have to let people talk to get things out of the way, but I am preparing for my next step, that I suppose he feels pretty apprehensive of strangers, but how would he feel this time if I were to talk with his doctor? I don't care whether he says yes or no, because I am trying to keep his attention, and then attempt to get a picture of what has been accomplished and what looks as if it could be accomplished, letting it sort of hang. Then—"If you don't quite agree with this, I still think the doctor ought to know something about my impressions, so that if he agreed, things could go right on." That I take quite a lot of time to do. I like to get the idea of continuity, and I am not hesitant about bringing out the hospital directory and saying, "Hm-m, yes, I know two or three people there and I will get in touch with them," and then I add, "You are in good hands." I want to spread an attenuated relationship until he has built something up.

This being transacted, I arouse myself and say, "But look here, this goddamn shoving around ought to bring useful things to your mind. Let's get all we can out of this while we still have an hour or two. What the hell, nobody is down. This is unquestionably unfortunate, but let's profit from it." If I can get him to do this, that is, in its way, a sort of powerful underpinning for the notion that I previously put to him in another connection, that the sooner he is better, the sooner he will be saved from having his life kicked around.

The last thing I would like you to think about is: How do you part with a patient? There are real opportunities there, and being a person who cannot express—well, the fewer words I use to express feeling, the better it gets across with schizoid obsessional people—and my actual parting with patients who have been taken out has been mostly wordless, with the reminder that I would see them at least for a moment in the near future.

I want to say one last thing about this visiting, which, God knows, is pure philanthropy on the psychiatrist's part. I had at Sheppard, a great treasure, a patient who had struggled through certainly two years, and maybe four years, of merchant service, despite very serious schizophrenia, and who finally blew up and was extraordinarily assaultive. He was snapped through two marine hospitals and one other hospital to Sheppard in less than ten days after his psychosis was recognized due to his beating up the ship's complement of officers. He did very well in the course of human events, and his father, for financial reasons, had him transferred to St. Elizabeths. I went through very much the performance I outlined to you, but when I telephoned St. Elizabeths next day I learned that the patient was very seriously disturbed, a great problem because of his assaultiveness. Well, I knew the admission ward over there, and so I went to Washington and I had him brought down to the office I used to use in the Receiving Building, and then I shooed away the supervisors and the guards that came with him. The supervisors looked worried, but then they remembered that I was sort of crazy and they stayed outside. I said to the boy, after grinning at him for a moment, "Dudley, you are terribly on the wrong beam. I know this place. As a matter of fact, I think a great deal of two or three attendants on that ward. They are extremely useful to patients. What the hell has gotten you mixed up?" Well, he talked, I don't know just what he said, but he was no longer combative, and before very long he had parole and presently was discharged to his home, from which I heard from him for about ten years. He never actually recovered from his schizophrenic state, but he lived at large under rather clever circumstances. I should say that his continued freedom was based on three factors known to me. One was that he was able to buy a rice farm where he lived a remarkably solitary life in the very deep South, where the Negro help were not human enough to worry him.* Second, his developing, on the basis of a hunch we had discussed, a great interest in singing in the church choir. He had a good voice, and excellent reasons for needing to use it, and singing in a choir is not too personal. The final fact was that he maintained this very tenuous contact with me, a contact in which I never heard from him unless he was deeply disturbed. I would get the goddamnedest hodgepodge letters that were as psychotic as anything he had ever produced, and I would reply saying that I was glad to hear from him and that I hoped things were going as well as usual, and then months and months, and then another psychotic letter, and I am sure I continued to be some tenuous reassurance that he was not as crazy as he thought. When he was really upset he would embalm it in writing and send it to me. I survived and that was reassuring to him. Also this move took him out of the family environment.

I am through with this unless there are any questions or comments anyone would like to make.

* See "Comment," p. 230, for discussion of this passage.

A series of questions * has come out of your discussions, and I greatly appreciate the interest which is reflected in these questions. I only wish to express my regret that I have had no opportunity to organize any way of answering them, but some of them are good enough so that we should discuss them and get your views on them.

[QUESTION 1: *What is the fundamental difference in approach to the handling of schizophrenics in contrast to that of psychoneurotics and others?*]

The first of these questions is on the fundamental difference in approach to the handling of schizophrenics in contrast to less ill patients. There is a fundamental difference, I suppose. That is, there is a difference which seems almost fundamental. The handling of all patients, that is, the useful handling of all patients, depends on one's establishing some kind of genuinely communicative situation. One does that for various reasons, the most obvious of which is that one can come to understand how the patient's past has led to the unfortunate present. One can usually so manipulate the present state, when one understands the past, that the unfortunate hangover from the past is seen to be wholly unnecessary. Whereupon the general principle manifests itself that people do try to get as much out of life as they can, and when they see that something is unnecessary, overcomplicated, or disastrous, if it does not still seem vitally important, they abandon it. One has to establish communicative situations because no matter how good your historical data is, you still don't know what the living patient before you has made out of that experience reflected in this historical data. Historical data is vastly useful in orienting yourself, but it is not to be taken as reflecting what the patient knows about himself. Many grave disorders appear both in historical data and in accessible data in a patient's memory.

To establish a communicative situation with any patient, one has to so manipulate things that anxiety about your reactions, your views of the patient and so on, will gradually be allayed.

* Because of the patient's departure and the possibility of insufficient clinical material for discussion, the seminar participants had asked Sullivan for permission to submit questions in advance for consideration. The actual questions are indicated in brackets in the text; some had obviously been submitted in advance and some arose during the seminar.

This is very much more difficult with schizophrenics than it is with some other patients, but it is always quite difficult. It is the first phase of all psychotherapy, and we will have some comments about it again and again as we deal with the questions.

Quite a misleading and still indicative statement about the difficulty of the schizophrenic is that almost all of them have come to believe that they have very poor judgment about other people and that if other people seem interested in them, favorably interested in them, that interest is either fraudulent or due to ignorance of the patient. In other words, it will die as soon as the stranger discovers what the patient is like. The more paranoid the tendency, the more the patient will think something is being put over. In any case, exceedingly little grounds for easy development of trust and confidence in the physician exist.

There again, the difference seems to me to be of degree. The patient who plunges into psychotherapy as some hysterics do is almost as difficult, excepting that here it is the patient that is putting something over on the doctor. The good communicative situation cannot be established with miraculous speed.

Since the schizophrenic, insofar as he is lucid and therefore capable of communication, is convinced that either you are mistaken in thinking him worth the effort, or putting something over on him, needless to say all your earlier operations have to be oriented at this level, and as these patients are often quite subtle in their capacity for inference, one has to be rather sharp in foreseeing possible miscarriage of one's efforts in establishing communication.

I must say that I always think of the difference in terms of the exquisite nicety with which one has to establish the doctor-patient relationship with schizophrenics and the comparative relationship that one can use with psychoneurotics. I might as well say that in later years I have found myself entirely unable to draw any sharp line between the obsessional way of life and the schizophrenic. A great many people who utilize an obsessional way of life are thereby saved from any necessity for schizophrenic disaster, but some of them are not, and one occasionally sees patients, I have seen several, in which there are schizophrenic episodes when the obsessional way of life cannot protect the patient adequately from interpersonal pressure. So I believe that as psychiatric theory improves, we will be able to combine incipient, that is catatonic, schizophrenia, and the substitutive obsessional states. I might remind you that one of the really deeply disturbing ways of onset of schizophrenia is a rapidly deepening compulsion neurosis in the young, and we have again in the Sheppard material a patient who was really an outstanding teaching case of intense obsessional neurosis for years, who then rapidly passed into what ultimately was a bitterly paranoid schizophrenia. He did not come out. He was not actually a patient of mine, which just meant that my initial interview with him presented such an extremely unpromising lot of material that I felt more interested in others.

[QUESTION 2: *What is to be accomplished in the initial interview with patients?*]

The next question pertains to the initial interview. I am going to be very depressing about that. In the first place, I have given two or three courses on the psychiatric interview, but more unfortunate for you, I have just finished three lectures in a course on the psychiatric interview, and my life has been characterized by an extreme unwillingness to do the same things over again until I have recovered from the first effort. I actually don't believe I could whip myself into saying, in a few minutes, anything that would not be strikingly misleading to you.

I will say that I think the psychiatric situation begins with the first look at the patient and the patient's first look at you, and I have in general found it pretty important to establish a basis for relationship. In other words, with ambulatory people, enjoying freedom, who come to me under their own steam, I expect them to set up in the initial interview a sufficient cause for seeing a psychiatrist. They don't have to tell me what ails them, maybe they don't know, but something that justifies my functioning as a psychiatrist. Where people do not come of their own volition, or are deeply disturbed, I nonetheless do that myself. I want, before we have parted for the first time, to have put on the record that there is a real basis for the relationship—which I regard as that of someone who is more or less of an expert, however less, with someone who needs expert services.

The reasons for that are many. It does not indicate any need on my part, which differs from the patient. It is a mood I have been driven to, to save time, to get things done. If the patient can, I expect the patient to set up a cause for seeing me, and if the patient cannot, I will tell the patient what I see as a cause. That, needless to say, with disturbed schizophrenics, threatens a war from the beginning, but I am not inclined to quarrel about anything and it is difficult to have a war if the other fellow has no position you can attack. I have expressed what I believe to be true. If it does not suit the patient, I am not asking him to agree, I am telling him what I think. The wars have not necessarily continued.

There are a good many people to whom I have never been of any particular use, but in my experience, this is a useful part of the initial interview.

[QUESTION 3: *Ask for Dr. Sullivan's old write-up on the initial interview which is particularly for schizophrenics and in which he deals entirely in terms of the catatonic schizophrenic.*]

The next question is again on the initial interview, with comments that my work is available. I am not quite sure what this pertains to, especially the part which says that this is entirely in terms of the catatonic.

There may be some among you who are not familiar with my views on schizophrenic ways of life. Very simply it is this: That incipient schizophrenia cannot in any phase be distinguished from uncomplicated catatonic states except in the degree to which certain phenomena are conspicuous, but the processes and disturbances of living seem to be identical. In uncomplicated catatonic states, even though they last for six or seven years, this essentially schizophrenic type of disturbance continues to be what is going on. As long as that is the case, one of three courses of events can happen, often with most dramatic suddenness. The patient can start out of the catatonic state, and with remarkable speed become practically safe in the general community, if not active; in comparatively rare cases he can be more of a going concern than even before the illness. With equally dramatic suddenness, in fact rather greater suddenness, the patient may withdraw, whatever that term means, in a kind of unearthly discouragement of interests and come to a way of life with remarkable speed, in which the securing of satisfaction from the crudest, most elementary type of zonal needs is his major living. This is the hebephrenic dilapidation. To my way of thinking no one begins a hebephrenic, but there is a joker in this. I do not believe that insidious deterioration should be called a schizophrenic way of life. I have a strong suspicion that insidious deterioration may prove to be an obscure kind of organic disturbance. Just what, I don't know, and I don't care, because I have found no technique by which one could do anything with them and therefore I am not talking about it.

What I am always talking about is preferably a patient in whom there has been a fairly clear incident of eruption of schizophrenic process. These people are almost invariably under much tension before this happens. I don't care how long they have been disturbed in their living, but I mean where eruption of dream processes into waking contact with reality is sharp, can be set in time. Those are the ones I am talking about. Not the people who drift off into pseudophilosophizing and gradually fall apart.

The third relatively dramatic event that can befall a person in the incipient, or catatonic state, is a paranoid maladjustment. Not paranoid ideas and feelings, if you please—these ideas of influence, of hostile and destructive influence, are as much a part of schizophrenia, or the schizophrenic way of life, as are such disagreeable delusions in your dreams. But when the tension, as it were, is very considerably reduced by fastening it on more or less specific external enemies, more or less real enemies. How unreal they can be is well reflected in a famous Sheppard patient who was persecuted for many years by John Doe, John Doe being a quite transcendentally real person. When in the catatonic state one achieves this massive transfer on to the environment, real or fantastic (and remember that the environment is always relatively fantastic, even to you, colored by your past and your interests), then the paranoid maladjustment has occurred; the hebephrenic dilapidation and the paranoid maladjustment are both bad news. There are very few abrupt recoveries from them.

I believe it is very hard, in therapy, to reverse these changes. Therefore the essential problem in the psychotherapy of schizophrenics is to get them early and so guard your operations as certainly not to necessitate one of these unfortunate changes, and, in fact, insofar as it is humanly possible, to arrest them. And arresting them can sometimes be done quite dramatically. After the Reception Building [at Sheppard] was opened, we had a youngster who showed impressive evidence of a switch to hebephrenia, which was reversed apparently so that he was discharged not awfully long afterwards. Against our advice, the family took him home, and he came back in a few weeks pretty well established in a catatonic state, only to recover from it dramatically as soon as it became perfectly clear that our advice could be carried out and he could go to a distant place with relatives and get away from the repressive parental situation. I am willing for you to say that under pressure he could renew his psychotic state, which, however, could be withdrawn when the pressure disappeared. To me, this is one of the very occasional instances of being able to interfere to arrest hebephrenic deterioration or dilapidation. And don't kid yourself about this deterioration. That hebephrenics are pretty much centered on zonal satisfactions can be demonstrated; but you can find a great deal of human personality in hebephrenics, too, only it is not good for anything [once the dilapidation has taken hold].

[QUESTION 4: *What about patients who do not talk, cannot talk?*]

That is a perfectly excellent question. It pertains to patients who do not talk readily, and I must say I don't seem ever to work with a patient who did not talk readily very long. A general principle is the easier the discussion, the better the therapy. We expect things that are going to count for very much to have anxiety pretty close to them. We say that the skill of the psychiatrist is to some extent manifested not by his avoiding anxiety, but by his mapping the areas which are colored by anxiety, and showing some reasonable discretion when he is stomping around there. As I say, if the patient can say nothing, I can still establish my view of the situation. I can talk at him, but one might well notice that if a patient is so disturbed that he utters nothing and shows many other symptoms of being thoroughly catatonic, you can't just assume that he is like an audience in a movie, perfectly in touch with what you choose to present to him. The trick of getting anywhere with these thoroughly tied up people, mute, incontinent, and things of that kind, is that one talks to oneself and to them, that is, at them, with careful regard to any clues that one can get as to the degree to which they are attending.

What one sees is organized to the best of one's ability to impress the true relationship—that is, that one has had the misfortune of becoming upset in the mind, that one is in a mental hospital, that the speaker is supposed to be more or less understanding and useful in clearing up these upsets. That it is clear that the patient cannot believe that a great many of these things are so, that the patient instead feels that some terrible disaster has occurred to him or perhaps to the whole world, that it may be extremely hard to believe that this is a mental hospital, that the people working on the ward are friendly and trying to be helpful, but when one can notice these things, he will find that they are true.

This is a hell of a brief note that I toss out to give you an idea of what one talks to oneself and at the patient about. One attempts to talk when the patient seems capable of hearing. One hopes that that which the patient heard will be relevant enough to the patient's mental state so that it awakens some interest, and then one attempts to educate the victim of a profound disturbance to an awareness of how he can begin to pin down a little of that, and that is to me one of the things that seem to be transpiring. If one has a fortunate situation, if the ward personnel is fortunate, if the classification of patients is careful, and if one gets at this before the patient has become simply convinced by accident of this and that, you sometimes make remarkable impressions along the general line I have indicated.

There is another Sheppard instance that went dreadfully to pot due to the intervention of a moralist. This boy came in combative, quite terrified and exceedingly disinclined to say anything, but not mute, and by spending an hour and a half with him in the room to which he was admitted, I got him to undress himself and lie down in bed instead of having a running fight to have it done, and the outcome was that of a quite good contact. I had to go away on one of my extracurricular activities and came back to find him completely settled in a paranoid development from which he never emerged. There had been a fatal incongruity between my approach and the approach he got in my absence, and if you think I sound bitter, I am! They have enough to contend with without interference by the superior hospital organization.

[QUESTION 5: *What might have been done with the seminar patient, and what mistakes were made?*]

The next question pertains to Dr. Kvarnes' patient and asks about what was not done and what mistakes were made. Memory does not serve me in that way. I can offer you nothing, but we might go on to the next question which follows it closely.

[QUESTION 6: *Ask Dr. Sullivan about his formulation of the homosexual panic in young male schizophrenics, and the value of a permissive environment, as well as the role of homosexually oriented attendants in handling these patients.*]

This is of great interest to me. Kempf's conception of homosexual panic, like almost everything Kempf has done, is to be taken with the utmost seriousness. Kempf was a splendidly disposed and a great and gifted psychiatrist. As to the theory, Kempf's theory and mine are notably different and our successes and failures have been most strikingly in different areas. I think I have had rather better luck than Kempf with patients who might be said to have had homosexual panic, even if he invented the term. I heard it referred to yesterday as "Kempf's Disease."

In this culture, as doubtless in certain others, many young folk find it necessary, if they can, to dissociate from any access to awareness, certain impulses, covert processes, fantasies, and so on, pertaining to zonal satisfactions. These may be the anal zone, the genital zone, or the oral zone, and sometimes the visual zone. Where dissociations have occurred, the pressure of loneliness and lust combining in the adolescent transformation of personality often leads to failure of this dissociation, and when there is a failure of all dissociation, the consciousness is rather abruptly flooded with extremely unwelcome material. The least that can happen is the eruption of what we call morbid cravings. These cravings represent imperative and horribly unwelcome desires for certain zonal satisfactions. So far as I know they may pertain to any zone of interaction with the environment, but it is not at all strange that in this particular culture, at least, and at the time when lust is the force that destroys the successful dissociation, the zonal needs take on sexual coloring, and that, in the slang, is homosexual craving; at least it can exceedingly easily be led to take that formulation. That failure of dissociation indicates a strong predisposition to a homosexual way of life, is, so far as I am concerned, entirely ungrounded bunk. There is no way of demonstrating any reasonable possibility of that, no way of demonstrating anything about it.

What about the permissive environment? Due to certain idiosyncrasies of personality, I feel at no particular disadvantage in dealing with homosexuals. I have, in fact, due to those circumstances, discovered that homosexuals have one of thirty-two different types of problems. It always carries a great many quotation marks. Some of those thirty-two seem to be entirely resistive to any technique which I have invented. Many of them are quite easily handable. The one thing I can say about homosexuality is that if you very carefully eliminate therefrom the psychopathic personalities, you have people who are at least amenable to a calm discussion of the worries of people who fear they are homosexual. To that extent it is not so much a permissive environment as an educable environment. They do not have loathing or dread or fear of this, or paranoid ideas about the doctor when the doctor tries to tell them what might be done, and certainly they do not suffer from appalling disgust reactions when they see certain performances of patients which often call out such reactions in the most benevolently disposed of the other sort. So that so far as I am concerned, what is probably meant by "homosexually oriented" attendants has been very helpful indeed in building up a hospital organization.

A thing you might not immediately realize is that in this environment, which I finally felt was worthy of being tried, there was extraordinarily little and brief concern with homosexual cravings. That gives, too, another light on a hint I have thrown out already, namely, that there is a pretty close connection between obsessional substitutive processes and schizophrenia. Much of the energy that destroys a good many young schizophrenics, drives them into paranoid maladjustment or hebephrenic dilapidation, arises because something that is really substituted for something else is treated by the environment as appalling, horrible, shameless, what not, instantly to be recovered from if possible. Those of you who have tried, or anyone who has tried to treat obsessionals, have discovered that dealing with obsessional content is as perfectly useless a performance as a psychiatrist can engage in. The same holds for a good deal of schizophrenic content.

I am going on because I will weave something of it in elsewhere.

[QUESTION 7: *What would be the further course of the interview with the seminar patient? So far it had been a subtle and differentiated form of reassurance. Would it go on like that? Did Dr. Sullivan intend to go beyond that and what were the long-range therapeutic objectives, and what about some interpretation?*]

Here is a long question which I believe is one of several bearing on the further course of treatment—on long-range therapeutic objectives, such as later on some interpretation. This last question startles me a good deal because it tells me that in the mind of someone interpretations are something other than what Dr. Kvarnes has been doing, and so I want to talk about that first.

There are interpretations which consist of something like this: What ails you is that this woman has projected an inverted Oedipus reaction in you because she looks like your mother—always, of course, coupled with about forty thousand words to make everything clear. That interpretation, I wish, might die without a trace.

Interpretations are, if they are anything except morbidities in the psychiatrist's lack of acquaintance with what the hell he is trying to do, and a certain lack of appreciation of how to do such things with other people—interpretations are the presentation of hypotheses for further investigation. A very simple way of doing interpretation is by asking questions. "Well, it might be that—" and "I get the impression that perhaps—," etc. If the patient by any chance says "Yes" or "No," that is extraordinarily unsatisfactory, and even very sick people have heard me say somewhat irritably, "This is a question. I don't want you to say yes or no. Discuss it. Good God, it can't be as simple as yes or no. Talk about it." So far as I am concerned, that is an absolutely adequate statement of interpretation. It is presenting an approximate hypothesis for exploration by and with the patient, and if by chance the patient thinks the hypothesis is a good one, the psychiatrist should be warned.

One learns a great deal over the years, and one thing is that a markedly obsessional person is moved to do a great deal with inappropriate hypotheses, so the more interpretation they are offered, the happier everybody is—that is, the more insincerity and less anxiety, the less progress. To a certain extent be warned that that may be the case with schizophrenics. A thoroughly wrong hypothesis heaved at a sick schizophrenic is evidence that he is again misunderstood and of no interest to the psychiatrist, but in any case, the notion that you, from your acquired divinity, can tell a person what is the matter, ought really to be adjourned. What the psychiatrist can do is to help people discover what is the matter, and the more the psychiatrist knows and the more agile a fellow he is, the more he is using what are often called interpretations to build up an understanding of the patient's past life, limitations and ability which will be dependable—that is, which is so probably significantly correct that the patient will have no occasion to doubt that he has that much grasp on himself and living.

For people like me, a questioning way of doing these things works very nicely, but for heaven's sake, disabuse yourself of the idea that you can tell anybody what ails them in a fashion that will be simply helpful to them.

As to the long course of treatment, all that I could say is included in what I have just said. Under some circumstances I can tell you what I think is going to happen in the next two or three weeks of treatment and be right more frequently than pure chance, but for me to attempt to excogitate how things will go more than two or three weeks in advance is something I could not undertake. I have never fancied myself as a therapist. The only particular respect I pay myself is that sometimes I have been able to discover what I have been thinking about and find that my life experiences seem to have supported the idea and that it could be used by others. So far as treatment is concerned, I don't claim to have the word, but I do know that with my work with patients all I am concerned with is that we shall always, if possible, be dealing with something that is significant, troublesome, or disastrous to them, and that their personality will direct a useful course of exploration as long as I am insistent that we must explore usefully. Where we will go, I don't know.

One aspect I ought to underwrite. Pretty often movements of personality, after the therapeutic situation has been established, which is often a matter of months, precipitate severe anxiety, and sometimes indicate to me that they will soon move to a point at which there will be very severe anxiety. That is guessing, but it is a guess so disturbing that I intervene. I don't permit patients to go wherever their personalities move them if I see it is going to precipitate intense anxiety. For that reason, in dealing with some supposed psychoneurotics, and a good many obsessionals and schizoid people, when hints have appeared which indicate to me that if we go very much further we will be in the midst of a lot of schizophrenic content, at those times I have intervened in a discouraging fashion, which, with me, can often be, "Yes, yes, I know, but what about so and so?" Literally cut off the process as if bored, not with the idea that we don't want to deal with it sometime, but that we will be more cautious in our approach. The general theory is that they will present the needs that bring them to psychiatry, but sometimes pressure leads them to present them in a manner disastrous to the situation.

[QUESTION 8: *What do you do if you get stuck?*]

I want to talk about reassurance, but I want to talk about getting stuck, too. I will express about 10 percent of what I have in mind.

The major advantage when one gets stuck in extended psychotherapy is to review where you have been. You often discover that you become unstuck in the process. You get stuck because you have participated in something that came to an absolute block from anxiety or from the prospect of intense anxiety. I can't tell you how to do it, but sometimes you can undo that by reviewing the immediate past and announcing that you see you were barking up the wrong tree, or something of that kind. You withdraw with a humble acceptance of your mistake. I can't tell you how valuable acknowledged mistakes have been in psychotherapy in my past; but in general in all therapy, if the thing bogs down, then it is well to review where you have been. It is sometimes well to review the whole thing anyway in the privacy of your office, and then review it with the patient, because some people have a wonderful faculty of leaving out things that don't suit them. But a succinct review unsticks a thing.

[QUESTION 9: *With schizophrenics would it have gone on pretty much the same, or would you get stuck in your therapy finally if they were unable to accept enough of reassurance?*]

And now this other question about reassurance. I think what you mean by reassurance are the sundry little movements that have been discussed here and that I perhaps have suggested at times with regard to Dr. Kvarnes' establishing his relationship with the patient. Those movements are for the most part addressed to two goals. One, to define and establish the doctor-patient relationship; the other, to define and establish the worth of the patient as a person. That is, not that he is a marvelous person, but that he is enough of a going concern to be very worth the effort that it will take to get well. The reason for the first, which could be called subtle reassurance, could be reduced to certain honorable characteristics: that you have a good doctor who could be some good to you, who could help you to overcome ingredients that every patient brings to you, such as the very widely held notion that a person ought to be ashamed if he needs a psychiatrist—that everybody ought to be able to handle his own mind. Well, to that extent you might say that the patient needs some reassurance about being a patient; the rest of what little he will get said on this point arises from the fact already stated, that you are always moving in the immediate environment of anxiety, that insofar as the person's self-system is intact and functionally effective, it will block any exploration that causes increased anxiety, that it will introduce all sorts of operations to protect the self-esteem of the patient from projected low appraisals in you. One has to play with the self-system to a certain extent to lull it, as it were, to the point that something else can happen. I don't know how many have had this experience but when therapeutic situations are well established, patients will sometimes say—this happens only occasionally—astoundingly revealing statements which in many ways look literally as if they had slipped by, because they are not led up to and not followed up. It is very discreet indeed for a psychiatrist to realize that this is the beginning of the manifestation of a very powerful part of the patient to get to mental health, and not clumsily to leap on this fortunate accident, but under no circumstances ever to forget that it occurred. When things are slipped by the self-process that way, they are pure gravy, but cannot be dealt with then. You have got some valid and important information but it is intolerable to him in the existing situation. We play with the self-system to a certain extent to literally remove an enemy from our way. Sometimes these accidents happen. With young psychiatrists, they like to deal with immediate things, under which circumstances you are bound to have a mess and to get nowhere. Sometimes you have the whole thing bitterly denied, wiped out, and skillfully avoided.

The apprehensions we all have to discover in the course of becoming a person are never particularly on the side of the therapist so that a good deal of what you seem to feel can well be called reassurance is calculated to facilitate the patient's personality in getting important material across to me, and the only way I can facilitate that, except by being alert, is by skill in avoiding unnecessary anxiety and, as it were, dissociating myself from the most traditional aspects of self-function. If a patient says to me, "Well, you must think I am terrible" and I don't feel this is just hysterical drama, but really means something, I am apt to say, quite passively, "About what?" as if I had not heard anything about such a notion. Quite frequently, just because my reaction has seemed so astonished and annoyed, they tell me, and to that extent I have gotten somewhere in getting the self-system out of my way. That is, I am no longer a suitable target to hang that on, and to that extent I expect that some material will begin to come forward in that area.

[QUESTION 10: *What can you do with obsessives?*]

Believe it or not, you can improve their living very considerably. It is rather lamentably a slow process, but not seven or eight years as it recently was in some areas.

About obsessives, I think I would advise any younger therapist to try to isolate a real problem, which would scarcely be told you, by the way, and try to keep at that, because obsessive people are past masters at substitutive processes, and this makes it pretty hard.

A classic example: A patient comes to me because she is having a great deal of trouble with her mother. We worked eight and a half or nine months, during which time we cleared up a practically fatal difficulty with her husband, whereupon she went elsewhere to get the difficulty with her mother cleared up, with high mutual regard of herself and me. I thought a great deal of the patient. She presented a problem. It was a very real problem. But it was not the killing problem, which gradually appeared because we kept at work, because we did not get lost in everything as we went along.

Another patient came to me because of a classic obsessive complaint. She got into difficulty with another obsessive in the place where she worked and she wanted her technique improved. In a year and a half, I think, we shed a good deal of light on the extreme struggle over who could destroy whom between this patient and a third obsessive, with whom she lived. The trouble in the office proved to be just a substitutive one, not of overwhelming importance in the life situation.

> [QUESTION 11: *What does Dr. Sullivan think of his role, specifically with the patient, related to that question about subtle reassurance? What he gets to be if that reassurance holds any weight? He has not had anything to say about his relationship to the patient except once or twice in answer to questions which the patient might put to him, or statements the patient might make concerning him.*]

This question is practically answered in the psychiatric interview course. I have come to define my role as that of expert with client. Nothing more and nothing less, but to be expert in psychiatry. I have to handle the patient in a fashion that works. It is nothing that I will fight about but I insist that this is my role. Because I set up this role for myself, I have been able to avoid two of the great evils that complicate psychotherapy. I learned to avoid the first by a ghastly disaster, and that is, do not permit anybody to develop transcendental expectations of you. Another patient is in a state hospital because I permitted that boy to develop transcendental dependency. All I have to offer is skill, and as the years roll over me I find it is best to offer just that. That does not necessitate rebuffs or anything. The relationship of psychiatrist to patient is that of expert to client. The expert has continuously to act like an expert. I can't take time out and act like a damn fool. I can't be lover and friend and whatnot, unless I expect to devote the rest of my life to that patient, and even that does not work out well.

Because of increasing firmness in holding to that type of relationship, the solution of the transference, resolution of the transference, which is so important in certain psychotherapeutic problems, has, I think, in my case, usually preceded the appearance of the transference. Just as when the gay and wealthy woman patient gallops in and announces, after two or three interviews, that she is madly in love with me, she hears me muttering in my corner, "You may find it a little difficult in my case, baby." We have obsessional enough processes and if you do try to be the good father or mother or some damn thing, it is welcome, and I have no doubt when you get bored with it, or can't get the patient to pay for it, then it needs some attention, but if you go to a lawyer to have some business handled, Christ, he doesn't have to resolve the transference at the end of the transaction. If you go to have your watch repaired, you don't have to fall in love with the watchmaker. People come to me to have difficulties in living untangled—that is what I do. Sure they are interested. Who the hell is not, and I think well of them, but no—no, not that! I am glad to have a question about my role. It is, insofar as I know, a person who keeps track of what he is supposed to be doing, and it is not getting involved in anything except transient disorders which require being dealt with, and I toss out another hint which might be relevant to homosexual panic. Not uncommonly with schizophrenics, with extreme chagrin they announce some desire for genital intimacy with my person, to which it is traditional that I say, "I know I would enjoy it, but it would gum up the work terribly and the work is more important." They sometimes try to pursue it under pressure, but my pose is unalterable. "Sure, I think zonal pleasures are all right, but I am selling expert service and not having a good time." It works if you get used to it. I may add that I go to considerable trouble to let them know that I would have no objection at all except that it would interfere with the work, and I mean it, what the hell!

[QUESTION 12: *What about the idea that it is sometimes valuable to break through the useless defenses that a person puts up and push him into a frank psychosis? Is that ever advisable?*]

That is a hell of a good question. It is a question I have not considered seriously for years. It has a corollary you hear in mental hospital circles, that the patient will be worse before he is better, and a great many of them become much worse, and some of them better. I have actually quite often ventured to smash security operations, leaving the patient in a pretty damned grave condition for a little while. I am very happy to say I have not done that intentionally in any case where I was not able to part with them at the end of the session with them feeling distinctly relieved at the venture. That tells the whole story. If you are sure you can get away with the thing, then—before you have to go away or before the patient can get away—then, if you are sure enough of what you are doing, why not? We are attempting to treat, and if you can smash the self-system process and get something done, the patient feels fine. They may think you are a little tough, but that doesn't do any harm. In general I am scared to death when other people plan these things. It is not that I have so much certainty about myself, but I have less certainty about others. There are times when the picture that you get shows that the patient will progress into deeper psychosis, and they do that very thing, and I wish we could get to the point that we did not let people suffer psychoses very long, but we haven't.

When it comes to clinical judgment of "Is his defense useless?" I tell you you have got to know a good deal about the patient because the mere fact that such a defense would seem useless to you is anything but information about the patient. If I say yes, I think it is sometimes valuable, I must add, but always a matter of very, very serious clinical judicial processes before it is carried out.

[QUESTION 13: *At one time Dr. Sullivan referred to the guilt feelings of masturbation, and having never, myself, been subject to any guilt over masturbation, I would like to know what the guilt is, from where it arises, and what some of the reactions of the patient are to this.*]

I simply have to discharge my feeling of good cheer that someone of the colleagues has had no problem about masturbation. The only justifiable problem that I have ever encountered about masturbation is that insofar as lust is discharged by oneself, one of the strong but troublesome drives to relate to others is thereby discharged, and therefore, insofar as lust is useful in bringing about the evolution of adequate interpersonal relationships, the problem is increased. But the guilt about masturbation comes from the very early moral training, just as all guilt comes from early training. That training causes the person to feel that insofar as they "pull the pud" they are unworthy of man's estate, or are disbarring themselves from reward in the hereafter, whether it be a happy marriage, a sane old age, or the heavens of the Christians. The trick is that these self-system processes—that is, afflicting of oneself because one is ruining the hereafter or acting like a child—are not capable of suppressing lust. Under the circumstances they simply add a fantastic superstructure of self-depreciatory, obsessional ruminations to a personality already heavily freighted otherwise. Otherwise, why does masturbation go on being a great problem? This superstructure practically guarantees that it will because the self-system is primarily organized for skill in avoiding anxiety. When ingredients become mixed in about how unworthy one is, naturally one is in a bad way.

I will repeat, I am not trying to be facetious, but a vast number of people in their early training have been taught to feel haywire about their genitals, and vast numbers of people have been trained later to feel pretty haywire about genital relationships with others, and so to a psychiatrist who never had any guilt, it would really be worthwhile to have a series of searching discussions with suitable ones of his colleagues who have, because it is a problem that will appear again and again in psychotherapy, and it is never helpful to a patient to discover that his psychiatrist, his expert, is utterly unacquainted with an aspect of life that is hell to the patient.

[QUESTION 14: *It might be interesting to formulate some question about constitutional and cultural factors in the development of schizophrenia.*]

Constitutional and cultural factors in the development of schizophrenia. To that I subscribe one hundred percent, but it has been a hard week. I feel really utterly incapable of doing anything with it. About constitution: if you are really interested in constitution, I will tell you I had in the Sheppard material only one male patient who was obviously of Kretschmer's pyknic build, but of the patients I had there was a remarkable distribution away from the ectomorph according to Sheldon's classification.

I, myself, more as a wisecrack, have at times said I believe a strikingly linear, that would be ectomorphic, tendency toward rather long bones seems to me quite possibly to be based on early vigorous thyroid activity. The curious relationship of thyroid function and severe anxiety suggestions that perhaps a study of unwanted children would show them to have a rather high metabolic rate early in life and the epiphyses functioned vigorously. This comes so near being idle thought that I don't want you to take it very seriously.

Cultural factors have an enormous amount to do with the schizophrenic way of life. Certain disastrous courses of development, which means incorporating culture into personality, could happen to people of certain constitutional peculiarities without their developing severe obsessive or schizophrenic phenomena. I would not know, but I have little difficulty in understanding the incidence of schizophrenia in some patients who still were accessible for study, and it is quite adequately accounted for by their experience and the stress of the situation into which they move, without reference to a factor of peculiar vulnerability.

[QUESTION 15: *Fundamentally, what is a psychotic reaction?*]

For many years I have written about mental disorders, mild and severe, and the effort there has been to suggest that degree was pretty important. From the standpoint of interpersonal relationships as the subject matter of psychiatry, the discrimination of what is psychotic would come pretty near from where it does —namely, that which other people think is psychotic. In intensive psychotherapy, one meets—and hears and even sees—with surprising frequency, behavior which is perfectly of a piece with some of the psychotic pictures. The point is, it is, we hope, always transient. Psychoses have broken out in intensive psychotherapy. Psychotic pictures, those things that others call "psychoses," seem to include patterns and processes that are not particularly novel—nothing new, nothing out of ordinary human developmental experience. But the bitter attempts to reach goals into which these processes are fitted are often so strikingly impractical in the world of people, that it is thoroughly unsafe [to continue the attempts]. The unsafest thing is for the patient to go on talking about them. Because I don't know how many people have in this way hurt their possible recovery from schizophrenia—a recovery that consists of thinking the environment is not against you but keeping your mouth shut because they just don't understand. In the psychotic episode you go on talking and get a lot of people convinced you are nuts. So separating from others may actually be very helpful to the psychotic by cutting off his opportunity to produce a record. Quite a number of people fail to recover because they have such a record to live down.

I would say this—that a psychotic episode is the appearance of a pattern of living which is so hard on the environment and so impractical in terms of achieving any desirable goal that one is no longer safely at large. We do recognize certain of these patterns, give them special names, but what we often overlook is the fact that essential parts of these patterns are transient episodes in psychotherapy of some people, and in the living of everyone; the difference between nightmares and certain catatonic situations is negligible, and actually in some people we see literally a working diagram of what it would be like to be schizophrenic when a person wakes from a nightmare and is unable to compel reality to take place. You wake up and the bureau keeps on being some troublesome part of the dream and you have to get up and walk around before you can get it to become the bureau again. That is a neat instance of what it is like to be catatonic. That might be a useful hint to you—the fact that the patient is convinced that you are a terrible enemy might simultaneously overlay quite clearly

that it is not so, that you are a fairly well-intentioned and sometimes useful doctor—which is the same as in the nightmare. You
know the bureau is there but the trouble is it just won't be a
bureau. It is not that you think the bureau is a dragon, but have a
schizophrenic state of mind for the moment.

Comment on Fifth Session,
Twenty-five Years Later, April, 1972 *

RYCKOFF: This completes the whole business, the patient has
left the hospital?
KVARNES: Yes.
RYCKOFF: And the seminar continued?
KVARNES: No.
RYCKOFF: Let's make a prediction as to what has happened to
the patient. I somehow felt this guy was headed for recovery,
even with some of the bad things that may have been happening
to him around that time.
KVARNES: What do you think happened to him?
RYCKOFF: I think he got stuck in some other kind of therapy in
another hospital, that the father would have pressured for some
kind of results. When I said I would expect him to recover, I
think that would be in spite of the somewhat destructive interaction that was going on between him and the family—I felt, for
example, that this boy had an unfortunate capacity to appear to
be sinking down into fearfulness, passivity, helplessness, in such a
way as to put the father on, as to make the father anxious.
KVARNES: Make the father feel a goddamn fool.
RYCKOFF: Make the father feel impotent himself, and part of
the abruptness of this was this kind of interaction between the
boy being sick and helpless and fearful and the father getting
edgy because of his own concern and helplessness and having to
move into action. I think that would have characterized the period after leaving you, whether the father got foolish enough
to push him into some other kind of bad therapy or not.
JACOBSON: I see a similar kind of thing but I question the recovery. The kind of recovery I can see is the guy coming to
live at home and having some undemanding job and living an

* John Dillingham was not present during the first part of this meeting.

isolated life, protected by the father, who thinks, "You are a very passive guy and we will take care of you."

RYCKOFF: Well, I think that's possible. By recovery I don't necessarily mean full recovery, moving right ahead with his life.

KVARNES: I can tell you what my unguided, gratuitous fantasy has been about this guy all the way along. I have gone on the assumption that he went back to law school, finished law school, and is now practicing law quite successfully——

RYCKOFF: Member of the state legislature maybe?

KVARNES: Two things come into this. One, I was very busy denying the severity of his illness; he was complaining about that. I couldn't really deal with the full impact of schizophrenia at the time anyway. And this is just part of that denial. The other thing is that I think that there was, and I did respond to, a lot of strength in this guy. As we assemble the story it is hardly the story of a helpless critter.

RYCKOFF: That's what I thought. I also think that it is hard to overestimate the effect of these wartime experiences on someone who is sensitive and shaky anyway. And I think that he had never resolved them. When he got into the hospital—it was about three years or so after those experiences?

KVARNES: It was 1946.

RYCKOFF: It may have been within a year. I remember at St. E's fellows like that would come in by the score. They would be real sick for a number of months—three, six, maybe as long as a year maximum, and they would really pull themselves together and go on out, getting no therapy at all there, but they would essentially make a good recovery. They would get all the panic out of themselves somehow and pull together.

KVARNES: I would guess that if this kid was able to negotiate the hospital stuff——

RYCKOFF: Get by the treatment if he could, he'd recover——

KVARNES: If he didn't get too much shock or that kind of stuff and made enough of a recovery to get outside and get away from the family, he'll have made it, and if there was still a total entanglement with the family, I suspect he got sick and stayed sick.

RYCKOFF: In this kind of case the family is both a source of pathology and also a strength. He comes from people who have some resources, both parents, and he's not the kind of patient who has a psychotic episode and really has nothing outside to sustain him.

KVARNES: Another way of saying that I suppose, too, is to talk about people recovering when they got back to their pre-illness state of health. That would fit this guy. He did have some state of health prior to the illness. I have some patients who are offended by that kind of idea because they never had any health to start with.

JACOBSON: He was at Sheppard for about six months?

KVARNES: Yes.

RYCKOFF: He was young enough so I wondered whether he might really still be working out essentially adolescent turmoil and problems.

JACOBSON: That's a possibility.

RYCKOFF: Pretty scary form—a schizophrenic form.

KVARNES: It does sound as if the crisis that he was trying to negotiate was the heterosexual behavior crisis that he really wasn't prepared for—that that activated the homosexual concerns and panics. But he doesn't impress me as a homosexually oriented kind of person, so that it's more panic about the heterosexual than it is attraction to the homosexual. And there were enough successes for him to go on so that time may have helped him to negotiate that.

RYCKOFF: If you can get patients unhooked from the expectation of success, say, aspect of sexuality—from the idea that they are going to have to succeed—then it is possible. Part of the recovery process is an increased tolerance for his own inadequacy or his own uncertainty about the whole business. I think nowadays, in this interval of twenty-five years or so, there is more tolerance for that. You don't have to be sharply successful in the sexual business.

JACOBSON: Of course Sullivan makes that point in therapy too, over and over again, of staying away from this central life-and-death issue for him, building up the self-esteem in other areas so that that can be managed.

KVARNES: There are a couple of interesting things in here, I thought. What Sullivan does is to provide a treatment situation of an expert-client relationship. He says, "I have come to define my role as that of expert with client. Nothing more and nothing less, but to be expert in psychiatry." And further,

I have to handle the patient in a fashion that works. It is nothing that I will fight about but I insist that this is my role. Because I set up this role for myself, I have been able to avoid two of the great evils that complicate psychotherapy. I learned to avoid the first by a ghastly disaster, and that is, do not permit anybody to develop transcendental expectations of you. . . . All I have to offer is skill, and as the years roll over me I find it is best to offer just that. That does not necessitate rebuffs or anything. The relationship of psychiatrist to patient is that of expert to client. The expert has continuously to act like an expert. I can't take time out and act like a damn fool. I can't be lover and friend and whatnot, unless I expect to devote the rest of my life to that patient, and even that does not work out well.

Because of increasing firmness in holding to that type of relationship, the solution of the transference, resolution of the transference, which is so important in certain psychotherapeutic problems, has, I think, in my case, usually preceded the appearance of the transference.

RYCKOFF: The resolution of it precedes the appearance of it?

KVARNES: By which he means that some therapists, instead of allowing the transference relationship to develop, analyze it immediately upon its appearance and so it never develops in the sense of a transference neurosis.

RYCKOFF: And he's advocating that?

KVARNES: He's saying in effect that the way he functions is to deal with the patient in such a fashion that the full transference never develops. Then he goes on, "Just as when the gay and wealthy woman patient gallops in and announces, after two or three interviews, that she is madly in love with me, she hears me muttering in my corner, 'You may find it a little difficult in my case, baby.' "

RYCKOFF: Don't know what the hell that says.

JACOBSON: I don't know what the hell that says either.

RYCKOFF: He knows he's not lovable, among other things.

JACOBSON: What he's referring to is the earlier spot that links up with that, "Due to certain idiosyncrasies of personality, I feel at no particular disadvantage in dealing with homosexuals. I have, in fact, due to those circumstances, discovered that homosexuals have one of thirty-two different types of problems." Now what the hell is he saying there? What are the idiosyncrasies of personality he is talking about?

KVARNES: The mythology about Sullivan has something to do with being a homosexual, functioning as one, or something like that. The data are awfully sparse. I don't know of any instances of acknowledged homosexual relationships.

RYCKOFF: I think that no one knows, but it does seem more like a myth, since you would assume there would be some evidence.

I think that what he is alluding to there is the fact that he found himself one of the few people who was genuinely at home in this area—that is, he was not put off by homosexuality. He could stay with it and share the experience of what homosexual existence was like, I think to a greater extent than many other people at that time. Or even now, for that matter—it's not easy to stay with that kind of thing. I think he was sort of bragging about that.

JACOBSON: Bragging about it in that kind of way would tend to develop the myth.

RYCKOFF: One of the phenomena about Sullivan is that despite this vague myth, no one really wants to know, and no one pushes the point.

KVARNES: But actually I think that in the revival of interest in Sullivan which I certainly experience—the William Alanson White group in New York is busy with it and something is going on here in Washington—there has been a time interval and a lot of this has sort of settled down and become sort of "so what" data.

RYCKOFF: I agree with you, that kind of stuff is not going to be important about Sullivan.

KVARNES: But that is the kind of question that gets asked, "Was Sullivan a homosexual?"

JACOBSON: And was he schizophrenic?

KVARNES: And was he an alcoholic? I'm afraid what a lot of people do with that process of applying a disparaging label is that they then unfortunately discount the person and his work—a lot of this type of discounting of Freud occurred when the evidence of his own psychoneurosis came into the picture in the various biographies.

RYCKOFF: But that's why that kind of question is asked; it's easy to discount the person's ideas when you say somebody is homosexual, schizophrenic, alcoholic.

JACOBSON: There is the other side of that, though, which is trying to understand what it takes to be able to understand other people—you have to be one to know one.

RYCKOFF: That's another myth about Sullivan. That he could understand the sick ones because of his proximity to schizophrenia.

KVARNES: Let me take a shot at these "labels." That Sullivan had strong schizoid and obsessional features in his personality I don't think anyone would dispute. As far as I can determine, there was no schizophrenic break requiring hospitalization or treatment in his adolescence. His history from medical school on is well documented. That's all I can say about the myth of "Sullivan's schizophrenia." Concerning the homosexual label, it is true that Sullivan never married nor apparently could he tolerate being around the hysterical type of woman. As I said, I know of no evidence of homosexuality as practiced by Sullivan. I can't help wondering whether his formulation of how the male arrives at adolescence emotionally unprepared to assume the male role in an intimate relationship with a woman * didn't pertain to Sullivan himself. As far as the disparagement about "alcoholic" goes, as I understood and remember it, Sullivan had had a couple of coronary accidents, which probably accounted for his taking small drinks of brandy throughout the day in his later years. In all the gossip I never heard one account of Sullivan's being drunk. So I think this unconventional pattern of nipping on the brandy got incorporated in some people's need to cut him down. Goodness knows, he was irascible and cutting enough to have hurt a number of his colleagues' feelings.

JACOBSON: Let me try a different kind of thought. One of the things we haven't talked about very much is what influence this had on you in treating that case, because Sullivan says very little directly about what you are doing or ought to do. In the beginning he says, start getting more information, but except for complimenting you frequently, reassuring you often, there isn't any interaction between you and him about the therapy itself.

KVARNES: No, but he says something about using the "third-person" method of communicating with a schizophrenic, and I had already done a little of that and his comments solidified that process and I went on using it.

JACOBSON: That's the kind of thing I mean.

KVARNES: Also, the very valuable business about apologizing for genuine mistakes. Around the time of the seminar I said something to a patient about putting her in sleep treatment—what I thought was a quite benevolent proposition. The idea was that we were going to try to get her to regress to an infantile state in the sleep treatment, then gradually bring her back out through

---

* See Case Seminar III, pp. 118-120.

the experience of "good mothering"—i.e., to have her needs for affection amply met by the nurses and therapists. When I told her about the sleep treatment she went into an absolute panic and attacked me violently. I didn't see it coming. I couldn't figure out what I had done, and then this seminar helped me to recognize what I had done. I had really made a severe attack on her security and she was afraid that she was going to get into some kind of assaultive treatment again like the shock treatment. And she reacted as she had to the shock treatment. I should have known that. I went back to her and told her that I had made a terrible mistake and that I had thought about what it meant to her. She wasn't communicative, but she heard me; the tension subsided and she consented to go ahead with the experiment. I couldn't hold to the process, however, as it gradually got clear to me that I was trying to "mother" the patient and I wasn't at all up to the requirements. I could document in many ways the origins of all kinds of orientations I have from my work with Sullivan.

JACOBSON: I can see why, because you have mentioned any number of times something you learned about what an interpretation is. It is in here where Sullivan says in effect, you guys are talking about interpretation as if what Dr. Kvarnes has been doing is not interpretation. He says, "Interpretations are the presentation of hypotheses for further investigation." And I've heard you say that more than once.

KVARNES: At that point I had the notion that as the youngest "superior" psychiatrist I was going to have to come on with all sorts of phenomenal formulations, and God, that was a very powerful support that Sullivan gave us at that juncture, for we were all puzzling about our roles as psychoanalytically oriented psychotherapists.

RYCKOFF: Wasn't that part of the confusion that came with psychoanalysis, that interpretation had to do with finding something unconscious or buried?

KVARNES: The utilization of such concepts as penis envy and Oedipus complex.

RYCKOFF: That's where Sullivan is so beautiful here. He positions himself, I think, in terms of his interpersonal theory, but it's also squarely in ego psychology. The whole thrust is that we've got to get this sick guy, this disturbed, frightened, anxious, panicky guy back into the realm where he feels that he's understandable to himself and others—that he's back in the realm of the comprehensible, and everything you do has to help move him in that direction, reassure him that it's possible. The so-called analytic interpretation does the opposite to people like this. Make a remark about penis envy, you increase his load of anxiety a hundredfold. I think there is a great deal in this. I'm tremendously impressed even with the little details, the real feeling Sullivan has for how you do this, how much he's aware of what the patient may be aware of, how alarmed he is inside, how much he takes into account, how he gives these little examples of how he frames the question or a comment he talks about, detouring any anxiety-provoking stuff. That's a kind of teaching that I think is very much needed.

JACOBSON: A kind of skill hard to come by.*

KVARNES: I find a lot of memories come back with this. For example, I remembered Sullivan's remarks that when you get into a jam with a schizophrenic patient and really don't know where the hell you are, you can go to the bathroom. Excuse yourself— he doesn't have to know why you are doing it. Step out of the picture a little bit and you get away from it. That's a very useful device, and a lot of scared therapists would sit glued to their chairs, trying to figure out how the hell to last until the hour is over.

JACOBSON: That is just another reflection of one of the themes in Sullivan that is so damned appealing, and that is the acceptance, the charitability, toward one's self, and his weaknesses and humanity and common sense.

RYCKOFF: I think you are talking about one of the key parts of Sullivan's genius; I think he had a clarity of vision about these things, a capacity for simplicity, that is really quite striking. When you think of this way of handling a schizophrenic as contrasted to the analytically oriented school that's all involved in obscure matters of transference, of talking the schizophrenic's language and so on—Sullivan sees in this a mixed-up human being who needs to be reclaimed into the world of comprehensibility where things become understandable and to get out of the terror he is in. That seems to me to be such a nice approach, an approach that's becoming much more common. He has a particular talent for doing that. I would like to be able to specify what the ele-

* John Dillingham arrived at the meeting at approximately this point.

ments are in his viewpoint that make it both so lucid and so simple and so do-able. Even Kvarnes got to be doing it in the course of this case.

KVARNES: I think one aspect that shows up in this work is his ability to make insightful observations about himself in these somewhat recondite or usually untalked-about things, and then to generalize from that on the simple presumption that this is a human experience. This is what you guys [Dillingham and the Metropolitan Mental Health Skills Center] call the "use of self" in the helping process. That's how Sullivan understood the schizo-prenic phenomenon.

There is a sentence in here I want to just call your attention to, I'm sure you all saw it. He's talking about how he would handle the patient being transferred to another hospital. Says:

Try to accomplish that on the basis of knowledge and esteem for other people. What I have actually often done—perhaps partly because in the old days the convenient thing to save money was to transfer patients from Sheppard to St. Elizabeths . . . —is to say that I would like to sort of pass on some of the profits from our work, that the patient might not be perfectly clear on, and that I would look in in a day or so and talk with his physician if that suited him, the patient before me. I let him fizz awhile because I have to let people talk to get things out of the way, but I am preparing for my next step, that I suppose he feels pretty apprehensive of strangers. . . .

That's a wonderful little statement said in a somewhat whimsical way—why you have to let people talk to get things out of the way.

DILLINGHAM: Also, again what you were saying, the humanness of his situation, that he does have an agenda and it's all right for him to have it; he doesn't give in to the tyranny of the patient or the process—lying in wait, as it were.

KVARNES: One other application of that, Stan. Is it possible that this process could be studied in the education of kids? Because I have a hunch that that's exactly what could be done to get kids to pay attention to their work—that is, get this other stuff out of the way before you go on presuming that you can teach them. You've got to give them some time to let that out.

JACOBSON: Of course, and that's Jones's * notion about dealing with anxiety-provoking material, that you deal with the anxiety

* Richard M. Jones, *Fantasy and Feeling in Education* (New York: Harper & Row, 1968).

in order to get the debris out of the way before going on. You don't attempt to either repress it or eliminate what might be anxiety-producing; it has its values.

KVARNES: Far more often what happens is that the attempt is made to repress it, to force the teaching onto the unready mind. Then when it doesn't happen, the kid is "lazy," or "he doesn't pay attention," or he's "careless," or God knows what other insinuation is made about his learning. And his self-esteem drops another fourteen inches. That simple phenomenon is not understood by ninety percent of teachers.

DILLINGHAM: What happens is what we see in this patient's childhood—very early he learns an elaborate kind of pretense of being attentive and so forth, always having the feeling that he never has read anything; he really feels like a poseur.

KVARNES: Yes, that's one of the devices a kid puts on—the demeanor of a student.

DILLINGHAM: I noticed one of Sullivan's references in another place to peers—Negro fieldhands—not human enough to bother. Was that sarcastic, or did he feel that way?

KVARNES: No, no. I think what he is saying there is that that particular patient was so divorced from intimacy that he could only deal with that kind of stereotyped relationship; in the South of that time there was enough stereotyping so that Negro fieldhands could be dismissed as not quite human, and there was no threat of genuine intimacy for this schizophrenic in that situation. That's not an expression of Sullivan's feelings, I'm sure.

DILLINGHAM: I couldn't tell—it sounded very uncharacteristic—but there was that whole earlier section about the whorehouse in Panama and the probable impact of sexual relations with a black whore.

KVARNES: Well, that was twenty-five years ago, and for a schizoid guy to cross the color line at the same time that he was venturing into sexual experiences could overload him.

I'd like to go back to Sullivan's notion about how the transference works in his kind of treatment, as compared to, say, treatment approaches that try to bring out the child in the patient during the treatment, and in the transference relationship. What Sullivan says in here would discourage that kind of thing.

RYCKOFF: I think Sullivan would treat it as something to be avoided, as pathological.

KVARNES: And that's a core question, I think, in the whole field of psychotherapy.

JACOBSON: Let me see if I understand this. Do you get out of what Sullivan says something to the effect that he would interpret the transference as he sees it developing?

KVARNES: Or he would move in such a fashion as not to encourage the development of the transference distortion. He would try to put it in a here-and-now relationship between doctor and patient.

RYCKOFF: He's simply being consistent, if you mean by transference something that's distorted. If he can anticipate a distortion, can sense it, he obviously will try to move in such a way as to correct that, to clarify from the beginning. He doesn't believe in getting himself immersed in the serious distortions of the schizophrenic who has a wall around him. He tries to set up a frame of reference which is going to get the schizophrenic out of this world of distortion and panic and into his world. Seems to me that the notion of transference is that you do let something pathological develop in order to see what it is, and once it's become established you then deal with it or you interpret it.

KVARNES: One of the reasons for the "neutral" therapist, the "neutral" analyst, is that if you don't make a lot of interpretations, don't make a lot of correctional statements, the transference distortion develops, and you get a full-grown transference representation of the therapist. Then he can start to resolve that by distinguishing who he is from what the patient thinks he is.

RYCKOFF: This point always fascinates me, because in some ways it is very much like the stimulus deprivation experiments. What's called transference is the response of the individual to an empty situation, to a nonperson who's sitting there. The question in my mind is, how do you know that that's pathology? Maybe it's a desperate attempt to inject something into a situation that appears threateningly empty. And so my notion of transference is kind of modified. I feel that in order to clearly delineate what's distorted in the patient's attitude toward you, you do have to give him guidelines—you have to establish some kind of reassuring actuality within certain limits. So that all I am saying is something like this: If you assume, as classical analysis does, that everything is transference—patient walks into your room and anything he says is interpreted as transference—I regard that as a realm of insanity. The patient says, "I like your picture," or, "The room is too hot"—you immediately begin to see that as his transference distortion. If you react to everything he says in those terms, I think you have created an insane situation. If you go through some process of establishing a reasonably realistic contact with the patient, and then within that, distortion comes in—he brings in all kinds of other stuff from way out in left field—then I think you are on sounder ground. I think that delineates it as transference. Do you get my point?

JACOBSON: That I don't understand, because, for example, if the guy comes in and says the room is too hot, it *is* transference. I mean, the room may be objectively too hot, but his manner of dealing with a too hot room carries with it something that's stylistically characteristic of him.

KVARNES: Not the same thing as transference; I don't think so.

RYCKOFF: All aspects of his thought then would be considered transference, everything would be transference.

JACOBSON: Freudians wouldn't argue with that.

RYCKOFF: That's what I am saying; that's a kind of nutty idea. Because if everything is transference, then nothing is transference.

JACOBSON: But Freudians would say that everything is over-determined, that there is a transference element in it.

RYCKOFF: How do you distinguish a transference from a non-transference element? How do you set up a situation so that that distinction comes out?

JACOBSON: But to go back to the case itself—it's not a dramatic case in which a hell of a lot happens. It ends as Sullivan says all schizophrenic cases end—either with death or pneumonia or parents taking them out of the hospital.

KVARNES: Well, like a lot of human behavior, it sort of just peters out.

DILLINGHAM: Still, I think the seminar is fascinating, but its fascination is increased in geometrical proportions by your sitting here telling us what effect it had on other people and why everybody was so quiet and whether Sullivan was being sarcastic or gentle when he said this kind of thing—that beautiful line toward the end when they said, "What kind of mistakes did Kvarnes make?" and he said, "My memory doesn't work that way." What comes through very clearly in what, as you say, is not a very exciting case is that you have a great teacher working.

KVARNES: One of the things that impresses me is the demonstration of how Sullivan could take a kind of scared, vague comment and do something to strengthen a weak signal, saying, "What I hear you saying, the point you are making, is an important one," even if the student isn't altogether clear about the point he is making. That is a damned useful technique in teaching and in therapy.

JACOBSON: He also uses such occasions to tell you something about schizophrenic process and the whole communication process.

KVARNES: Some of his contributions were very long passages to listen to, yet I was absorbed from the very beginning to the end of the things because every so often Sullivan said something that recaptured my attention, either by a vivid word—like "loathsome"—which makes you think, or by a clause that you have to pay attention to our you'll lose the thread or a particular insight. He is very good at that. If you read it aloud you can get a better sense of it.

DILLINGHAM: His technique of using the aside you can't get unless you are listening.

KVARNES: Why don't you read something aloud, Irv?

RYCKOFF: When he asked the test question, "What do you do when some disastrous intervention like this occurs?" everybody gave some kind of an answer—sympathize with the patient, cuss the parents out, one thing and another. Then Sullivan began to speak. [Ryckoff reads passage in which Sullivan first comments on setting an example of desperation and rage so that the patient can feel free to become furious at being shoved around, and then speaks of conferring with doctors at the patient's new hospital.]

RYCKOFF: In referring to talking to the patient's physician at the new hospital, he excuses himself with the patient, by implying that he is not going to tell the doctor what the patient is able to tell the doctor himself, but some things that the patient himself hasn't quite noticed. And throughout he's acting, he makes it spontaneous while being careful and rehearsed. He's got all these ideas and gimmicks lined up, how he is going to handle it.

JACOBSON: What do you make of the substance of that business? From my experience with institutions, my feeling is that it's risky to give the patient so much reassurance about continuity because there's a good chance there isn't going to be any.

KVARNES: Can you do what he says he can do—do you know "a thousand psychiatrists"?

JACOBSON: Even if I did, so what? Even in the best of circumstances it is difficult.

RYCKOFF: You mean even Sullivan couldn't do it?

JACOBSON: That's right.

RYCKOFF: That is right, he may know doctor so and so at St. Elizabeths and put in a word about his patient, but neither Sullivan nor anyone else could predict what kind of experience his patient would have. When he gets on a ward with different patients, nurses, you don't know what happens.

KVARNES: I really don't think that is what he is concerned about.

JACOBSON: But if the reassurance he is giving the patient doesn't work, as it is likely not to, doesn't that make the patient feel more hopeless?

KVARNES: Your argument answers itself. That is, if he provides a bridge that makes a patient enter the hospital with a somewhat more accepting attitude, it makes it possible for things to happen. And second, if it goes bad, it would have gone bad anyway; he could be blamed, but he would be blamed anyway, some way or other.

DILLINGHAM: I think there is a third issue there, that one of the goals he is setting, which he sets very early in that discourse, is that the patient should somehow have a sense of what was accomplished at Sheppard. This gives him strength that he wouldn't have if he went through the thing completely disorganized. He can capitalize on it, he can say, I got that far with somebody—regardless of the kind of help he gets in the next situation.

KVARNES: There's a message in there that says, "I want you to understand that I regard what we did as serious work."

RYCKOFF: Another aspect of it that I heard was reassurance on a very general level, in spite of the fact that he makes it personal by saying, "I know so and so," and "You are in good hands." He is saying to the patient: *"You and I were able to make sense of the situation here. You are going to another hospital. People over there are sane people too. It is possible to make sense with them."* If you read it as a personal guarantee, of course he is way off base. But if you read it as a general statement that any other hospital is also run by people who are not totally out of their minds, there is a possibility that you can continue this kind of process that makes sense.

JACOBSON: Which leads to the other part I was thinking of, that this puts a lot of faith in the patient.

DILLINGHAM: I think it is interesting to think in retrospect about expressions about Springhill. He obviously didn't think a god-damned thing could happen there. Sullivan either is a hypocrite or else he does believe this whole other level of reassurance.

JACOBSON: That's an interesting question. If he heard of a patient who was going back to Springhill and going to get shock treatment, what would he say?

KVARNES: But he is saying, I know a couple of people there and I will go talk to them. If you do that you are at least setting up some hope that you are going to avert disaster. I think we have proved the point. Did you sense anything different as you read it, Irv? Fact is, you didn't read it like Sullivan would have said it; I heard the difference.

RYCKOFF: The voice lends the appropriate weight to the clauses. Maybe this is what makes it a little difficult to read. In many of the earlier passages, he really follows two or three different tracks simultaneously. One is that very often he seems to be talking about the necessity of getting facts, of getting history. But the next thing I feel is that he isn't doing that, that he is using that only as a way of establishing the important thing, which is a sense of communication and understanding with the patient. He doesn't give a goddamn about who said what and where. Then, the third thing he is mixing in—and I think he does it character-istically—is that he is teaching, he is conscious of the teaching technique, he is trying to get something across.

And maybe that's why he lectured so much. You can do all those things together. When you write, you are not teaching at that moment. You put something down, you are expounding something which you have thought out and which is being put down for posterity. The whole question of teaching and tech-nique disappears when you sit down to write. I think he found the appropriate form.

Afterword

The patient identified as Bill in this seminar was transferred to a Veterans Administration hospital in April, 1947, stayed only four days, and was immediately hospitalized in a large urban psychiatric hospital. Because of the depressive features of his illness, a series of fifty-four insulin shock treatments (ten of which were combined with electroshock) was instituted. The self-depreciatory, depressive, and suicidal talk disappeared, and Bill was discharged four months after admission.

During the next two years he took postgraduate courses in sociology and market research, living at home with his parents. In 1949, Bill's brother married, and soon afterward Bill met Ruth, a friend of his brother's wife. He and Ruth dated frequently and were married in 1951. Ruth worked to support them while he continued his studies. Their first child was born fifteen months later, followed by a second one after another eighteen months. Bill worked at three separate jobs relating to market research. When it was learned that a third child was on the way, Bill and Ruth decided that it would be desirable to live in a less urban atmosphere, and moved to her hometown in the Midwest, where Bill worked in her family's business. In Ruth's words, "We were very happy there. . . . We moved into a large farmhouse on the edge of town. Bill so enjoyed having a garden and a lawn and he was entranced with the children. . . . He organized the PTA at the new school where our daughter attended the first kindergarten class . . . was active in local politics, president of a community association. He made many friends and was a success at his job."

Around 1956 three events occurred in the patient's life: Bill's father died, a fourth child—a son named for Bill's father—was born, and Bill lost his job, presumably because of management pressure for not attending to his responsibilities. Bill had been spending a great deal of energy and time supporting Ruth's candidacy for an elective office. Gradually, erratic behavior—such as grandiose expenditures of money while his debts were mounting, suspiciousness, and hostility—became more evident. Because of his increasingly threatening and psychotic behavior, Bill returned to New York and was hospitalized in a Veterans Administration facility. He remained there from 1958 until his death in 1975.

During the VA hospitalization there were many suicidal attempts, including one in which he seriously slashed his wrists while on leave at his mother's home, and another in which he slashed his throat while in the hospital. Throughout the seventeen years of hospitalization he was essentially depressed and withdrawn, and made little effort to recapture a healthier existence. During a 1968 visit from Ruth, by then divorced, he expressed concern "that the children see a psychiatrist regularly," although the children have matured quite satisfactorily.

His death followed a heart attack, the last of a series he had suffered during his years of hospitalization.

Bill's wife, on reading the seminar report, wrote:

. . . some comments on his attitudes toward sex might be helpful. We were intimate with each other for about a year before we married. He initiated our first time (I was almost totally inexperienced) and from then on we were in the sack every chance we had until we married.

On our wedding night he went out and walked, never came to bed, and I believe that my memory is correct that he couldn't have sex until after our honeymoon. I was very hurt and upset and angry. Then after we were back in New York, we had an active sex life again. But I remember one Sunday afternoon something happened within himself, he became so carried away that he was terrified at "losing himself," and I wonder, looking back, if he ever really relaxed again.

It was an unwritten rule that I must *never* initiate sex. If I tried to it was absolutely no dice. In my inexperience I thought that this was how girls ought to be. . . . He would talk about sex as an intellectual subject, but never discuss it personally. . . .

There was a brief affair with the wife of one of our closest friends. . . . I mostly resented it because I felt cheated. I wanted sex so much more than he did. He told me that I had "a stronger sex drive," but I think that he was afraid of losing control again. . . . I do remember resenting the only-once-a-week pattern he imposed on our marriage and that I was too naïve to express my resentment.

The last six to eight months we were together, when he quit working and became so terrified of everything, there was no sex.

I'd like to add one last word of tribute to Bill's brother and to his wife, who provided the details of Bill's life since 1947. Although burdened by the futility and tragedy of Bill's life, they have themselves grown into open, sincere adults, compassionate and concerned about Bill, but with a forward look to their own lives. However painful the review of Bill's history may have been to them, they have been fully cooperative and encouraging. Obviously, any discomfort over the personal data in the seminar has been overridden by the hope that the presentation of Bill's history may be of some help to psychotherapists and patients alike.

R.G.K.

Index